From a Life of Adventure

of Adventure

The Writings of

ERROL FLYNN

From a Life of Adventure

of Adventure

edited and with an introduction by

The Writings of ERROL FLYNN

TONY THOMAS

CITADEL PRESS   Secaucus, New Jersey

First edition
Copyright © 1980 by Tony Thomas
All rights reserved
Published by Citadel Press
A division of Lyle Stuart Inc.
120 Enterprise Ave., Secaucus, N.J. 07094
In Canada: General Publishing Co. Limited
Don Mills, Ontario
Manufactured in the United States of America

Library of Congress Cataloging in Publication Data
Flynn, Errol Leslie, 1909–1959
   From a life of adventure.
   1. Flynn, Errol Leslie, 1909–1959.   I. Thomas,
Tony, 1927–   II. Title.
PN2287.F55A28   1980   818'.5209   80–11519
ISBN 0–8065–0690–3

He was one of the wild characters of the world, but he also had a strange, quiet side. He camouflaged himself completely. In all the years I knew him, I never knew what really lay underneath, and I doubt if many people did.

ANN SHERIDAN

ACKNOWLEDGMENTS I am grateful to a number of people for their help in putting this book together. Particular thanks are due John Hammond Moore, the author of *The Young Errol*, for the use of some of his material and some invaluable illustrations. I thank Earl Conrad; the reference library staff of the College of Lake County, Illinois; the Round Lake, Illinois, Public Library; Bob Matzen; Basil Courtel; Paul M. James; Neil Stannard; Rudy Behlmer; Eddie Brandt; and especially Rick Dodd, the owner of a splendid collection of Flynn photos and memorabilia. But mostly I thank my friend Trudy McVicker, without whose help and encouragement this book might never have come to be.

TONY THOMAS

Contents

Errol Flynn—Enigma

"I DON'T REALLY KNOW why I write, unless it is to prove something to myself. Before I became an actor, I nearly died of starvation trying to sell my stories. I suppose that compulsion is still part of me and always will be. Sometimes I ask myself why I bludgeon myself into spending late night hours at my desk. I've never been able to give myself a satisfactory answer. I've just *got* to write, that's all."

Errol Flynn is not likely to be remembered as a writer. The celluloid image he carved for himself as a swashbuckling hero, abetted by his private life as a roistering cavalier, obliterated his chances of being taken seriously. Such was the apparent gaiety of his lusty life that not even his fans were prepared to show much interest in any claims he made to the more restrained and intellectual facets of his nature. But he did indeed have those facets and he did indeed manage to do a fair amount of writing in his lifetime. Not enough to qualify him as anything other than a part-time professional but enough to prove that he had some genuine talent with words and phrases, and especially with the telling of tales. In fact, as a tale-teller he was a veritable Baron Münchhausen—but more about that later.

He was an incredible man. Which is not to say that he was an entirely admirable man. He wasn't. Errol Flynn was rather like a statue that overwhelms the viewer on first impact but upon examination is found pitted with blemishes—and yet still commands the attention. He was the most beautifully heroic actor in the history of the movies, possibly because fate made a mistake and placed him in the wrong century. Flynn was Don Juan, Robin Hood, the Earl of Essex, General Custer, Captain Blood and

Gentleman Jim Corbett. James Thurber's Walter Mitty never had a better personification.

Most of all Flynn was very, very lucky. His pre-film life had qualified him for nothing in particular. His great good looks and charm had enabled him to skim across the surface of life and he had not bothered to acquire any trade or skill. He was an adventurer in the literal sense of the word, a man who lived by his wits and by the skin of his teeth, and with much evidence of casual morality, high-handed treatment of acquaintances, and even a bit of larceny here and there. Years later he would capitalize on it all with a twinkle-eyed reference to his "wicked, wicked ways." And he was adored by millions because of it all. He lived, or seemed to live, the life of a man who flaunted all the rules and won.

But there was a great deal more to Flynn than this. A truly satisfied, successful man does not become an alcoholic and a drug addict by the age of forty and burn himself out at fifty. Behind the Flynn bravura, which he never in public let down, was a lot of dry rot. Inside the rollicking rascal was a serious man screaming to get out. He allowed himself to become a kind of amusing phallic figure and he laughed about it, along with everyone else. But it is highly probable that it resulted in a sense of self-disgust that contributed to his decline. Flynn was a more sensitive and insecure man than his dashing image led people to believe.

Sometime in his later years he remarked to a group of friends, "I think I'm going to have to give up something I've always had a passion for." They laughed because they naturally assumed he was talking about women. He then explained that what he was referring to was writing, which had become too difficult for him. But Flynn, keenly aware of his image, saw the joke and laughed—and kept on drinking.

He was never given much credit as an actor and yet, as every actor knows, to be convincing as a swashbuckler requires quite some talent. Few critics paid him compliments until 1957 when he appeared in *The Sun Also Rises.* They said he was good as Mike Campbell, the bankrupt, charming gentleman drifter. He was indeed good but what he was actually playing was himself.

One scene in *The Sun Also Rises* is particularly touching and revealing. It takes place in a hotel room in Pamplona after several days of riotous fun have come to an end. Jake Barnes (Tyrone Power) comes to see Campbell and finds him sitting on the edge of his bed with a bottle and a glass in his hands. Barnes asks him how he feels and Campbell replies with a flourish, "Never better." They talk; Barnes declines a drink and leaves after a while. As he goes through the door, Campbell raises his glass and says, "Bung ho, old boy." Barnes looks back with concern and quietly replies, "Bung ho." The camera then moves closer to Campbell as the smile leaves his handsome but puffy, bleary face and he puts his head in his hands. What we see is a lonely, spiritually desolate man. *That* was Errol Flynn, age forty-eight and two years from the end of his life. Those who knew him at that time, and cared, could only ask themselves how a man who seemed to have it all—beauty, physique, intelligence, wit and ability—allowed it to slip away so soon.

Despite his Irish name and a generous amount of blarney in his makeup, Flynn was a Tasmanian, born of Australian parents in Hobart on June 20, 1909. His mother, Marelle Young, came of a seafaring family and claimed as one of their antecedents Midshipman Young of *H.M.S. Bounty* fame. They had in their possession the sword owned by Fletcher Christian, which doubtless fired the imagination of young Errol, who, according to his mother, was a lively lad and loved to dress up and play people like Robinson Crusoe. His father, Professor Theodore Thomson Flynn, had just been appointed to the faculty of the University of Tasmania and would, within a few years, become a greatly distinguished marine biologist. He would also be given the post of Director of Fisheries for Tasmania, and when seen around the harbor and waterways of Hobart, he often had his young son in tow.

The ocean would become the great love of Flynn's life. He frequently said that it was only when on the water or in the water that he felt truly at ease with the world.

In view of his father's career, it was not unusual that Flynn should acquire a fine knowledge of the sea. But he also inherited his mother's love for the water, although he seldom gave her credit for it. She was a champion swimmer and had the boy in the sea while still an infant. Marelle was an attractive, spirited lady and Flynn obviously took after her side of the family, a fun-loving, enterprising lot, quite different from the reserved, academic mien of Professor Flynn. But Errol claimed that his rapport was with his respected father and not with his mother. In later years he would seldom have a good word to say about her, claiming that she was extremely severe with him, and she in turn would tell reporters that her famous son had been a "nasty little boy." Their lack of rapport doubtless had some bearing upon Flynn's peculiarly ambivalent attitude toward women.

Flynn was clearly not the product of a happy home. Both parents objected to living in Hobart, which they considered dull and provincial, compared to Sydney, where they had both spent much of their lives. The Professor was away from home a great deal of the time, mostly on research forays or for periods as a lecturer at other Australian colleges, leaving his wife and son to their battles. Flynn's sexual curiosity manifested itself at an early age, perhaps even at seven, when he swapped views of genitals with a girl of the same age. When found out he was thrashed by his mother, who, according to Errol, referred to him as a "little pig" for a long time thereafter. It did little to abate the boy's increasing curiosity about girls.

Errol was healthy, large for his age, very good-looking and well aware of it—and quite rebellious. The contempt for authority and established order, which would endear him to multitudes some years later, would appear to be almost congenital.

Although intelligent, he was not a good scholar. He rather arrogantly considered academic studies boring and chose instead to have as good a time at school as he could, which included excelling in sports and athletics. With his looks, his physique and his charming manner, everything came fairly easily to young Flynn. This resulted in a major flaw in his character—laziness—and that flaw would dog him all his life. It would prevent him from truly excelling in the things that were important to him, like writing. As an actor he rarely worked hard at a role; his immediate and long popularity made it easy for him to give pleasingly glib performances. It was an attitude that began in his school years.

Flynn was put into good schools in Hobart and when his father was posted to do research and lecturing in London in 1923, he was enrolled in a boarding school for a year or so. He appar-

ently saw little of his parents during that time and in his autobiography he wrote with some loathing of that period, claiming
that it was a dismal, Dickensian experience. However, when he
returned to Hobart in the summer of 1924 to start high school,
he donned the natty wardrobe of an English schoolboy, complete with Eton collar and smug manner. Now fifteen and six
feet tall, he could best any boy who challenged him, and he was
prone to dating older girls. His school work would continue
to be uninspired but his prowess as an athlete would advance
rapidly.

By October of 1925 young Flynn was a Tasmanian tennis star,
with accounts of his skill written up in the papers, but by the end
of that year he had been ousted from school. Even his credits on
the tennis courts could not save him from his pranks. Among
them: dropping ice cream on the heads of teachers and smear-
ing syrup on the steering wheel of a teacher's car.

Early in 1926 Flynn was enrolled in a renowned Australian
school, The Sydney Church of England Grammar School, well
known Down Under as 'Shore.' His father's standing in academic circles was surely the only reason for the acceptance.
The pattern remained the same—excellence in sports, with a
marked skill in boxing, and almost no interest in formal subjects,
although he did reveal some ability in English composition and
essay writing. By August of that year, however, Shore too decided it could do without the presence of handsome, ingratiating
young Errol Flynn. He had seduced the daughter of the school's
laundress. And there was also talk of his having lifted a little
money from the guest of a fellow student. It would not be the
last time such a charge was made against him.

In later years Flynn would claim that he was virtually abandoned by his parents when ensconced in these private schools.
Possibly he felt they didn't send him enough pocket money,
which in view of his love of fun, might be true. But he seldom
admitted that he had a raft of relatives in Sydney, including dot-
ing grandparents, who were generous to him. This unwillingness
to acknowledge help and assistance given him was unfortunately typical of Flynn all through his life. Some of his warmest bene-
factors, for example, fail to get any mention in his
autobiography.

Flynn's expulsion from 'Shore' took place a couple of months after his seventeenth birthday—and that was the end of his schooling. After the death of his famous son, Professor Flynn would admit that there was never any likelihood of Errol following in his academic footsteps and that school for him was simply a place to let off steam and have as much fun as possible. But in the latter part of 1926 the young blade was forced to face reality for the first time. He was qualified for no profession and he had no money. His father was in England and his mother in Paris, one of several periods of separation. Flynn clearly had not been the product of a happy, well-balanced home. He had no brothers but one sister, Rosemary, ten years his junior, of whom he had seen little. All of which contributed to the "loner-drifter-dreamer" nature of Errol Flynn. On the positive side, he was the product of a fairly good family and had the earmarks of a gentleman; he spoke with fairly cultured accents and his charm and humor made it easy to make friends. He moved in the social strata of Sydney, even though he really couldn't afford to. Through the influence of friends he was able to get a position as a clerk with the shipping and merchandising firm of Dalgety and Company.

Flynn was with Dalgety for a little more than a year. He enjoyed life with his society friends and made an impression with his athletic prowess, particularly as a boxer. He entered the New South Wales state amateur boxing competition and did well for himself. His style and skill were well covered in the Sydney newspapers. But there was something amiss in his lifestyle at this point—he simply couldn't earn enough money to keep up with his chums. Flynn resorted to a little light crime—lifting funds from the petty cash account—but he was caught and fired. Since Dalgety and Company were not about to provide him with a reference, he found it difficult to get another job, and after a few weeks hit upon the idea of heading for New Guinea, where tales of gold strikes were luring many young men from all parts of Australasia. Presumably one of his relatives provided him with money for the boat trip.

Errol Flynn arrived in Rabaul on the first of October, 1927. Ideas of proceeding to the gold fields soon fell by the wayside; the fields were extremely hard to reach through the wild terrain, the native tribesmen were dangerous, it required money and equipment, and, most dampening of all, tales of success proved to be greatly exaggerated. Flynn heard of an opening in the government service and applied. He was accepted as a cadet, to be trained as a patrol officer, with the provision that he could supply character references from his school and from his last employer. He informed the authorities that he would have to send for such papers and they took him at his word, but when no such papers appeared he was relieved of his post. His period as a cadet lasted less than two months and in the following two years he would get by with a variety of jobs, mostly as a clerk or laborer around Rabaul and as an overseer on copra plantations. He also spent time as a sailor on schooners in New Guinea waters, doing some pearl fishing and recruiting native labor. He would do a fair amount of recruiting over his New Guinea years, an activity that was within a stone's throw of slave trading and one step short of the law. Flynn, of course, enjoyed anything that thumbed its nose at authority. He also enjoyed shocking people years later with tales of his days as a "blackbirder" or "slaver," as a man who rounded up natives at five pounds sterling per head for work in the gold fields and plantations.

After two years of adventuring in New Guinea, and contracting the malaria that would dog him all his life, Flynn returned to Sydney. He had had a good time, but at the age of twenty he was still no nearer to any kind of trade. He resumed his social whirl but work was very hard to come by. His parents were back in town, and while they were happy to see him again they were far from pleased with his footloose, profligate ways. What was to become of their handsome, charming son? Errol still showed no signs of career interest. Indeed the only strong interest he developed at this time was a yearning for a fifty-year-old yacht named the *Sirocco*. The vessel had a colorful history in racing and she had long been a familiar sight in Sydney harbor as a pleasure cruiser.

Flynn acquired the *Sirocco,* but not in the manner he described in his autobiography, which claims he bought it with funds accrued from his gold mining claims in New Guinea. In actual fact it was his mother who bought it for him, presumably to give her boy some means of making a living. Rather than use it for the purpose of making money, Flynn decided to take off on a great adventure. With three friends—Sydney socialite Rex Long-Innes and two Englishmen, H. F. Trelawney Adams and Charlie Burt—he set out to sail the *Sirocco* up the Great Barrier Reef to New Guinea. This is the trip he wrote about in *Beam Ends*. It was a far from wise venture to be undertaken by four underqualified sailors in an ancient ship, but it was the kind of challenge Flynn loved.

The cruise of the *Sirocco* took the better part of half a year—a very leisurely, haphazard cruise at that—and not long after arriving in Port Moresby, Flynn decided to return to Sydney. By the end of January 1931, he announced his engagement to a girl he had known for several years, Naomi Dibbs, and it seemed as if the rover was about to settle down. But his errant ways got the better of him and by April he was off again to New Guinea, this time enticed by news of the fortunes to be made in the growing of tobacco. With a little money of his own and a lot of money from associates in the area of Port Moresby, Flynn took over a plantation a few miles away, up in the hills and near Rouna Falls on the Laloki River. Flynn managed the affair well enough and took time off to join his pal Trelawney Adams, who was running a trading schooner up and down the coast. For about a year and a half Flynn's life was somewhat more substantial and orderly than his previous two-year fling in the islands. He claims to have done a great deal of reading, and it is at Laloki that he began putting pen to paper. His success at having material accepted by the *Sydney Bulletin* no doubt gave him a moral boost.

The life of plantation manager eventually palled on Flynn, particularly as it turned out to be far less profitable than he had imagined, and by the end of August 1932, he could be seen once again carousing with his friends on the beaches of Sydney. Whatever frame of mind he may have been in—perhaps getting a little weary of being footloose—fate was about to step in and make the enormous change in his life that would lead to fame and fortune. He was spotted by John Warrick, a film actor who was also the casting director for Cinesound Studios in Sydney. Producer Charles Chauvel was looking for someone to play Fletcher Christian in his production of *In the Wake of the Bounty* and Warrick thought Flynn might fill the bill. He did indeed.

Flynn would later elaborate on his discovery, claiming that Chauvel had seen photos of him in the papers due to his being ship wrecked off New Guinea, but it was simply a matter of Warrick noticing Flynn on Bondi Beach and thinking that this striking young man would be right for the part. Flynn would also claim that Chauvel took him to Tahiti to film on location but the fact is that Flynn's three weeks of employment, at a wage of just a few pounds, took place in a modest Sydney studio. By the time the film was shown, Flynn would be long gone from Australia, and about the only immediate good his debut as a film actor did was to improve his social life.

No other offers of movie employment came his way and once again Flynn was wondering about a means of livelihood. Prospects must have seemed bleak and depressing to him at that time, because he resorted to theft. In *My Wicked, Wicked Ways* he admitted to stealing jewels from a lady he identified as Madge Evans, a married woman with whom he had a fleeting affair. He rationalized that since she was wealthy and since he intended to simply "borrow" them until he got on his feet, he would swallow his self-respect and play the gentleman thief, à la Raffles. In his autobiography he claimed that the jewels were later lost and that he was never able to locate the lady again. Both claims are dubious. However, his theft was immediately detected and the police tried to locate him. He was searched as he settled in the cabin of a ship about to head north from Sydney, but nothing was found. He sailed to Brisbane and from there made his way up the coast, doing odd jobs, to Townsville, where he sailed—once again—to Port Moresby.

Flynn arrived in New Guinea at the end of December 1932, and in the next two months managed to sell whatever interests he had in the island—mostly his partial ownership of the Laloki plantation—and took up the one trade at which he knew he could make some immediate money: recruiting native labor. He wrote about these adventures in a notebook which was eventually lost. Years later he would recall these days to friends in Hollywood and almost everyone thought he was lying, albeit beautifully.

By the end of February 1933, Flynn had gathered sufficient funds to take his leave of the islands—for the last time. He made his way to England via a number of ports, and in one of them, Colombo, he wrote his father a letter saying, "I think I am going to try to make a career of acting when I arrive in London. I feel that is what I want to do and where I may make my fortune." Professor and Mrs. Flynn were now living in Belfast, Northern Ireland, where the professor had accepted a post at the university in 1931, which he would hold until his retirement in 1948.

Errol Flynn went about becoming an actor in much the same manner he had tackled other enterprises—with a bold front and the air of a man who knows his stuff. He invented a list of credits for himself, the only genuine item of which was *In the Wake of the Bounty,* which, fortunately for him, had not shown up on British screens. Thus the "Aussie movie star" was able to get himself a job with the Northampton Repertory Company, whose staff and actors may have been surprised at his lack of histrionic skill but were more than impressed with his personality and his ability on the sports field. He stayed with the company for a year and a half, and it is to Flynn's credit that he applied himself to learning something about the craft of acting. But he clearly knew that his future as an actor was not on the stage but in films, where his looks and personality would make it much easier to get ahead. By sheer persistence he got an interview with Irving Asher, manager of Warner Bros.' Teddington studio, who took a chance on Flynn and gave him the lead in a low-budget mystery called *Murder at Monte Carlo.* It was during the production of this "quota-quickie" picture that Asher recommended that Flynn be sent to the main studios in Burbank, California.

Flynn turned up in Burbank in January 1935 and did little for half a year except play a couple of small roles—and court and marry French movie star Lili Damita, whom he had met on the boat coming from Europe. Damita was working for Warners and she was doubtlessly a big factor in promoting her handsome young husband at the studio. He was then twenty-five, eight years younger than she, and their marriage lasted a stormy, squabbling seven years. He would speak bitterly about her in later years, mostly because of the severe alimony she clamped on him, and he would never allow that she had been helpful to his early career. However, Damita was successful in having some of his less flattering comments excised from the first edition of *My*

Wicked, Wicked Ways. During their marriage she was cautious with reporters about commenting on her husband, although it was common knowledge in Hollywood that she was tempestuous and sometimes violent, and that the Flynns were battlers. But she would occasionally admit that he was not a very demonstrative man and that, amusing and charming as he was, there was a perverse streak in him. In a magazine article, Damita said, "He loves to annoy people in childish ways. He knows their weak points and plays on them. He is a liar, too. You never know when he is telling the truth. He lies for the fun of it." They were not comments that endeared Lili to his fans but in the light of later knowledge about Flynn, she was very likely speaking the truth.

Errol Flynn's erratic patchwork of a life took a dramatic turn in the summer of 1935 when Warners took a huge gamble and cast him as the lead in *Captain Blood.* His overnight success in that swashbuckling classic is part of Hollywood legend. Few actors have ever rocketed to stardom so swiftly and made such a deep and lasting impression, or revealed such a natural talent for publicity. The publicists at Warners found themselves with the peculiar problem of having to play down the background (and foreground) of an actor, instead of having to invent one. Most of the publicists thought he was lying when he related his days in New Guinea and Australia. Flynn lied, or went along with *their* lie, that he was an Irishman; presumably he was easier to market in America as Irish rather than Aussie. With his name and his parents living in Belfast, it was a facile lie to support. The publicists did their best to cover his indiscretions (drinking, brawling, and loving in excess) but barely knew what to do with the letters that arrived from people Down Under and in the islands who informed them that their star owed them a lot of money. To his parents he was a rather painful pride, especially to his father, whose achievements in biology made him one of the foremost men in his field. After Errol died, the professor admitted that his son was an enigma. He would smile a little wistfully and say, "There was all sorts of publicity, a lot of it bad. But Errol didn't mind. He thought all publicity was good. Sometimes we protested it, but it was no good. He would laugh it off."

Flynn's first seven years in Hollywood were his best. Most of his films were expensive features which brought Warners a solid return on their investment, particularly if they presented Flynn as a dashing, costumed hero. At this he was without peer. His Robin Hood, for example, is so persuasive that perhaps that it might have been Flynn in a former life. Flynn was, whether or not he realized it, a personification of Byronic romanticism.

Things came easily to Flynn in his early years in Hollywood, including trouble and controversy. He was forever bothered by men who wanted to find out if he was as tough as he appeared on the screen—they usually found out he could handle himself well enough—and by women eager to discover whether he was really sexy and amorous. Just how great a lover he was is open to question; he garnered a reputation as a ladies' man but evidence suggests he allowed the impression to build in order to foster publicity, and that he was in fact not a seeker of female company except for sexual gratification.

Despite his bravura façade, Flynn was easily embarrassed by personal questions and always warded them off with quips. But it became increasingly hard to do as the Second World War wore on. His movie heroism caused him some discomfort when critics wondered why such an apparently fit and brave man was not in uniform, as so many of his fellow actors already were. He had in fact offered his services to the government but had been turned down. He was medically fourth rate, which in itself was an embarrassment. Neither he nor his studio wanted the public to learn that he had developed a heart condition, that he had recurrent malaria, that he had had tuberculosis, and that back in New Guinea he had suffered from gonorrhea. Even at the height of his fame Flynn sometimes collapsed on the set from overexertion. And yet this was also a man who performed beautifully on the tennis courts and in the water; a total contradiction.

David Niven, who was one of Flynn's earlier Hollywood friends and fellow-carousers, left to join the British Army in 1939 and did not return until six years later, following a solid military effort. He would sometimes see Flynn in the years that followed but they could never fully resume their friendship. "I think Errol suffered because he didn't go off to war with the rest of us. It bothered him but he didn't show it, in fact he rarely betrayed his seriousness, he hardly ever unburdened himself. It would have been better for him if he could have, instead of living behind a façade. Errol was a many-sided creature."

If Flynn inwardly worried about his lack of war effort, it was hardly apparent to his fans, who were not bothered by the disparity between his screen heroism and the real world. Perhaps it was because his image was that of a man of former times. The press, particularly the British press, would razz him about winning the war all by himself, but he actually appeared in only five films which had anything to do with the war. Ironically, the best of them, *Objective, Burma,* caused him the most embarrassment. He was excoriated in England for appearing as an American soldier in a film about the largely-British war campaign in Burma. It was one of his most restrained and convincing performances and one that few people in England saw because the picture was taken out of circulation after only two weeks of British play. But the damage had been done, and he endured Burma jokes from then on.

But a lot more damage, inner damage, had been done Flynn before the Burma picture. In November 1942 he was summarily yanked out of his playboy dream world by a court order. Flynn was arrested and brought to trial on two charges of statutory rape. He was acquitted but his image was irrevocably changed, and tarnished. The highly publicized trial, front page news for months, was considered a kind of wartime *divertissement.* At the end of the trial the judge said to the jury, "I have enjoyed the case, and I think you have." Flynn obviously didn't enjoy it and he paled visibly during the five-week ordeal. Had he been found guilty he would have faced imprisonment. Not that he intended to subject himself to that indignity. He later admitted he had arranged with a private aviator to skip the country in case of conviction. His acquittal was greeted with cheers. He emerged from the courtroom beaming like a schoolboy. As for his self respect—he claimed that there were times when he sat alone in his bedroom with a loaded gun in his hands. But it seemed to his friends and fans that the trial had made little difference to the breezy Errol; it would take some time before they noticed that his drinking had increased and that he was dabbling with narcotics.

Flynn lived for sixteen years after the rape trial. As time went by he would look back and realize what a turning point it had been in his life. By 1942 most of his finest films were behind him; those that followed were of varying merit, few of them really good. The flaws in his nature had begun to catch up with him. Lack of discipline was the fatal fissure; he had rebelled against his mother, his teachers, his employers, his wives, and even himself. The hedonistic Flynn gradually smothered the cerebral Flynn. He resented the reporters and the comedians who fed off his image, yet he did little to change their impression of him as a superficial celebrity dedicated to fun, sports, girls, and drink. Yet, according to his second wife, Nora Eddington, whom he married after the rape trial, he was embarrassed by attention: "He was rather shy and he didn't know how to accept a compliment. He was worried by autograph seekers; he would get red in the face and stammer." It was during this marriage that it became apparent that Flynn had become addicted to narcotics. "He said he had no intention of becoming an addict. I believe that. It's just that he was a born adventurer, he had to try everything, every challenge had to be tackled. He enjoyed the sensations he got from drugs but I don't think there was any doubt in his mind that he could stop any time he wanted. But he didn't—he went on and on—and I think that's what killed him."

Flynn's great escape was the ocean. If he was anything, he was a sailor. One of the first things he did in Hollywood was to buy a boat, a ketch which he named the *Sirocco,* after the one he had owned in Australia. But the *Sirocco* came in for some juicy publicity because of the rape trial and he got rid of her. He looked around for something bigger and better, and settled for a 120-foot, two-masted schooner which could be sailed or power driven. He named his new prize *Zaca,* the Samoan word for peace, probably hoping he would find it with her. In 1946 he sailed her down the Mexican coast, through the Panama Canal and into the Caribbean. He and his crew became lost in a storm and drifted toward Jamaica. He put into Port Antonio, on the northeast corner of the island, without knowing where he was— and it turned out to be one of the happiest twists of his life. In Jamaica he found an island that was an idealized version of New Guinea—friendly natives instead of savage ones, a tropical climate that was benign instead of lethal, and something that reminded him of the South Seas but with no unpleasant associations. Flynn soon bought property around Port Antonio, including the whole of Navy Island, and set up a coconut plantation, a cattle ranch and a home. For a while he also owned the Titchfield Hotel. The waters were perfect for sailing and skin diving, and he became a local character. In Jamaica he felt at home and it was where he intended he should be buried.

But to support his lifestyle on his boat and in Jamaica Flynn still needed the income of a movie star. He had long quarreled with Warner Bros. about his image, feeling they exploited him as a costumed hero, but the attempts to put him in other kinds of films, in light comedies and dramas, simply did not bring gold to the box office. His image was set. In 1949, in an effort to recapture the old Flynn screen glory, Warners cast him in *Adventures of Don Juan,* with a large budget, sumptuous sets and costumes, and plenty of swordplay. Vincent Sherman was assigned to direct the film; not having worked with the actor before, he was warned by other directors to be prepared for problems with drink, tardiness and much waiting around during production. He recalls: "At the beginning of the picture he told me he knew I had heard about his drinking, and he wanted to assure me he wouldn't drink on this picture. He said he'd give me all the cooperation he could in making *Don Juan* a great film. I found him charming and sincere, and I think he was serious. The first ten days he was marvelous, he was never late and he knew his lines. One day he called me into his dressing room; he had a bunch of clippings on the table. He said, 'Have you seen these?' He had just opened in New York in his previous picture (*Escape Me Never*) and the critics were very unkind to him. In essence they said that if Flynn wasn't on a horse and shooting in a Western or a costume picture he was pathetic as an actor. I read these things and it was embarrassing to do so in front of him. He sort of made fun of them, kidding, but inside I could see he was terribly hurt by these reviews. He was covering up. Two days later he came on the set completely drunk, and for the rest of the time he was drinking on the picture."

Flynn's casual approach to his work increased the budget of *Don Juan* by at least half a million dollars. It remains, however, one of his better performances, possibly because he understood the character of the part, knowing, like Don Juan himself, that the reputation of Great Lover is something of a joke and a bit of a bore. Flynn had a talent for comedy which was seldom given scope, but this Don Juan was plainly a triumph of tongue in cheek. Vincent Sherman finished the film with warm feelings for Flynn despite the problems he had given him. "It was hard not to like Errol. He was a man of great humor and charm, and he had real merits as an actor—yet he made fun of the whole business of acting. Few actors have ever been able to wear costumes and handle a sword as he did, with such style and conviction, and yet if you pointed that out to him he was insulted. He didn't really appreciate himself."

Despite their differences, Flynn and Warner Bros. set out on a third seven-year contract. With this one Flynn demanded even greater latitude. He wanted, and got, the right to make films for studios other than Warners. His first away from them was *That Forsyte Woman* for MGM. It co-starred him with Greer Garson, and she remembers him with affection: "He presented, out of his artistic and creative imagination, with no assistance from anybody else, a believable and most interesting portrait of Soames Forsyte, so completely different from anything else he had done that it made one realize what potential he had as an actor. It's a tragedy that he didn't live longer. There was a great deal more to Errol than people supposed; more than this rather two-dimensional figure, swashbuckling, rascally, and a great man with the ladies. I'm sure he never bothered any woman who didn't want to be bothered, because he was a gentlemanly soul and a great charmer, much more cultured and erudite than people supposed. He had a very light-hearted wit, but most of all he was a romantic."

By the time he was forty, Flynn's power at the box office was over. *Adventures of Don Juan,* which is now viewed as one of his best efforts, failed to make the impression Warners had hoped, and from then onward they cut back drastically and gradually moved to sever their contract with him. The critics were fairly civil about his work as Soames Forsyte, but the public showed little interest. Already he was heard to make quips about death. Director Raoul Walsh, who was to be one of

Flynn's pallbearers, recalls that in 1950 the actor was told by a doctor he had only a year or two left. Flynn called Walsh to his home and asked for advice. Walsh recalls, "I told him to give up drinking. He started playing tennis and swimming again. Then I went to Europe, and when I got back I found he had been drinking heavily."

Flynn's appearance began to change when he reached his forties. There was a slight and gradual coarsening of the face and a deadening of expression in the eyes due to alcohol and drugs. He was unable to perform as athletically as before. But perhaps the biggest change was mental. Flynn continued to put up a brave front but there were signs of despondency and bitterness. By his own standards he probably considered himself a failure. His popularity had waned and he had failed to win much attention as a writer.

Despite his inner contempt for his image as a swashbuckler, Flynn went along with it because he realized it was about all he could do to make money. In 1954 he decided to make a film of his own and to do it with style and class, with no interference from people at Warner Bros. He chose *William Tell,* set up production in Italy, and budgeted it at $860,000. Half of this was his and half came from Italian backers. After the company had filmed about half an hour of usable material, his backers informed him that there was no more money on hand. Flynn now found himself in the direst of financial straits. Production on *William Tell* was halted and never resumed, and various members of the cast and crew sued him for back salaries. It was also the time when the United States government chose to remind him that he owed back taxes amounting to $840,000.

This predicament was largely the fault of Flynn's business manager in Hollywood. The man had just died, but before dying he admitted to misappropriating funds, and to losing Flynn's money at gambling. To appease his creditors, Flynn began disposing of some of his properties—his house on Mulholland Drive in the Hollywood Hills, his cars, and some of his valuable paintings. Two things he clung to and refused to surrender were his estate in Jamaica and his yacht. Flynn was always very cagey about money. He took the precaution of carrying gold bars on the *Zaca,* in case of extreme travail, and after his death it was found he had more investments and bank accounts than he had admitted. But in late 1953 Flynn was hard put for cash.

The *William Tell* fiasco brought to an end one of Flynn's closest friendships. Bruce Cabot, in the years prior to his going in the army in 1942, had been among the handful of hard-drinking, hard-playing buddies with whom Flynn most preferred to spend his leisure time. When Cabot returned after the war he noticed a marked change in Flynn, which he thinks was partly due to his coming under the influence of John Barrymore and his coterie. Flynn admired Barrymore enormously, and Cabot claims Flynn took on some of the mannerisms of the older actor. Some of Barrymore's illustrious friends were drug addicts and this is how, in Cabot's opinion, Flynn became hooked. Flynn, mostly for fun, had tried marijuana, cocaine, and almost all the narcotics—opium, heroin, morphine. Said Cabot, "Eventually it was the heroin that got him. And even then he lived ten years longer than most who took what he took."

With the collapse of the *William Tell* project, Bruce Cabot, who had been hired to play the villain, sued Flynn for his salary, claiming he had received nothing. Flynn bitterly resented it and the two never met again. Cabot later claimed that what he sued was Flynn's company and not his former friend. He believed that Flynn's business judgment had been sorely affected by his drug addiction and that the incident was part of a much larger tragedy—the gradual decline of Flynn. "Dope is like termites. It destroyed him the way termites destroy a building, and it was a pitiful thing to see. You couldn't put your finger on it but you could see it happening. His associations changed. He didn't take the care he used to take with his appearance or his performances. Dope destroys the fiber of a man, the character, the reliability, the self-respect. With Errol it was the saddest case I've ever seen."

Flynn's home for most of the period from 1952 to 1956 was his yacht, which he sailed and moored in the Mediterranean. His drinking was heavy and continuous; had he not been a lover of swimming and sailing, his health would have been even worse. In this period he occasionally went to England to make films and do television, and in late 1956 he was invited back to Hollywood to make a film called *Istanbul*. He had assumed his association with Hollywood was over and accepted the offer from Universal in the belief that the film would be shot on location in Turkey. Some things about Flynn may have changed but one hadn't: his love of travel. He would go anywhere in the world, especially if it was a place he had never before seen. *Istanbul* turned out to be shot entirely on the back lot at Universal. It was a mediocre picture and Flynn knew it—but it was a turning point. It brought Flynn back into focus on his old stamping grounds and resulted in a renewed interest in him. Everyone in Hollywood remarked with regret on the sad manner in which he had aged so rapidly, and yet—there was still something about him. A few critics even commented that his world-weary appearance gave him a credibility that he had never had before. This opinion was not lost on Darryl F. Zanuck, who decided to take a chance on Flynn as Mike Campbell in his filming of Hemingway's *The Sun Also Rises.*

Flynn himself was dubious about his ability to play the role and Patrice Wymore, his third wife, tells of having to talk him into doing the part. It meant accepting fourth billing, behind Tyrone Power, Ava Gardner and Mel Ferrer, and it was a hard pill for him to swallow. He had never before been a supporting actor. But the result was an amusing and touching performance that won him the best notices of the film. There was some talk of his being nominated for an Oscar, which didn't materialize, and much talk of his "comeback."

However, it was clear that Flynn's career had a new lease on life. Warner Bros. called their prodigal idol back to the studio, after a five-year absence, and made him an offer he couldn't resist—to play John Barrymore in their filming of Diana Barrymore's confessional best seller, *Too Much, Too Soon.* The critical consensus was that Flynn was by far the best thing about the picture. Commenting on Barrymore during production Flynn said, "We have some things in common; we both owned boats and we made a lot of headlines. He was unlucky in his emotional life and destroyed himself. Perhaps I have had a little better luck." The comparison went deeper than that, whether Flynn realized it or not. Sadly, he seemed to tread exactly the same path as his idol, except that it took Barrymore sixty years to burn himself out and Flynn only fifty.

As his career picked up, his marriage to Patrice Wymore ran down. He made his usual flippant remarks about marriage, such as, "They marry me—I don't marry them," but on some private occasions he was heard to say that he envied people who were truly happily married. When Wymore said, "I wish I could hate him but I can't," she was speaking for a great many people whom he had treated in cavalier fashion but who found it hard not to be swayed by his charm and his humor.

While making *Too Much, Too Soon* he met the fifteen-year-old girl who would be his companion for the remaining two years of his life. Beverly Aadland was playing a bit part in *Marjorie Morningstar* at Warners when the eagle-eyed Flynn spotted her. She had been a model and dancer for several years and looked older than her age—not that Flynn cared at this point. Beverly was a bright, lively girl and as Flynn said, "She amuses me." The two were almost inseparable from then on; he said he would marry her but it seems doubtful. He could hardly have been unaware of his rapidly declining health, not to mention the fact that he would first have to get divorced.

Offers of work came to Flynn, but they were always for the parts of "once handsome but now alcoholic and decadent" fellows. He unwisely accepted an offer by his friend Huntington Hartford to appear in Hartford's stage adaptation of *Jane Eyre*. Flynn lasted a few weeks for the tryouts in Detroit and Cincinnati and then quit. He claimed the play was poor stuff but the fact of the matter is that he was incapable at this time in his life of memorizing lines. He reduced the play to a shambles with his use of prompters calling the lines from every angle of the set. Fortunately Darryl F. Zanuck came to his rescue and rushed him off to Africa to star in *The Roots of Heaven.* It would be his last major film. Early in 1959 he would produce a film of his own in Cuba, *Cuban Rebel Girls,* but it was a pitiful effort, best forgotten. There would be a few television appearances but they, too, would be rather painful because of his physical and mental health. In the last year of his life his body began to deteriorate quickly; Flynn had been a sick man for many years, although he had always managed to present an agile, buoyant appearance. As he approached and passed his fiftieth birthday, it all started to collapse. In Vancouver, British Columbia, on October 14, 1959, a heart attack brought his life to an end. The autopsy revealed a multitude of contributing factors, not the least being a near-absence of liver and kidneys. The doctors remarked that it was incredible that Flynn had lived as long as he had.

Incredible, indeed. An incredible man—a sort of Tasmanian Till Eulenspiegel. Flynn had thumbed his nose at just about everything. He had endeared himself to millions, even though some of them realized that he was a rogue who had invented his own rules and treated people in a very high-handed manner. He was a mass of contradictions. In fact, it is possible to take almost any viewpoint on Errol Flynn and prove it with evidence: that he was delightful, that he was dreadful; that he lived marvelously, that he lived foolishly; that he was a good actor, that he wasn't; that he enjoyed his wicked, wicked ways; that he didn't, and felt a little shame. Amusing but poignant, brave but lacking in confidence, talented but lazy. A man of intellect but a sensationalist. Paradoxical, complicated, unfathomable.

Perhaps the most contradictory thing about Flynn is that while his life was viewed as a great success by his admirers, reinforced by his firm place in movie history, he was also a failure. The word "failure" doesn't sit very well with his image. The laughing cavalier, sailing the seas in his own yacht, having endless fun and limitless access to beautiful, willing women—how can that be termed failure? Difficult. But this was a man who admitted toward the end that he would rather have written a few good and lasting books than to have made all his movies. Did he have sufficient talent as a writer to warrant such a sad regret or was it his actor's sense of drama seeking sympathy for something that might not have been?

The reader of the following pages is invited to arrive at his own conclusions.

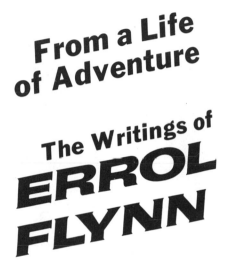

From a Life
of Adventure

The Writings of

ERROL
FLYNN

PART ONE

New Guinea

ERROL FLYNN SPENT a total of four years in New Guinea and those years were the source of much of the material he would write about. All three of his books contain items about his days in the area of New Guinea, and it was while he lived there that he started his career as a writer. What he would write about the island, its people, and its terrain would prove that he had an exceptionally good eye for detail and a most retentive memory. He also had a flair for coloring his tales with dramatic exaggeration; Flynn would raise a great many eyebrows in Hollywood with his yarns. A lot of people would assume it was all invention but there were a few who found out for themselves that there was truth in the Flynn claims. These would be men who were stationed in New Guinea during the Second World War and who, upon returning to Hollywood, would be able to face the actor and confirm what he had told them—and more. They would discover that some of his exploits were a little shady and that there were ex-acquaintances who did not speak too well of the famous man.

Someone who had occasion to probe Flynn's background in New Guinea is John Hammond Moore. Dr. Moore, an educator as well as author, became intrigued with the Flynn story while living in Australia. One bit of information led to another and another, and Dr. Moore finally decided on a complete job of detection. The result of his investigations ended up as a book, *The Young Errol: Flynn Before Hollywood,* published in 1975 by

Angus and Robertson, Sydney, Australia. In the introduction to his book Dr. Moore writes:

> *In August 1970, while trying to teach American history at a university in Sydney's sprawling suburbs, I attended a professional conference at Port Moresby in Papua and subsequently took a short tour of the New Guinea highlands to the north. Even before I left the Moresby area I began to hear bits of Flynniana. The pattern was always the same—at the Rouna Falls pub near Errol's old tobacco fields, in Wau where he worked as an air cargo clerk, at Lae where he delivered labor recruited from the surrounding hill country, and so on. Flynn departed in 1933 owing much money. When he became a famous Hollywood star his old pals wrote seeking payment, but instead each received a glossy autographed photo from the publicity boys at Warner Brothers.*

In Dr. Moore's opinion, no matter how wild and improbable Flynn's yarns there was a basis of fact in them. "Nearly all of the events described were experienced by Flynn himself or by someone he knew well. And frequently one can pinpoint the true source without much difficulty." The files of the *Sydney Morning Herald, Hobart Mercury, Rabaul Times* and the Port Moresby *Papuan Courier* were the primary sources of his Flynn probes, plus lists of ships' passengers and interviews with those who knew him in those years.

Just when Errol Flynn began to think about writing professionally is difficult to gauge. Despite his poor track record in school, he was obviously a young man of superior intelligence with a love of literature. The one area of schoolwork in which he apparently did fairly well was English composition. Even his earliest letters show a flair for expressive phrasing and a feeling for words. His first period in New Guinea, 1927–29, produced nothing in the way of writing. Seemingly it was a period of adventuring; he was, after all, a lad of eighteen, nineteen, twenty.

There would be another period of going back and forth between the island and his family ties in Sydney, but in the middle of 1931 he had his first stab at actually settling down to a job, running a tobacco plantation. This clearly left him with a lot of time on his hands, and he claims that it was a time when he did much reading of great books—and possibly a little reflecting on purposes in life. However, it was his position in the tobacco business that resulted in his first major published letter. Like other Papuan tobacco growers, Flynn was hard hit by the stand the Australian government took about colonial crops being allowed into the country and competing with Australian output. He found that he could not sell his tobacco in Australia, despite Papua's being a part of the Australian Commonwealth. Flynn voiced his displeasure in a letter published in the *Sydney Bulletin* on July 20, 1931:

Dear Bulletin:

Papua is one of the natural homes of the tobacco plant, and, as Papua is part of the Commonwealth and is in receipt of a yearly subsidy of $40,000 from the Federal Government, the obvious market for its tobacco is Australia. But the market is closed by a prohibitive tariff. Within the past eight months the Papuan Government twice made representations to Canberra on behalf of a pioneering tobacco-growing concern, asking for a preference over foreign countries. It was pointed out that Papua is part of the Commonwealth, supported by the Australian taxpayer, and that a reasonable preference would perhaps mean the beginning of a large and profitable industry; also that Papua, with the bottom fallen out of two staple commodities (copra and rubber), is urgently in need of a new industry. The reply in both cases was identical—the matter was being given consideration. They have apparently been considering it ever since, for the Papuan Government has heard no more of the matter. Meanwhile the pioneering concern has produced a splendid crop just behind Port Moresby, which is being sent to the English market, as the growers can no longer afford to await the decision of the procrastinating authorities in

Canberra. It would be a nearsighted policy should the fact that the tobacco was grown by black labour prevent those responsible from assisting Papua in every way possible, when that country is being expensively supported by the Australian taxpayer. And particularly when, as in this case, the assistance would not harmfully affect Australia, which is still and must be for years a large importer of leaf.

Yours,

Errol Flynn (Papua)

EDITOR'S NOTE: It seems unlikely that Flynn's letter to the *Bulletin* did much good about the plight of Papuan tobacco growers. But it did mark something of a turning point in Flynn's life; he had been tinkering with the idea of being a journalist and now he had the opportunity to see something of his in print. It inspired him to ask the editors of the *Bulletin* if he might be their New Guinea correspondent. They were obviously impressed sufficiently with his letter-writing to agree. It was not a salaried position. He was invited to send in occasional pieces, describing life and customs in the islands. These he did under the name of "Laloki," which also happened to be the name of the plantation on which he was an overseer at that time. "Laloki" was to write only seven pieces for the *Bulletin** but they were a good start to a writing career. Merely to have something accepted by that popular Australian weekly newspaper was considered an accomplishment in Down Under literary circles.

THE RESULT OF the pourri-pourri seance in Port Moresby at which medicine men enjoying great prestige among the surrounding tribes failed to bring a dead dog back to life, should have been a moral victory for his Ex.† But the Papuan sorcerer is an astute opportunist. The chief pourri-pourri expert suddenly remembered that the medical officer, invited to satisfy himself that the dog was dead, had touched it with a stethoscope. That, of course, cleared up the mystery of the dog's refusal to come to life. Every reasonable native

---

*Permission for use granted by *The Sydney Bulletin*.
†Presumably a reference to His Excellency, the Governor of New Guinea.

knew at once that the medical officer had applied a powerful counter pourri-pourri. It is unfortunately true that the
magicians were given presents of rice and flour—a not unusual instance of official stupidity. If these natives did not
return to their village and exhibit the rice and flour as proof
that the Government was much impressed with their prowess, then they're not the pourri-pourri men I take them for.
They ought to be able to live on their reputation in ease and
luxury for the rest of their lives.

December 2, 1931.

KILLING A TURTLE in New Guinea is a horribly messy
business. I once came upon several natives about to dispatch a 600-lb. specimen. The turtle was lying on its back
on the beach, helplessly flapping, and my cook-boy, Mai-
Iki, squatted nearby, kindling a fire on its stomach. Bellow-
ing loudly I rushed to the rescue, scattered the fire, and, in
honest rage, was about to inflict grievous bodily harm on
Mai-Iki. Deciding, however, that he knew no better, I sent a
boy for my revolver, and, while awaiting him, discoursed to
the assembly on the evil of cruelty to animals. To my an-
noyance Mai-Iki wanted to debate the matter. "Master," he
said earnestly, "this fella he no savvy die quick time. S'pose
you shoot 'im he no die." "No?" I said, "you watch," and
pumped three rounds from a .32 into his head. To my cha-
grin the turtle showed no sign of having noticed anything
unusual, and did not even interrupt the slow pendulum-like
movement of its head from side to side. Rather staggered by
such unconcern I fired three more rounds, but with the same
result. The thing seemed slightly bored with the proceed-
ings and certainty displayed no resentment. "Bring akis!"
(bring an ax) I shouted desperately. "Cut off head belong
'im." That was done and the turtle, I thought, was out of its
dreadful agony. But when, to my amazement, the headless
body continued to breathe through the severed windpipe, as
though losing a head was an everyday occurrence, I threw
the towel in. "All right," I told Mai-Iki, "go ahead and kill it
anyway you like." He remade the fire, and when the tissue

was no longer like leather cut the flesh around the edge and removed the stomach shell, leaving the inside exposed. It was such an uncanny sight to see the heart pumping and everything else apparently working to schedule that I repaired to the house for a drink. Even when I returned several hours later the turtle wasn't quite dead.

January 27, 1932.

THE KUKU-KUKUS WERE the cause of many unpleasant alarms to the party of Europeans who for the last year have been prospecting in the headwaters of the Taveri River in Western Papua. The white men never slept, ate, worked or performed their toilet without a revolver close at hand. When contact could be established, safety-razor blades were found to be the best "trade," but at first six wax matches would buy 20 pounds of native food for carriers. These, however, the Kuku-kukus soon eschewed, due to the fact that they would immediately strike the matches one after another, to the immense delight of their relations, and then have nothing left to show for the food they had sold. When the used matches failed to ignite a second time they regarded it as a callous swindle and demanded the return of the food; this being refused an ugly situation was barely averted. Culturally the Kuku-kukus are still in the Stone Age. Tools and implements are all made of stone, and the clearing of a few acres of timber is arduous toil. It takes them a week to fell one tree, two feet in diameter, so that when they first saw a steel ax in use, one man completing in a day what would take them a month to perform, they were overcome with astonishment. But later on their surprise could not be compared with that of the Europeans when two mysterious Kuku-kuku implements were found. A steel axhead, presumably stolen, had been cut through and the two halves thus procured were fastened with lawyer vine to handles formed like the figure 7. The result was two adze-shaped implements, and these, with other tools which were found, made from shovels cut in pieces, greatly intrigued the Europeans, who wondered how these primitive people had contrived to cut steel. It was concluded that the steel had been sawn or rather worn through with incredible patience by means of a length of lawyer vine and sand, a conjecture which, if correct, will make the ant, which has long survived as a model of industry, appear as a futile dodderer beside the Kuku-kukus.

April 13, 1932.

THE MEDICAL OFFICER was making a visit of inspection in the village of Hanuabada, near Port Moresby, and was confronted by a deaf and dumb native. That native had been as garrulous and able to hear as well as any other Papuan a week or so previously, so the medical officer inquired of the village constable, how he became affected. "Well," answered the gentleman cautiously, "I understand it was a punishment for blasphemy. The man would not listen to the talk of Tau, the missionary, and one day, in Tau's presence, he tore a page from the Bible to use as cigarette-paper. So Tau said he would ask God to strike him deaf and dumb. And God did." The medical officer, who realized he was up against a case of pourri-pourri, sent the sufferer to hospital and there gave him the only possible treatment for his trouble, counter pourri-pourri; and was gratified to see an immediate response. In fact, so sedulously did he cast his spells that the man was completely cured in the course of a day. Later the medical officer learned that the pious Tau had once sought the afflicted one's sister in marriage, and met with a refusal. Tau no longer interprets the Gospel in Hanuabada.

May 25, 1932.

THE MOTUAN LANGUAGE is singularly lacking in vituperative possibilities, but it has one good, very good, word for that purpose. Call a Papuan a "Goiaribari" and you heap upon him the nth degree of loathing and contempt. The

Goiaribari people are by far the lowest tribe I have ever come across. In addition to being filthy in all their habits, and eaters of snakes, snails, and crocodiles, their treatment of their womenfolk relegates them to a cultural status little above that of the beast. A Goiaribari will prostitute his wife and daughter to anyone for three sticks of trade tobacco, sell her outright to the highest bidder, or hire her out by the week or month. It is necessary that young men of this tribe about to marry should first do some brave deed. This is how he usually qualifies: he purchases from her father, who knows exactly what will happen to her, a girl about twelve years old, and then gathers around him six or seven cronies. The party, armed with spears, stone axes and other weapons, journey into the bush for a week or longer. The girl is, for several days, subjected to unmentionable barbarities. Then, at last, the stalwart braves form a circle about her and, at a signal, all rush in to hack and batter her to a pulp. She is then cut into small pieces, cooked in sections of bamboo and eaten. Such a case occurred only a month ago and the murderers are still at large.

June 15, 1932.

A PAPUAN WALKED into a trade store in Moresby, planked three shillings on the counter and demanded a "pyblo." "A what?" inquired the European storekeeper. "What's it like?" The customer explained that he was to appear before the magistrate that afternoon to engage in litigation for the return of his wife, who had deserted him for another, and he wanted to weight the scales of justice as much as possible in his own favor by buying a "pyblo," which, he felt confident, would serve that end. "Yes, but what is this pyblo?" insisted the storekeeper. "Show me what it's like." "This one book, Taubada, 'nother kind book—too strong! Before time I see one Taubada go along courthouse. He got case. First time he go inside courthouse he stand up, he take this one pyblo in his hand, he smell 'im—all right, he win this one case. Ah, 'nother kind book, this one." The explanation sufficed, and the storekeeper sold him a Bible, an old one, whose efficacy was claimed to be enhanced by age.

August 17, 1932.

ONE OF THE OLDEST yachts in the world, the *Sirocco*, is lying at anchor near Port Moresby in Papua. She was built by Ford in 1881 at his shipyards on Sydney's Circular Quay for E. W. Knox, of C.S.R. fame. Oldtimers remember when, with her blackbearded owner at the tiller and generally one small boy as crew, she developed speed that was the pride of the waterside. She sailed for thirty-four years before her original sail plan was altered. Her then owner cut several feet from the topmast, shortened her booms and discarded four tons of lead ballast. She sailed as well as previously, and continued a successful racing career for eleven years. When nearly fifty years old she was bought by a New Guinea planter, who sailed her to Papua, taking five months for the journey from Sydney. Her subsequent history included a collision with a coral reef, but she was repaired and is now destined to be a diving-tender, in the bêche-de-mer industry.

October 5, 1932.

EDITOR'S NOTE: The final two pieces of Flynn's contribution to the *Sydney Bulletin* were probably written in Sydney, since he left Laloki late in the summer of 1932 and returned to the Australian city. The October 5 piece is curious in that Flynn failed to mention that he was the New Guinea planter who bought and sailed the *Sirocco*. But it certainly gives a positive answer to those who were to read his *Beam Ends* and wonder what really happened to the old yacht.

During his last period in New Guinea, the end of 1932 and the first three months of 1933, Flynn kept a notebook. The writing does not suggest that it was intended for publication, except possibly when later revised and expanded. He lost this notebook before leaving the island and it was found in a hotel in Salamaua in 1935. For various reasons the notebook never found its way to him. But excerpts from it began to turn up in newspapers in Australia and the islands after his death. His autobiography, *My Wicked, Wicked Ways,* provoked a lot of comment— and quite some protest—in the lands Down Under, mostly from a few people who had been involved with him and felt that he grossly exaggerated some of his adventures—at their expense. As a consequence, a few passages were deleted from the second printing of Flynn's best seller. The lost notebook then became quoted in articles dealing with the autobiography, notably in the *Pacific Islands Monthly* in November 1960, in which journalist Stuart Inder gave his version of the somewhat mysterious Flynn saga in the South Seas.

Flynn's New Guinea notebook is a fascinating insight into his activities. It begins at the Sattelberg Lutheran Mission, not far from Finschhafen on the northern coast of the island:

Sattelberg Mission, 13th Jan., 1933.

Arrived here at 5 P.M. after leaving Finschhafen this morning at 10 A.M. Broke journey half way at Yermen to give my boys time to cook some rice. Carriers would not carry beyond Yermen so paid them off and sent to Yehu for a new lot. Cost of carrying very high in this district—they all know what money is. Sattelberg is 3,650 ft. above sea level but commands wonderful outlook over the sea—I can see Umboi Island from here—it must be 80 miles away.

Queer lot, these Lutheran missionaries. For the main part they are Germans but there is a sprinkling of Australians of German parentage. Father Helbig (a lay helper, one of six people at the mission) met me and gave me this room—very comfortable and I'm dog weary and a bit footsore as is usual on the first day out.

Coloured prints of Christ are regarding me dolefully from every angle in the room. He is portrayed in a large variety of postures. Rebuking (or confusing) the Elders, who have the longest and whitest beards I've ever seen; conferring blessings, etc. Why is it that Christ is never shown smiling? He must have laughed sometimes. The prints are old though, probably done twenty or thirty years ago when gaiety of any sort was still regarded as sinful.

Sattelberg Mission is the health resort for rundown and enervated missionaries. They're sent up here for a month every year to get the benefit of the excellent climate. I spotted a pretty girl when I came in today so I'll have to shave tonight. Three days' growth is no good even for a recruiter to wear. She's the little Dutch sister, I suppose—hope she comes to the table tonight. (There were three lady helpers at the mission, all unmarried: Clara Helbig, Jutta Keysser and Marie Uke.)

These missionaries treat their womenfolk like dirt. I stood up last night when Karchner's wife came into the room at Finschhafen and only succeeded in embarrassing everyone present! It was a quite unprecedented occurrence for the entrance of a woman to be more than curtly acknowledged by a sort of grunt. The idea is for all the men to sit down and eat what the women bring in at odd intervals. When in Rome do as the Dagoes do, thenceforth I kept my seat and grunted.

They sing grace in German before every meal. I very nearly laughed aloud last night at a young Bavarian, newly arrived in the country, who was making the bravest effort to lower the tone of his naturally high falsetto voice. He had fully a dozen hairs in his beard.

Long day's march tomorrow—hope to make the Hube country in four days from here. If the rain holds off may make it in three. If it doesn't I won't be able to cross the Waria River, perhaps for a week. Thank God I brought 2 bottles of O.P. rum and the Bible, and will thus have both drink and something to read. Have often wanted to read the Bible—I believe it is very entertaining and instructive. There goes the kai-kai (dinner) bell. Hungry lot these missionaries, so I'd better get along or the board will be cleared.

14th.

Stayed at Sattelberg today and rearranged my equipment for cheaper carrying. The paramount luluai of the District Selembe came up to see me this evening. We had a long discussion, with Wasange and Tutuman, the two tultuls, being present. (A luluai was a headman or chief confirmed by the territorial administration; a tultul was a native government official and interpreter in a village.) The old man is a very distinct personality, quite a superior type. He has agreed to help me recruit after, no doubt, making extensive inquiries about me from my own boys, summing me up by the text of our talk and the added incentive of Kyle's message brought by Tutuman. He has agreed to send out three tultuls in different directions—Tutuman to go to the Waria River, Inge to go to Mape, and Sambar to the beginning of the Hube country. They will meet me at Fior Village in four days time (Saturday).

Fior, Wednesday, 15th.

Left Sattelberg after lunch at 2 P.M. and arrived at Fior at 4:30. The track is about the best I have found inland and very beautiful besides. Crossed three mountain streams, each one dammed up at the crossing into crystal-clear pools. Bathed in the last one; first bath in three days. These pellucid pools were typical of New Guinea's specious beauty. They were fed by a sparkling stream flowing over bright limestone and fringed by capiac palms and coconuts. Several varieties of orchids were flowering among the surrounding undergrowth.

I sent carriers on ahead and shedding singlet and shorts leapt joyously into the cold water and lay there, lazily enjoying the rare sensation of a plunge bath and admiring my surroundings. As I lay there floating I noticed what I took to be innumerable small black twigs attaching themselves one by one to my body, but took little notice of them. Then horrible thoughts occurred to me. I jumped up hurriedly and found my fears realized. I was covered in leeches who obviously hadn't had a square meal in months.

Luckily I had matches with me so spent an hour burning them off, a proceeding which was watched with keen interest by some ten boys who had come back along the track to find me. If leeches are removed by any other method except

burning their tails to make them release their hold, a tropical ulcer will almost invariably form on the spot. I now
looked like a leopard, after dabbing myself with iodine on
the bites.

Thursday, 16th, Fior Village.

The mission has obviously benefitted these people greatly
in a number of ways. They have good roads, twenty-odd
head of cattle bought from the mission and bred up from an
original three or four head. I know of no other natives who
own a herd of cattle. They also grow English potatoes, kohl-
rabi, tomatoes. This morning I bought twenty-four green
corn cobs, a dozen or so taros for a shilling; a pineapple and
half a dozen cucumbers were thrown into the bargain.

I think Wasange will get me a recruit here.

There is a little stream running right through this village
and the rest house is situated a hundred yards or so from
the village. Consequently I have no giant and irrepressible
native pigs and dogs to annoy me. I thought at first I might
get a little privacy too, but that is expecting too much. My
every action has been keenly observed by at least fifty
pairs of eyes ever since I arrived. But I'm very comfortable
here and waiting until Saturday is not going to be so bad as
I thought, particularly as corn, eggs and fruit are plentiful
and of course very cheap.

Was very amused last night. My three Aitape boys, being
in a strange country and having been used to finding enemies if they strayed a yard beyond their own hunting
grounds in Wapi, have been scared stiff ever since they left
the coast. An old woman brought them some taro last night.
Although very hungry they examined it dubiously and then
asked Wasange, who was sitting down outside their house,
"Are you sure this food is not poisoned?"

Wasange couldn't understand what they were asking at
first and they had to repeat the question several times.
When he did, he and the entire gathering burst out laughing
at my bushmen. With good cause, of course, as I suppose
this village has been peaceful for ten years or so. But it was

not a ridiculous question. After all, only two days' march further in, in the Hube, they would not stop at a small thing like poison if they thought there was something to be gained from it.

I hear there is some trouble in Hube over a woman. Two villages are about to fight, so the talk goes. If it's right, things couldn't be better for me. Am bound to get recruits, probably from both villages if there's a fight as they'll want to get away to escape reprisals later.

17th, Fior Village.

First boy this morning—good stamp of native, too. He'll look well leading an axe about, although he doesn't suspect it yet. He thinks he's going to be my cook. This is a very good omen—to get a boy from the chief's village means that I'll almost certainly get as many as I want from other villages.

Big "talk-talk" last night. The chief and his two tultuls came along and we discussed everything under the sun, including the late war, which appears to cause much amusement and astonishment. That all the white men should indulge in extensive fighting among themselves after having given them, the black men, the very strictest injunctions against fighting, with prompt and severe punishment for disobedience, must, I suppose, appear to them somewhat paradoxical. It must have chafed them a bit when they heard details of the Great War and were themselves prevented from carrying out those periodical raids and sorties against the neighbouring villages, which used to be their favourite occupation and hobby before we came along and told them they had to be friends.

18th, Fior.

Two more boys, making three now. Excellent going. Went down to the Bun River yesterday—very peculiar formation, mainly a sort of limestone bottom with no wash in the riverbed to speak of at all. Good-looking wash on both banks though with no overburden more than two or three feet at

any part. Will wash a few dishes down there tomorrow although it's very unlikely if there's even colours. I believe all these rivers were well prospected years ago by the German missionaries and others.

Have just finished reading *The Good Companions.* Wonderful. Can Priestley ask for anything more from life than that gift of expression? I felt I knew personally every one of those characters at the end. Especially Micham Moreton—if he had been drawn from old Simpson, ex-actor-manager, now sandalwood king of Papua, he couldn't have been described more faithfully.

Three more boys tonight.

19th, Fior.

The rush has set in properly. Tutuman came back with seven boys, which makes thirteen and I'll have two more tomorrow.

As all my boys come from the purlieus of this district, all the old men of Fior decided to read me an address. It was rather amusing. The entire village gathered round me while I sat in the middle of the circle on a tucker box. One old greybeard then got to his feet and began to harangue me in forcible but quite incomprehensible terms as he spoke in his own language.

I however nodded solemnly at each pause and later had his speech interpreted. He said in effect that Fior had given me all their young men and I must look after them well. He enjoined me that I must not sell any of them and when their time had finished must bring them back myself, and then I would be given new boys to take their place. He then wound up by stating that although he was talking to me in strong words, I must not think he was "cross"—and when I came would I bring him a dog? He then asked me, through the interpreter, if I would shake hands with him and I did.

20th, Fior.

Broke camp this morning having recruited sixteen boys (with my three Aitapes makes nineteen) and proceeded.

EDITOR'S NOTE: Flynn's account of the recruiting expedition ends with the above notation. But the notebook continues with observations on sundry things, mostly, it would seem, as notes to be used later for use in another form. The manner of note-taking suggests the work of a journalist. Ironically, since this notebook was lost, Flynn would have to rely on his memory when he came to write about his New Guinea experiences. His memory was good. But to get back to the notebook for a moment: it ends with some introspective ramblings upon his then philosophy toward life, and they are of interest to the Flynn detective because they give some insights into his plans for attacking life. It seems obvious that the years of being footloose and aimless are beginning to tell on twenty-three-year-old Errol and that there is an appetite for something more substantial. Seemingly his first point after leaving New Guinea was meant to be China. This never came about; he proceeded to England, with stops in places like Hong Kong and Shanghai. However, these were his views in early 1933:

I AM GOING TO China because I wish to live deliberately. New Guinea offers me, it is true, satisfaction for the tastes I have acquired which only leisure can satisfy. I am leaving economic security and I am leaving it deliberately. By going off to China with a paltry few pounds and no knowledge of what life has in store for me there, I believe that I am going to front the essentials of life to see if I can learn what it has to teach and above all not to discover when I come to die, that I have not lived.

We fritter our lives away in detail, but I am not going to do this. I am going to live deeply, to acknowledge not one of the so-called social forces which hold our lives in thrall and reduce us to economic dependency. The best part of life is spent in earning money in order to enjoy a questionable liberty during the least valuable part of it. To hell with money! Pursuit of it is not going to mould my life for me. I am going to live sturdily and Spartan-like, to drive life into a corner and reduce it to its lowest terms and if I find it sublime I shall know it by experience—and not make wistful conjectures about it conjured up by illustrated magazines. I refuse

to accept the ideology of a business world which believes that man at hard labour is the noblest work of God. Leisure to use as I see fit!

One can never become a skillful reader or acquire the ability to appreciate books, unless one first cultivates a keen sense of the relative value of things; for this sense is the quintessence of true education and culture. To learn what is worth one's while is the largest part of the art of life.

Time, for example, just one hour of time is far more important than money, for time is life. Whenever you waste your time over printed words that neither enlighten nor amuse you, you are, in a sense, committing suicide. The value, the intrinsic value, of our actions, emotions, thoughts, possessions, way of life, occupations, of the manner in which we are living—this is the thing to be determined; for unless we are *satisfied* that any of these things have true value, even if only relative, our lives are futile, and there is no more hopeless realization than this.

EDITOR'S NOTE: It is interesting to speculate on Flynn's reaction to the above entry had he been able to read it toward the end of his life. At the age of twenty-three and just about to depart New Guinea—never to return—and proceed to England with no definite plans, he would have no idea of the fame and wealth that would shortly be his. Was he true to the above stated principles? For a large part, yes. His contempt for big business and money would prove somewhat hypocritical, since he would earn millions and display a keen appetite for high earnings, and all it could buy. There would be nothing "Spartan-like" about Flynn's lifestyle as a celebrity. Whether he lived "deeply" is open to question but he certainly lived fully and widely. He did not fritter away his life in mundane detail and he surely tackled life with great gusto and little respect for conventions. True to his manifesto he did not acknowledge any of life's social forces "which hold our lives in thrall" and if he didn't quite find "what is worth one's while," no one can fault him for not trying.

One of the social forces for which Flynn had only a slight regard was truth. He held the belief that in the telling of a story, the effectiveness of the telling was more important than the factual content. Nowhere is this more apparent than in the first of his magazine articles based on his New Guinea days. Titled "I Have Killed!" and written for *Screen Guide* in early 1937, it takes enormous liberties with the truth—not so much with the facts of the material but with his involvement in them. Whereas his pieces for the *Sydney Bulletin* and the entries in his notebook may be taken as factual, "I Have Killed!" can be looked upon as only a nice bit of storytelling. Flynn, as we know, was never a patrol officer. And he makes one vital mistake in his first-person account—what he describes in this article actually took place in 1926, a whole year before he arrived in New Guinea. Be that as it may, it makes for a good yarn:

I Have Killed!

IT WAS THE damnedest-looking snake I'd ever seen!

I was basking in perfect contentment on the broad gallery in front of the patrol house, my mind a complete blank except for a vague wish that I could stay in pajamas forever, when I spotted the lout. He was about eighteen inches long, slim as a pencil and had a head like a carved coral rosette on the end of his brilliantly green body.

Now I am as susceptible to beauty as the next man, but when I saw that lovely little fellow slip silently out of the palm thatch and weave slightly in the air an inch from my face, I had but one thought—that the coast of New Britain is a devil of a place for a lone white man to be planted in. I hadn't been in the Islands long, but I had a healthy regard for the more deadly aspects of the local fauna, and I did what most men would do under the circumstances. I yelled.

Then suddenly a flash of silver light passed over my head and the coral rosette dropped harmlessly to the floor as the headless green body wriggled convulsively. Maru, my number one boy, stepped quietly out of the house back of me and silently went down to the beach to retrieve his knife. No word was spoken while I did my best to gather up the white man's dignity before he returned.

I was quite pleased with myself when he came back.

"That, Maru," I said with measured calm, "was nice work."

Maru didn't answer. He just went in the house and fetched me a glass of brandy.

It was a glorious Island day but somehow I felt it had

started inauspiciously—though, at nineteen, one is not much upset by premonitions. After breakfast I called the boys up for medicine parade, just to be doing something.

I was thumping chests, peering solemnly into clear eyes and taking temperatures in the manner of old-timers in the Papuan constabulary, when the sounds of running feet came along the path that leads, eventually, to Rabaul and the Commissioner's office. Long before we could see him, Maru had cocked his bushy head to one side and announced, "A runner, Master, from Govamin Howz."

The boys were just as interested as I was. After all, we'd been downcoast in the Nakani country for three weeks at this lonely post, the first one that I could call my own in the year I had been a patrol officer, and this was the first intimation that anyone knew we were alive—or cared. I'd felt rather badly about it. After all, I was an officer of the Crown and I felt that I ought to be doing something heroic.

However, I was soon to get all the action I craved and, as it turned out, more than I'd bargained for. The runner stood puffing at my side while I signed the chit and retired to my office to read it.

The message was terse but definitely to the point. A punitive expedition was starting immediately against a large tribe of natives, called the Kukus. Four white prospectors had been wiped out, foully mutilated, by this still untamed, savage community in the interior, and it behooved "Govamin" to take stern measures. The three constabulary posts along two hundred miles of coast, my own included, were to head inland at once, meet at a given point, and proceed against the tribe. The message concluded with a brief line to the effect that caution was to be used, as the tribe would undoubtedly be expecting just such reprisals. Frankly, I was elated. It was my first call to action.

With a great show of speed that I later regretted, I got my boys together, issued ammunition and supplies and got the launch into the water. For two days we headed upstream through indescribable heat, miasmal swamps, hordes of the deadly, fever-carrying anopheles mosquitoes and the countless miseries of the jungle marshlands. At length we came to a friendly village. After the usual interchange of gifts, we were put up in a highstilted guest-hut for the night. The whole village pretended complete ignorance of our mission, but there wasn't a man-jack among them who hadn't heard every filthy detail of the massacre weeks before word had got to headquarters in Rabaul. Some of the younger bucks had a distinctly quizzical look in their eyes as they surveyed the size of my party, thinking, of course, that we were all the "Govamin" forces going in to chastise several hundred wild savages.

I kept my peace and we shoved on through the jungle at dawn, leaving the launch in care of the chief.

The next day we met the main party and had a conclave. It was during this meeting over a smudge fire that I developed a complete distaste for the whole trip, which, in part, was shared by the two other white officers. The senior, Ralph Huston, scratched his red head irritably, loosened his collar in a characteristic manner, and proceeded to enlighten us. True, four white men had been ambushed in their own camp. But in my own opinion, they deserved it. They had committed several unpardonable sins, among which were encouraging their own boys to steal pigs, the pride of every native householder, food from the native gardens, and, to put it euphemistically, made advances themselves to the young native girls.

Obviously, in taming a wild and savage people, the dignity and, at least, the superficial righteousness of the white race must be upheld. The natives are nothing but backward children despite their ingrained disregard for human life. The worst cannibal, the most powerful head-hunter, is no more conscious of being vicious than the wild animals that throng his jungle home. With people such as these, the only method of taming that has been at all successful is a combination of showing a fine example, sticking to it, and punishing any infringements with stern impartiality, regardless of race.

Fine! ... so far as it goes. But in the case in hand, the whites had asked for what they got. They had callously broken every jungle law, the laws their own people had imposed, and the jungle had taken prompt retribution. So why, I wanted to know, bother with a punitive expedition against the natives? I was to learn then of the inconsistency that later drove me from the service. Every man to his taste, but this was not to mine. Again, the premise is the childishness of the native. If one tribe were allowed to get away with the murder of whites instead of filing a complaint against the offenders with the Commissioner, then the tenuous hold of the remaining handful of white colonists would be terribly undermined and wholesale massacre might well become the rule of the jungle day.

Therefore we went on with it, under oath to do our duty according to orders.

Several days followed of taut nerves, of silent, pressing jungle walls. Hourly we were conscious of unseen eyes, of imminent peril; every tree held a cluster of poisoned spears, every twist of the trail marked the possible scene of ambush. We were getting deep into savage country and the silence of the jungle was unnatural, forbidding.

The first definite warning came as almost a relief. A cry from the two native boys ahead brought the thin little column to a nervy halt, every eye trying to pierce the soft, green wall. Maru came running back, carrying a long-shafted native spear in his hand. It had been driven deep into the path, a none too subtle manner of saying, "It is death to come farther."

Huston blew his whistle, hand held high. He brought it down sharply, pointed forward. The small column moved on, slower now, each white carrying a revolver in hand, his gun-boy trotting at his heels with fresh loads and a rifle. We had three more gunners, natives, each licensed to handle firearms in the line of duty . . . six guns against—how many?

We were in a clearing when it happened.

There, directly before our eyes, lay four huge, bloated, headless bodies. White men, they had been, but now they resembled nothing more than immense feather-stuffed pincushions, innumerable spears protruding from the backs of the putrefying bodies.

It was a horrible way to see death for the first time.

Giving them as wide a berth as possible, holding hand-kerchiefs to our noses, we pressed on to the deserted village. The first step was the systematic destruction of the houses by ax and fire. After that our men had located three divergent trails going off into the silent wall ahead. We three shook hands, somewhat melodramatically I'm afraid, and split up into the original three groups, each taking a trail.

I was scared. I don't care who knows it or what they think about it, but, as my boys and I lost sight and sound of the others in following our blind little trail, my mouth was dry and my stomach a block of ice.

It was a horrible hour before they ambushed us. The air seemed thick with spears. Strangely enough, only one struck. A native soldier drowned in his own blood, his throat cut wide. The rest of us held fire, waiting for a mark, our backs crawling in anticipation of more spears. It seemed forever, but certainly was no more than a couple of seconds before there came a wild yell, and from the green burst the biggest, woolliest, scar-tattooed savage I've ever seen! He brandished a long, feathered spear in either hand and yelled like a fiend out of hell. I got to my feet, praying inwardly that they'd hold me, and covered him while I called upon him and all his followers to surrender. A stupid thing to do but regulation; and anyway, I hated to shoot.

I'd never killed before.

Guns? Certainly! That was fun, sport! I rather fancied my target work, but to drive that hot lead into a man, white or savage—well, it was suddenly quite different.

I hardly expected him to lay down his spear, knew instinctively that when he threw it would be the signal for his invisible horde to charge to the kill, but I waited, much to the frank terror of my boys. They'd have run, but there was no place to go. I leveled my forty-five at him. With a howl that I hear in my dreams even now he let his spear fly at me, the blood-lust in his maddening eyes.

Somehow he missed. The spear just went into my ankle as I pulled the trigger. He dropped like a pole-axed steer, half his head suddenly gone.

The bushes vomited men—but amazingly, on their hands and knees in supplication! I later learned that I'd killed their invincible leader and *pourri* (magic) man. Any other native wouldn't have mattered, but his death struck terror to their hearts. My magic had been greater than his—Colt's magic.

I don't remember much of that return trip.

The spear had been poisoned and the dead leader's magic had got me after all. Despite every precaution, jungle gangrene set in with incredible swiftness. They carried me back, out of my head most of the time, cursing and laughing, yelling and more than a little mad. With our party were eight native prisoners marching under guard to Rabaul and the gallows—object lessons.

I was invalided out of the service, at my own desire. Those natives swinging at a length of hemp because four weak-minded whites had violated their women, had spoiled my ardor for punitive expeditions. Granted that it was an exception to the rule but it was my first experience and I'd had enough. Anyway, the doctor said that what I needed was a long rest and sea air, to get the virus out of my blood.

I'd always loved the sea, always had some sort of a boat, if only an outrigger. And I had a lot of luck. They say Irishmen are supposed to be lucky, but I'm damned if I see it except in this one instance. The *Maski* was a trim little schooner, perfect for just that type of interisland trading, the miscellany of moon and monsoon, pearls, freight and the South Seas to sail in. Even her name, a Papuan word, described her. Roughly *Maski* means "Who cares?" I didn't. I was getting a grip on life again as I stood on her decks and watched my crew of Kanakas handle her, take orders from me even when I knew that they knew more about sailing an Island vessel than I'd ever learn!

There was one brilliant afternoon when I was lounging in the pub at Kaviang on the lustrous coast of New Ireland. My Kanakas were hard at work down on the quay loading a cargo of copra. Life seemed very fair to me that day. Two more trips as profitable as this one and I'd have the *Maski* paid for and money in the bank. The Islands, whimsical and enigmatical as any woman, were being good to me after all the grief I'd had as a patrol officer on that other island across the straits.

I'd just ordered another pint of bitter as a concrete method of showing my appreciation of life when a bar-boy brought word that a man, a Kanaka, was outside and wished the favor of speech with the great, kind and illustrious Master Flynn. Inasmuch as I was perfectly willing to agree to all those adjectives at the moment, I moved to the door on a floodtide of expansiveness. The boy was an old friend of mine, Allaman, chief overseer on a plantation downcoast owned by a pal recently up from Australia. Allaman had been up to Kaviang for a bit of a fling, was now broke, and his ladylove had found greener pastures. He was through with flings and women and wanted to go home, but the gods were frowning on him (heaven knew why!), home was far, and Allaman was without passage money, and Master Baily would have it in for him for overstaying leave. The worried overseer had contemplated taking his own life, until he saw the lovely lines of the *Maski* and knew that the great, kind and illustrious Master Flynn was near and would care for so good a boy as Allaman.

In short, could Allaman thumb a lift?

Allaman could. The sun broke through the heavens once again. Allaman dug deep in his torn pants, pulled up a shilling, and went straight to the native bar, there to extol the virtues of the great, kind and illustrious sons of the Flynns. Meanwhile, I repaired to the quay to start checking cargo and passengers.

I'd been pearling for a couple of months and had found it dull going; lonely work, that, with just a few boys, whom a white man must keep at his distance, and nothing to do all day but pull up basket after basket of shell. But I'd made a good profit and felt that I could afford the gregarious if less remunerative life of coastal work for a time.

The Kanakas had the copra stowed in the least possible bulk, leaving me room for the dozen-odd native passengers who were quite content to sit in a stinking hold till kingdom come, cooking their rice, eating their smelly grub and trusting blindly in their god and the captain, sometimes confusing the powers of both. I checked them in, got their papers, which were signed by their district commissioners along with their bills of health, without which they cannot travel by packet; told one old lady that she'd either have to have her sow tethered on deck or leave it behind, and was ready to push off down the coast. Just then Allaman, grinning stupidly, came lumbering down to the boat, saluted smartly, then stumbled and fell into the hold, where he lay exuding alcoholic vapors and silly chuckles to one and all.

The afternoon's sail was uneventful as we rounded the rough waters of Cape St. George. Dusk was just falling and I was drowsing contentedly on the after-deck, vaguely wondering if I ought to go to the trouble of putting my hand up to keep my pipe from falling out of my mouth, when, above the noise of the sea, there keened the scream of a woman demented. It snapped me so hard that I remember nearly breaking a tooth on the pipestem. As though it had been the conductor's cue for an anvil chorus of Salem witches, the entire hold broke out into such a wild shrieking, a retching, throat-splitting bawling that my hair prickled along the base of my skull.

I was halfway down the companionway into the hold when I felt strong hands grappling at my shoulders. It wasn't the grasp of hands nor the sickening noise of unreasoning terror below that stopped me in my tracks. I knew that for a Kanaka boy to lay hands upon his master presaged a new and terrible danger. I couldn't hear what was being said on account of the clamor below, so I stood where I was, straining my eyes into the murk. For years I've tried to erase that scene—in vain.

Two native women lay just below me, one with her head split open like a halved peach; the other, her throat cut and one breast hacked brutally off. As I stared, horrified, the body of a baby hurtled through the air against the forward bulkhead, with a horrid thud and dropped limp and all queerly asprawl to the floor. The rest of the visible passengers below were huddled together in one mass of seething, sensate terror, pressed against the hull.

His gibbering lips flecked with blood and froth, his eyes wide and glazed with madness, his hands slippery and red, Allaman, the native overseer I'd taken aboard at Kaviang, stood crouched above them, a restless ax swinging loosely. A lull in the screaming, throats unable to articulate momentarily, and I could hear Maru, my old boy, yelling in my ear.

"Amok! Amok! Allaman amok! Come back, Master. Back!"

I didn't need to be told that the poor beast who held the passengers in stark terror had fallen into that inexplicable madness that strikes heedlessly and without warning. The question was, what to do?

I tried calling to him, conscious of my own futility. There is no voice but God's to whom a berserker will listen. It would be plain suicide to go down and grapple with him, a giant by nature and now clothed with the mad strength of a dozen killers. I sent the trembling Maru astern for ropes. We made three nooses and, on the pitching deck of a small schooner, tried a technique similar to the one used in roping a raging tiger caught in a drop trap. It was utterly useless, but it served one purpose—it took Allaman's crazed mind off of his human victims as he sullenly evaded or chopped at the swinging ropes. But it was fast getting dark and this cat-and-mouse game had to be stopped. There were six more native women, some with babies, in the hold with Allaman.

Time after time I tried to put out of my mind the one solution, the ineluctable end to which I knew this dread game was coming. That end was securely strapped to my thigh—blue and deadly.

I waited until he circled under me, trying not to remember that I'd known that round black head ever since I'd come to the Islands.

The forty-five jerked viciously in my hand.

The next morning I buried Allaman on the island he loved so dearly. I'm afraid I was the only mourner. Kanakas fear even the grave of he who has been touched by the devil. From that day to this I've never carried a passenger. I liked and respected Allaman—the finest type of Polynesian, loyal, true and brave.

I've never been one to be ridden by mawkish sentiment, but after what happened that day on the *Maski* I was perfectly willing to try my hand at something else. I got a good chance to charter her to a sportsman in Port Moresby and snapped it up. In time I drifted back to Rabaul with nothing in particular on my mind and too much money for an idle man.

The inevitable nights in the pub followed until I met a grand old rascal who had drifted from one island and job to another from the first days of the White invasion. He was leaving for Sydney on the packet in the morning, having just returned from the brush. A few drinks and he was spinning yarns a mile long—the usual bush yarns that tourists gawp over in wonder and old hands just smile and wink at, with their beers.

But he told one that has always stirred me to interest no matter how many times I've heard it—the famous one of the hidden valley where nuggets of free gold the size of hen's eggs are ready for the picking. There's always a good reason why the discoverer hasn't gone back to make the millions himself. . . .

But I had nothing to do, so why not? Maybe I'd find a couple of ounces of gold or whatever else Old Lady Jungle had to offer. I took my time about it and outfitted. I tried to get some of my old boys back, but with the exception of Mari, I had to take on a new crew. A fair bunch of lads as ex-headhunters go, but Maru didn't like them. I never exactly learned to love them myself.

Off we went, going nowhere in particular, just "deep in" to see what we could see. We saw precious little of anything but mosquitoes, snakes and a few deadly flowers, but even they weren't of the kind that could be sold to collectors—a dull trip of early rains and no returns to speak of. I'd no idea where we were—just well in the interior and going by compass. There are no roads in that country, nor trails either, where every living thing must, of necessity, cover its own backtrack.

I'd gotten pretty well disgusted with the whole thing and started swinging around southeast where I knew the sea to be, when we found ourselves in a long slot of a valley with nearly perpendicular sides. Whether or not the natives were friendly in that section was a mystery. So far as I knew, no one had ever been there before—which usually means that strangers aren't welcome!

Our second day threading along the floor of the valley was pleasantly kept from monotony by the occasional sight of natives running along the crests above and waving at us to go back, even shaking their spears and making other inimical signs. The boys were of two minds about the whole thing, but supplies were running down, we were headed for the short way out, and I'd sooner have unfriendly savages in front of me than behind.

We went on.

The next day was even more interesting. Sudden landslides came from nowhere, fortunately not hurting us. We saw no sign of natives, but a volley of arrows seemingly from nowhere left little room for doubt about their presence. Maru was trying to keep the boys happy, but they didn't like it any better than I did—and not being white, didn't have to pretend nonchalance. They were in a funk and didn't care who knew it. Through Maru I tried to find out if any of them had any smart ideas, but like most frightened natives, their idea was to dig a large hole, crawl into it and pull it down on top of them, awaiting a merciful death in which they might retain their heads for the hereafter.

I don't like holes—or blind valleys, either.

We went on.

The next day we came to the end of the valley—and an ancient, jungle-grown ruin. Nothing spectacular, for, strangely, those hidden temples you read about are usually the effort of fecund imagination. That is, the ones with the gigantic begemmed idol and a fortune of gold lying handy for the taking. All the ones I've ever seen were just piles of slimy rock smelling badly of decay and bat guano. That's what this one was, but I knew we were in for trouble.

Natives are superstitious—even the "Mission Boys" like

mine. They give the kind padres great lip service, but they know things the padres don't about the jungle. They're hard-headed Christians, afraid of nothing when in town surrounded by white constabulary, but they're just scared black boys when they run across places presumably haunted in the jungle. They stayed with me that day because they didn't have any other place to go that looked safer.

The next morning we undertook to get out of there via a narrow, stone-walled defile. I pointed out to them with some pride that the air sweeping up the defile was not jungle air but carried with it the tang of the distant sea. It didn't help much. They felt the sea was too far away anyway, and who knows how many outraged ghosts had been risen by our passage through the ancient temple? I wasn't worried about ghosts, but I was concerned about head-hunting savages who had expressed their dislike for me and mine—and I was quite aware that I couldn't depend on my boys in a pinch. They were too green and frightened.

Well, it happened at the end of the defile.

They jumped us.

Yell? You've never heard anything like it unless you're fey and have heard the wail of the banshee of Gort na Clokamora! I sincerely felt that the end of Errol Flynn had come, and was wondering how silly my head would look drying on a ridge-pole. The boys, of course, gave one startled yell, dropped their packs and disappeared. Even Maru shoved my guns at me and muttered something about going after the boys and bringing them back.

In his eagerness he must have passed them at full speed.

I wish I could cut a dashing figure along about here, but I am afraid that all I can say is, when I pulled down on one big buck who was bluntly intimating his desire to separate my head from me, that for once I felt no qualms or emotion about killing. I just let him have it, full in the face, as he swiped at me with a massive ax. He missed. I didn't!

And that, amazingly, was all there was to it!

The rest of the tribe fell flat on their faces, their weapons discarded, and moaned in terror whilst I stood above them unashamedly shaking and preparing to sell my life dearly.

Of a sudden I realized that I was, almost certainly, the first white man they'd ever seen and that my gun had done the trick! One shot, a dead buck from the white god's finger of thunder and lightning, and the fray was over. I didn't wait for them to get curious about my immortality.

I disappeared.

I went down the back-track faster than I believed it possible for a man to travel, and kept going until my legs wouldn't hold me up. I fell underneath a tree and lay there sweating and gasping for breath, wondering what had happened to my boys.

Here I was, a lone white man with five rounds of ammunition, a compass and, to all intents and purposes, lost in the New Guinea jungle without my safari—so then it started to rain as it can rain only in the jungle! I was starved, felt that a cigarette would help. They were there, right in my pocket, but my trusty boys had run off with the matches.

It was the most miserable night I ever spent. I didn't mind being soaked to the skin and hungry, but I did want a smoke.

In the morning I staggered aimlessly and fearfully on, terribly conscious of being alone. Even my own scared boys would have helped. Four hours later I found those heroes eating and drinking and smoking gaily around a camp fire—my food, my cigarettes—they'd never expected to see me again, but their spirits were volatile and their sorrow momentary.

I joined them.

I had that cigarette.

I took a large swig of rum from the medicine chest.

I cleaned up a bit to preserve dignity.

I beat hell out of my poor, scared, six-foot savages.

After that, everything was very friendly again.

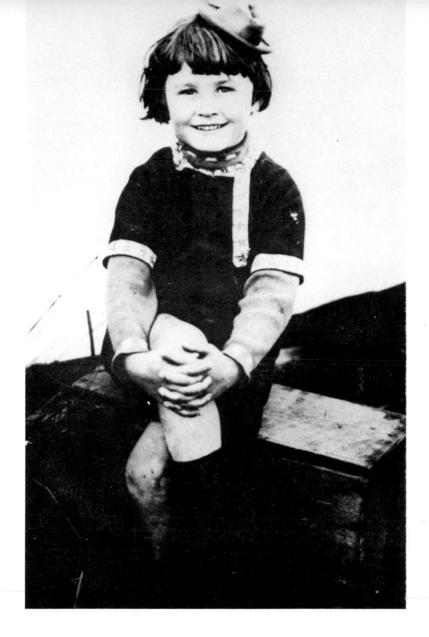

Errol Flynn at the age of four and a half, in the garden of his home in Hobart, Tasmania. On the back of this photo his mother wrote, "Errol always liked to dress up." Was he playing Robin Hood even then? *(Courtesy of Earl Conrad)*

The proud owner of the *Sirocco,* in a mock-heroic pose. *(Courtesy of John Hammond Moore)*

The seventeen-year-old Flynn, at the Kensington race course in Sydney in 1926. To his left is his good friend Ken Hunter-Kerr, who was a boon to Errol's social life. Then employed as a lowly clerk at Dalgety's, Flynn no doubt had difficulty keeping up with his society friends. *(Courtesy of John Hammond Moore)*

In Sydney in 1927. The woman on the left is Naomi Dibbs, to whom Flynn would later be engaged for a while. *(Courtesy of John Hammond Moore)*

A tennis afternoon at Burradoo, New South Wales, in 1931. Ken Hunter-Kerr is behind Flynn. Sitting beside him is Bradley Ryrie, the son of Major General Sir Granville Ryrie. Errol liked to keep himself in good company. *(Courtesy of John Hammond Moore)*

The captain and crew of the *Sirocco*, on their cruise up the Great Barrier Reef in 1930. To the left is Trelawney Adams; to the right is Rex Long-Innes, and at the bottom is Charlie Burt. *(Courtesy of John Hammond Moore)*

At Bowral in 1931. The pose would suggest ownership, but it was just a jest. It would be some years before Flynn could afford a car. *(Courtesy of John Hammond Moore)*

Flynn's plantation house at Laloki, New Guinea, in 1931. He supervised its building, and it was his home for more than a year. He was the plantation overseer at the time, and it was here that he wrote his first published articles. (*Courtesy of John Hammond Moore*)

benefit of the excellent climate I spotted a pretty goul when I came in today so I'll have a shave tonight. Three days growth is

This notation in Flynn's diary at Laloki clearly points up his normal interests. (*Courtesy of John Hammond Moore*)

BASAGE   Shoe Mandl.   lap lap.
          Singlet.
          Basket suit case
KARBU   Clothes blonga
TIRM BONG }
NINGJO   } lap lap. Singlet.
DOME   }
HOME (TOI-TUI) Striped costume — serge la
          man's blouse.   Salt
AILO.   Striped costume Trousers. — serge lap   man's Blouse.
BONIEVE   lap lap.
SAMBAR   Singlet   Umbrella 2 Bl
BELA.   1 serge lap lap } 2 Singlet.
BAU-U
MANSE   SASANG INER?
          lap lap   singlet
KANE   Beads
BUAMENG   Singlet. serge lap lap

On his third visit to New Guinea, Flynn threw caution to the winds and employed himself in the illicit business of recruiting native labor, considered to be one step up from slave trading. This entry in his notebook in January 1933 lists the "boys" he had recruited and the items he had given them as inducements, mostly, it seems, singlets (undershirts). (*Courtesy of John Hammond Moore*)

Errol Flynn's movie debut, as Fletcher Christian in Charles Chauvel's production of *In the Wake of the "Bounty."* Flynn was employed for three weeks in late 1932 for a pittance of a wage probably not more than ten pounds per week.

In early 1934 Flynn placed this advertisement for himself in the British theatrical journal *The Spotlight*. He was then at the Northampton Repertory Theatre; only his listing as the lead in the *Bounty* film is accurate. The rest is his invention. *(Rick Dodd Collection)*

ERROL FLYNN

FILMS: Lead in "In the Wake of the Bounty"
—*Chauvel Prods. Ltd. (American-Tahiti)*
"I Adore You"—*Warner Bros.*   "Third Degree"—*B.I.P., etc., etc.*

NORTHAMPTON
REPERTORY
THEATRE

———

Olympic Games
Boxing Representative

c/o "The Spotlight"
GERrard 3002

Photos : Sasha.   Height 6 feet 1 inch

Flynn at twenty-five, the lead in the British
B picture *Murder at Monte Carlo,* filmed at
the Warner studios in Teddington in October
and November 1934. After seeing the picture,
Warner Bros. brought him to California on a
six-month contract at $150 a week.

During the making of *Captain Blood,* the film
that rocketed Flynn to stardom, he clowns
around with his co-star Olivia de Havilland.
The chemistry between them would prove
potent.

Robin Hood, the quintessence of Flynn's film
image and legend.

On the back lot at Warner Bros. in Burbank, during the making of *The Prince and the Pauper* in 1936. With him is Bobby Mauch, who played the prince. The animal sitting on the tractor is Flynn's beloved schnauzer Arno, a dog who loved his master and tolerated no other human.

Lily Damita, the first Mrs. Errol Flynn, visits her husband on location during the making of *Robin Hood* at Chico, California, in November 1937. Their stormy marriage would stagger through almost seven years and produce one son, Sean. *(Rudy Behlmer Collection)*

By the late thirties, Flynn was truly a star tennis player in the Hollywood community. He had been an amateur champion in school, and as a celebrity he was a welcome guest on any court. But alcohol and drugs would eventually rob him of his vitality. *(Rick Dodd Collection)*

Flynn's family pay their first visit to Hollywood: sister Rosemary (a dozen years Errol's junior), his mother, Marelle, and his father, Theodore, whose own fame was gradually increasing (in marine biology). *(Rick Dodd Collection)*

Flynn was also a good horseman, and at a horse show in Washington in 1939 he accepted the invitation of President and Mrs. Franklin D. Roosevelt to ride their entry. Flynn greatly admired FDR and proudly displayed an autographed photo of him. *(Rick Dodd Collection)*

PART TWO

Beam Ends

ERROL FLYNN LOST no time in turning his fame as a movie star to his advantage as a would-be writer. In fact, his first two years in Hollywood account for a very large portion of his output. Seemingly his great success on the screen, which had prompted him to do something about his ambitions as a writer, resulted in gradually deflecting him from that purpose. Writing was hard work for him and acting was not. The vast income and the even vaster opportunities to enjoy the high life soon sapped Flynn's resolve as a man inclined to sit at a typewriter for long hours and sweat out stories. However, at the start of that celebrated career he did indeed spend some time pounding the keys. From that period came a stream of magazine pieces and his first book, *Beam Ends,* the title of which refers to the nautical term for sailing a vessel with more bravado than knowledge—by its beams. The book covers the half-year he spent sailing the old yacht *Sirocco* from Sydney to New Guinea in 1930. It was published in 1937 by Longmans, Green and Company and printed in condensed form in the November 1936 issue of *Cosmopolitan* magazine. It is this version here reprinted by permission of The Hearst Corporation.

FOREWORD: The Sirocco *was over fifty years old when I bought her, and with three companions, sailed out of Sydney Harbor to the South Seas. She was forty-four feet at the water line and cutter-rigged. We set out for New Guinea, three thousand miles away, having no clear idea of why we were going there beyond the fact that it was one of the far corners of the earth's surface unexplored and savage today, and seemed to promise adventure.*

After seven months we got there, surprisingly, for the remarkable thing about our seamanship was our appalling lack of it. If I took sextant and "shot the sun," my calculation of our position would, as often as not, locate the ship anywhere from the South Pole to the middle of the Sahara. When Trelawney took a sight, we at least had a chance of finding ourselves on an ocean; being a very determined fellow, he would never put down his pencil until he did get us on an ocean. Doubtless there is a providence for the purpose of protecting youth from its own folly. I can think of no other reason why I am now able to write the story of our voyage.

A FEW YEARS AGO, after a series of adventures in New Guinea and Australia that included a good sock in the jaw from a hard-boiled third mate, I walked one day into the bar at Usher's Hotel in Sydney, New South Wales, and became suddenly rich—not in wisdom or experience or anything valuable like that, but in hard, solid cash. Usher's is the famous place where foregather all the men from the South Sea Islands. Bend a leg on the bar foot-rail and you will hear many strange and wonderful stories. You will hear of encounters with unknown tribes of savage head-hunters, of close shaves in the New Guinea jungles, of good gold prospects found in the mountains of the Solomon Islands, or how so-and-so's canoe capsized in the crocodile-infested Sepic River, whose source no man knows.

The barmaids in Usher's are like familiar landmarks to the man from the islands. Yolande—she of the billowing bosom and the bar pump—owns a claim in Morobe, pegged for her by an admirer. She expects to get rich from it some day and retire. Alice will grubstake you to follow up a leader you may have struck in savage Aitape. She has never been anywhere near the islands but she knows there is gold in Aitape if only the hostile tribes don't make a pincushion of you.

It was Alice who told me of my luck. She had heard that an English company was interested in a claim of mine in the New Guinea gold fields. The claim was worthless in itself but, as it lay between two large leases belonging to the company, it interfered with development.

That same afternoon I sold it for five thousand dollars. The sudden transition from poverty to affluence was intoxicating—in every sense of the word. I wanted to cut my friend Trelawney Adams (known as the Dook because of his Cambridge accent) in on a large share but he would not hear of it. I wish he had, for a couple of weeks later I awoke clear-headed one morning and, taking a census, found myself the possessor of a yacht and about a thousand dollars.

It will always be something of a mystery to me how I came to acquire the yacht *Sirocco*. The Dook could shed no light on it. However, a friend named Rex helped to clear the matter up when he said he had been one of the guests at a party I had apparently given on board. He had, he said, tried to stop me from giving the owner a check but I insisted that nothing less than the yacht itself would serve for a souvenir of the party.

I hurried round to the bank, hoping against hope. But it was too late. The check had been cashed.

With Rex and the Dook, I went to see my pleasure craft. She was a cutter, about forty-four feet long and so narrow in the beam that you could lie across her. On stepping aboard, the first thing that struck my eye was a brass plate on the tiller post bearing the date 1881. Most yachts are considered ancient at twenty. Mine, I thought grimly, would only be the grandfather of them all.

Depressed by this added blow, I sat down on deck and wondered how I could cut my loss. The *Sirocco* was too big to ship aboard any of the little island steamers to New Guinea and would be of no use when I got her there. She had no cargo space and seemed to have a six- or seven-foot draft—far too deep for the reef-studded island waters. With the money paid for this ridiculous craft I had cherished plans to outfit an expedition to a place in New Guinea where I had once found gold prospects. If I sold her now, the most I could expect would be about a third of the price I had paid.

"Well, Admiral," said Rex, breaking in on these gloomy reflections, "where do we go from here?"

"You can open up a pore and go to hell," I told him. "Never mind about my movements."

Ungracious, perhaps, but the affair had soured me.

"I bet she can sail!" said the Dook. "She's got lovely lines." He was on the bowsprit looking aft and we joined him.

She looked her best from there: long, low and raking, built to slip through the water like a greyhound. I began to visualize her as she would look with full sail bent and a bone in her teeth. The Dook was right. With those sleek lines she would sail, and handle well, too.

"Why not sail her to New Guinea?" I murmured half to myself. "It would be a wonderful trip."

Rex smote his knee. "Right!" he exclaimed. "I always wanted to see the islands. When do we leave? Tomorrow? I'm ready any time."

"By Jove, so am I!" said the Dook.

"Wait a minute, you crazy nuts!" I said. "New Guinea is three thousand miles from here, and this boat will probably sink the minute she gets outside Sydney Harbor, And who in hell asked you to come, anyway?"

"I'm going home to pack a bag right now," said Rex, ignoring the irrelevancy. "See you later!" He jumped ashore and ran up the landing.

The Dook and I looked at each other. He smiled. "Damn good idea, don't you think? I'd better make a list of charts we'll need—navigation of this coast is awful if you don't know it. And we must have a chronometer and sextant."

He looked around. "How about putting in a steering wheel instead of the tiller? She'll handle easier, you know. Then renew all the running gear and buy a complete spare set of sails. Yes, we are going to need quite a lot of things."

"Perhaps we might get a few provisions too," I suggested sarcastically. "Money is no object. You know—a few tins of caviar and so on. And what do you think of the engine? Let's throw it out and get a new one, eh?"

"That's a good idea," agreed the Dook; "and we should take along guns and ammunition and fishing tackle. Then we'll need an outboard motor for the dinghy. As a matter of fact, we might as well have a new dinghy and some new—"

"Ah, what the hell!" I said. "Why tie yourself down to mere details? What do you say we get a new ship altogether?"

The Dook shook his head. "I wouldn't," he advised firmly. "I think she's a topping little ship. As a matter of fact, I'm extraordinarily fond of her already. Aren't you? You should be!"

I looked at him sharply, dismissed a quick suspicion and gave up. Some Englishmen are like that.

The Dook came of a seafaring family. His great-grandfather had founded the famous Green Line of clippers, long since defunct, of course, but well sung in the legends of the sea. It was not surprising, therefore, that the Dook numbered among other accomplishments the theoretical ability to navigate and a profound knowledge, also theoretical, of ships and the sea.

I also had a certain acquaintance with the sea. For a year I had been captain and half owner of a schooner in the South Seas, making a precarious livelihood by freighting copra and fishing for bêche de mer, the ugly sea slug so valued by the Chinese epicure, Trochus shell and occasionally pearls. I knew next to nothing of navigation, which with a native crew and pilot is an unnecessary accomplishment for inter-island work. Rex could distinguish one end of the ship from the other, but ask him to name them and you had him.

We were badly equipped for a voyage of three thousand miles of treacherous sea and coastal line in an old forty-four-foot harbor yacht. So Charlie joined the crew.

Charlie was a young Englishman from the Isle of Man who had just been sacked from a sheep station in the back country. He was short and stocky, wore his hair cropped like a convict and spoke like a judge, In fact, his whole attitude was judicial and solemn. He wandered aboard one day, introduced himself and said he had once been a half owner of the *Sirocco.* He and his partner had been forced by lack of funds to sell her to the shipyard where I bought her.

He seemed a nice sort, so I asked him if he would care to come along with us. He pondered the matter and then gave judgment to the effect that he would be glad to.

By the time we were ready to sail, a new semi-Diesel engine, fishing tackle, guns, provisions and so on had left me with only about twenty-five dollars on which to make a three-thousand-mile journey. None of the others had any money either. Funds to cover mishaps? No one cared! The spirit of adventure had us in a firm grasp!

We made about four attempts to leave, but each time something went wrong. The first time we were met by such a fierce gale outside the harbor that we had to put about. We waited a couple of days and tried again, but this time something happened to the engine. On another occasion we found we had forgotten to fill the water tanks. Finally our friends stopped coming down to see us off. When at last we sailed, it was in the dead of the night, unsung and without farewells.

The voyage nearly ended on the first leg, from Sydney to Port Stephens, a couple of hundred miles north. With all sails set and the engine running we were leaving Sydney Harbor, when the little ship dived into the first large headswell of the open sea. Another swell came on top of it; we went under that one too.

All attempts to make coffee in the galley were hopeless. The ship pitched and heaved and rolled; the seas came green over the deck, and there were ominous clashes from below. Then suddenly, after about five minutes of this, all was calm again. We had been passing through Sydney Heads, where the conflicting crosscurrents and heavy swell make an unexpected maelstrom which gives a small boat a quick but severe trouncing.

The surprise of the thing left us slightly dazed. The galley was a shambles. All the crockery was smashed and a lot of water had come through the forward hatch.

Outside Sydney Harbor there was a steady wind blowing hard with a rising sea. We bucked into it, the *Sirocco* making heavy weather.

The day seemed very long. Toward evening, the wind had become biting cold and was blowing a young gale. All I asked of life now was that the wind might drop and let us get on to the shelter of Port Stephens. But it kept up and the *Sirocco* continued to give her imitation of a porpoise.

Late the second night the engine suddenly began to misfire. How I cursed the folly that had led me to take an interest in the thing. Being the only one who knew its little tricks, I now had to go down and tinker with it.

It refused to respond either to curses or wrenchings. One of the cylinders had become choked with carbon. I stared at it with hatred, and then I caught sight of the bilge. The water in it was level with the floor!

Hurriedly I glanced into the cabin. Water was sloshing about on the floor with the motion of the ship. She was leaking!

I shouted to the others but couldn't make myself heard above the noise of the engine and the weather. Scrambling up the greasy companionway to the deck I found them huddled in the wheelhouse, haggard from sickness and lack of sleep.

"Hey!" I shouted. "We've sprung a leak! You get on the pump, Charlie, quick!"

For an hour we pumped in ten-minute spells without making any appreciable difference on the water. The pump was a hand-plunge type and soon ceased to work at all because of the continuous shifting of the water from side to side as the ship rolled.

We continued to pump incessantly all that foul night. We had to. With a few tons of water in her, the *Sirocco* lurched, rolled and staggered up into the headwind as heavily as a sodden log. At dawn I was seriously considering turning in towards the distant shore and trusting to luck to find some shelter on that bleak and stormy coast, but one glance at the chart showed that it was utterly impossible.

We appeared to have made no headway at all during the

night; the headland of Point Stephens was seemingly as far off as ever. Then at last the wind veered a few points to the east. By midday we were off the point and making a good five knots. An hour later we dropped anchor close to the small jetty in Port Stephens. The ship had over two feet of water in her.

Taking a tin of biscuits with us we rowed ashore and fell asleep instantly in an empty shed on the jetty. It smelt badly of lobsters and fish, but no one noticed that—not until next morning, anyway.

After a good hot breakfast, we began the job of cleaning the ship. Books, clothing, papers—all had been reduced to a sodden mass by the oily bilge water. It took a couple of days to get shipshape once more and, after scraping the carbon out of the engine, we hove up anchor and set sail for Coff's Harbor, halfway to Brisbane.

With a fresh, fair wind blowing from the southeast, the *Sirocco* bowled along in great style, the following seas catching up every so often and shooting her along on their crests. The engine was shut off and, with no sound except the swish and hiss of the water along her side and the occasional flutter of a sail, we felt the keen joy of sailing a hard-driving vessel.

Then, in the late afternoon, the wind began to rise and dark clouds rapidly overtook us from the south, threatening a strong blow and probably rain. At six we had logged ninety-eight miles in twelve hours—magnificent sailing for a vessel of the *Sirocco*'s size.

At midnight the Dook sighted a flashing light which he recognized from the chart as South Solitary Island, off Coff's Harbor. If I had just come out of a tomb I couldn't have been happier to see a light.

The entrance to Coff's Harbor is narrow and tricky, necessitating careful negotiation between a rocky headland and a small island at the mouth, and even more careful steering in. You have to keep two red leading lights directly in line. If you once let them get out of line, even slightly, you finish upon the rocks.

We rounded the island and began to search anxiously for

the first red leading light which would mean turning in towards the harbor. Trelawney spotted it just when I thought we must have missed it entirely. I took the wheel and hove to while the others stood by in readiness to take sail off.

It was pitch-dark but somehow we took the mainsail in, or rather, it took us in. It came down with a rush and covered the entire deck and the crew as well. The night became even blacker as we frantically struggled to free ourselves, expecting to hit the rocks at any moment. During that time the little *Sirocco* did everything but stand on her bowsprit.

As it was, just as we freed ourselves, a tremendous wave caught her beam on, crashing on deck with such force that I thought the main hatch cover would surely be smashed in. Fortunately, it held and I jumped for the wheel and once again headed for the entrance. With the sea shoving us along much faster than we wanted to go, we ran wildly for the narrow harbor mouth. So far, only the one leading light had been picked up; the other was not to be seen at all.

I went below to keep the engine in full reverse, in an effort to give the others time to find the second light. With only the one lead spotted I expected at any moment to feel the sudden lurch and crash as we piled up on the jagged rocks of the breakwater.

Being shut up in a tiny engine compartment under such circumstances is enough to give the strongest man a bad case of claustrophobia. It seemed an eternity before the other leading light was sighted. It had been hidden directly behind the first one all along! They were a long way off, but instead of being on the waterfront as we expected, they were set far back inland and we were almost ashore before we knew it.

Charlie saw the beach just ahead and bellowed down the companionway: "Go astern! Astern, you fool! We're in the breakers!"

"I am going astern!" I bellowed back. Then I waited for the crash with bitter calm. But slowly the *Sirocco* backed off, the engine for once going madly instead of missing. It was a narrow shave. We were practically on top of the line of breakers before they could be seen in the darkness.

We let go anchor without having the least idea of our position, beyond the fact that it was an exceptionally bad one. We pitched and heaved there all night, exposed to the wind and sea. In the morning we were surprised to find the *Sirocco* lying in the center of the fairway, only a few yards from the wharf.

We were four days at Coff's Harbor waiting for the weather to break. The harbor is a death trap in the southeast, being fully exposed to the fury of the sea.

For thirty-six hours we lay to with two anchors out and the engine running as a stand-by in case the cables parted. Most of the time was spent trying to contrive a means of making the wretched forward hatch watertight by nailing pieces of rubber round the coaming.

At last the weather broke. On a fine sunny day we left Coff's Harbor hoping never to see the place again. A fair wind was blowing from the southeast and the *Sirocco* scudded along at seven knots with as little motion as if tied alongside a wharf. If the wind held we hoped to make Brisbane the following day. Beyond Brisbane lay the sheltered waters of the Great Barrier Reef, where we could cruise along without fear of being caught by sudden gales. We had to choose our weather carefully. The *Sirocco* was far too small and unseaworthy to take chances.

During the afternoon the engine broke down, but even without it the ship made good speed. When the sun went down the wind eased a little but still kept the sails full. This was the first pleasant night we had spent at sea. We were able to leave the hatches open and sleep in the cabin without being half-suffocated by oil fumes. But it was such a perfect night, so warm and starlit, that I took my bedding on deck and for an hour or so watched the moon drift across the sky.

With the engine practically out of comission there was little chance of our making Brisbane. A cylinder was cracked and the oil pump broken; it could only be run for a few minutes at a time, as it then became red hot. A glance at the chart showed that the Richmont River, about eighty miles below Brisbane, was the most likely place to have it repaired. The Sailing Directions stated that the bar over the river was very dangerous at times and that the passage was narrow but had plenty of water on it.

I had never seen a bar and had no idea what it was like. When, at daybreak next morning, the Dook pointed ashore and said he thought that must be the bar, I could scarcely believe it. Three enormous lines of raging breakers lay ahead, bursting in mountainous foam. There was supposed to be a passage somewhere through them but the lines of surf looked uniformly unbroken.

In consternation we studied the Sailing Directions, hoping there was some mistake. There was no mistake. We were supposed to sail through those breakers!

"What's that signal on the flagpole ashore?" asked Charlie anxiously.

The Dook trained his glasses on it. "A black ball," he said. "Where's the code book?"

We looked it up. "Black ball," it read. "Do not attempt entrance. Bar dangerous."

"We've got to go in," I said. "We can't go on to Brisbane with a busted engine."

We started up the engine and went in closer but could not find the other beacon. The Dook said that if we trailed a length of grass rope out astern it would keep us from broaching to. He had read of this old trick of the days when sailing ships had to cross bars, and it was lucky he had.

All hatches were battened down and lashed. The *Sirocco* crept up towards a spot in the line that seemed to have a slightly smaller surf.

It was a tense moment when we reached the first line of breakers. Luckily, it was smaller than usual, and just then, through the glasses, Charlie picked up the second beacon, far over on the port side. I gave the ship full speed ahead and the Dook swung her over to get the two beacons in line. He barely managed to straighten her up when the second breaker caught us and flung the ship onward in a mad rush, with her stern high out of the water, bow down and rudder useless, the rope astern saving us from making the swerving broach that capsizes ships, small and large.

In the middle of the maelstrom of colossal breakers, the steering gear broke! The Dook promptly let go of the useless wheel and jumped to the short stump of tiller aft, using all his strength to bring her stern on to the surf. He undoubtedly saved us from crashing into the breakwater on the port side.

There were seven lines of breakers on the bar that day, the middle ones much larger than the others. By great good luck only one breaker came aboard. It was a big one. It swept over the deck into the wheelhouse and submerged everything, filling the Dook's long sea boots right to the brim. Intent on the arduous business of steering with a tiller about eight inches long, the Dook yelled frantically to Charlie to come and pull them off.

Even in those tense moments it was comical to see Trelawney sitting braced on the deck in running water, clutching the tiller in both hands, with his left leg stuck up in the air while Charlie heaved at the waterlogged sea boot.

With what relief we sailed into the calm water of the Richmont River! It was the merest fluke that we ever crossed that bar. Fool's luck, according to the pilot, who was waiting on the wharf to inform us of this fact among others of a more personal nature.

That day was devoted to some really serious drinking, and I awoke next morning to see one George, a youthful fisherman who had joined us at some indefinite period during the night, sleeping wheezily on the cabin floor. Next to him lay Frank, the convivial town-policeman, using as a pillow a parcel containing three lobsters. These were immediately turned over to Charlie to convert into a curry for breakfast.

The journey from Richmont River to Brisbane was so good that I don't remember many details of it. The engine gave no trouble. The sea was calm, the weather fine and warm. No one was sick and the *Sirocco* flew along with a bone in her teeth.

It is forty miles from the mouth of the Brisbane River to the city, all against a strong current, and it was dark before we made fast to someone's nicely painted boat mooring.

With more optimism than judgment, I had calculated on a week for the voyage from Sydney to Brisbane. It had taken us a month and I felt as though we had sailed halfway round the world instead of about six hundred miles.

We decided to stay a week or so in Brisbane to have the engine thoroughly overhauled. Brisbane is an uncomfortable city in the summer. The heat is stifling and even on the hottest day the citizens go about dressed in somber, heavy black clothes, which gives a new arrival the impression of having been set down in the midst of an undertakers' convention. If, however, the stranger ventures to don tropical garb, he instantly becomes an object of curiosity. The natives will stare at him in astonishment and even follow him around.

The Dook found in the heat a long desired opportunity to wear the new khaki pith helmet he had purchased in Sydney. But the unusual headgear attracted such attention that a bunch of urchins collected at his heels and followed him along the street, shouting: "Shot any tigers today, mister?" "Hey, mister, where's yer helephunt?" "Gawd's truth! 'E's come out without 'is gun." "Look at 'is 'at, will yer."

He returned to the ship in great confusion, and with the topee wrapped up in a brown paper parcel.

While we were in Brisbane, the Dook received an advance on his estate from his lawyers in Sydney, and this he insisted on placing at the ship's disposal. Not that anyone tried to prevent him. We were much too hungry. He also bought a new jib, to replace the one blown out off Coff's Harbor.

Finally we chose a fine day and sailed. A hundred miles north of Brisbane we came to a large island, Great Sandy. The scenery was beautiful on the waters between this island and the mainland. Little inlets, their gently rolling banks matted with gorgeous wildflowers in full bloom, sent forth gusts of perfume and offered a constant speculation as to what lay beyond. To the left, on the mainland, the country was flat, divided by little streams thickly sown with bright green water lilies.

In the late afternoon we were off the Mary River, and as the chart showed a small township just inside the mouth, I decided to anchor there for the night. On entering the river, however, we found the town had disappeared! There was no sign of human habitation, let alone a town.

Mystified, we sailed up and down the stream to look for it. The chart even gave the names of the principal streets. Having little more faith in the Dook's navigation than in my own, I thought we might be in the wrong river. But another look at the chart proved this was impossible. The only other river in the vicinity, the Burnett, lay many miles to the north and was quite thickly populated.

So we slept at anchor off that nonexistent town and at dusk the following day made Bundaberg, on the Burnett River. Here the mystery of the missing town was explained. It had been the proposed site for a new town and somewhat prematurely had been marked in detail on all charts and Sailing Directions. That was as near as it ever came to civic glory.

It was the annual Show Week in Bundaberg, and the town was in the throes of carnival excitement. Tall, bearded sheepmen from the western districts, in wide-brimmed hats and elastic-sided boots, rode through the streets on fine-looking horses. Others, with faces scorched by the sun to the color of a walnut, strolled about with the stiff gait of men unaccustomed to being out of the saddle, or gathered in circles to discuss the coming rodeo events.

Posters and placards decorated every shop window, announcing that the Tallest Man in the World had arrived in town, also the Fattest Lady and Zimmo the Limbless Wonder. The Chinese Giant was there too. Other posters said that Ned Wirth of Coonabarabran, the best rider in the world, had undertaken to remain on the back of Curly Bell's famous horse, The Devil, for three minutes, despite Curly's assertion on the same posters that no one in the world could do that.

Each man, the announcement continued, had bet heavily on the result and everyone was urged to turn up and see the battle. Forty Rounds of Boxing was to be an added attraction.

We decided to see Ned in action. The price of admission, two shillings, nearly deterred us, but it was worth it, though the big bet was obviously a put-up job. You will never see finer horsemanship than in these small rodeos in "out back" North Queensland towns.

The Forty Rounds of Boxing lacked in quality what they supplied in quantity, though the exponents all seemed consumed with the desire to inflict as much damage as possible in the shortest space of time. Several young men stepped into the ring and offered to take on anyone of their own weight. Actually, they were third-rate "pugs" engaged by Curly Bell to insure some competition. He would hold up a boxing glove and offer three pounds to anyone in the crowd who could beat the challenger and one pound to anyone able to stay three rounds.

Rex sat up and nudged me in the ribs. "It's a cinch!" he whispered urgently. "Money from home! Take him on, Skipper. Think what we could do with five pounds!"

I stared at him. "You're mad," I said coldly. "Take him on yourself."

"I would if I was his weight. And you're a boxer. Think of that cash! I'll tell you what I'll do—I'll second you!"

In spite of this added inducement I still managed to restrain myself. But as there were no takers and the offer was repeated, I began to think about it. Five pounds was wealth at the time. My only pair of shoes let water in through the soles; food was scarce, and we needed some oil for the engine. So I climbed into the ring.

Curly was surprised and suspicious. He probably suspected I might be some professional fighter out for a bit of easy money, but then he must have decided I did not look like one, for he smiled and offered me a dirty pair of shorts. When I declined those in the toughest and most contemptuous manner I could manage, his suspicions were aroused again and he went into a whispered conference with Cowper. That gentleman gave me a nasty look, spat on the ground and nodded.

The ring was cleared and time called. My opponent advanced, as I thought, to observe the ancient boxing tradition of shaking a man's hand before trying to knock his head off.

Instead, he knocked me flat with a right-hand swing. I stayed down for the count of seven, groggily conscious of having been foully wronged, then got to my feet and somehow managed to last out the round.

Rex helped me to my corner and, under the impression that he was reviving me, began to slap a wet towel over my face so that I could hardly breathe.

Encouraged by the hisses and boos of the crowd, I was lusting for bloody revenge at the call of "Time!" Cowper jumped right across the ring. I missed his chin, but the lacing of my glove made a gash over his eye which began to bleed copiously.

When you know the crowd is with you, it helps. I tore into him with everything but the kitchen stove. Outweighed ten pounds and with a badly cut eye, Cowper must have decided that I looked like lasting the distance, as he retired at the end of the second round to attend to the eye.

Every one seemed pleased except Curly. Rex collected the five pounds on my behalf and stood fingering them as I washed a couple of cuts.

"Nice work," he said. "Nice work. Didn't I tell you it was a cinch? I suppose you wouldn't mind lending me a couple of pounds out of this?" I said I certainly would mind. "I shed blood for that money. All you did was try to smother me!"

En route to Gladstone, our next port of call, we began to observe the first signs of the Great Barrier Reef. At low water, away over the starboard hand, the surf could be seen breaking in a rumbling foam on several patches of exposed reef near Breaksea Spit. As we proceeded, running fair before a light southeasterner with topsail set and all sails drawn taut, small tropical islands showed up on the starboard horizon and quickly dropped astern. There was no following swell and the *Sirocco,* lying slightly over to port, flew along with hardly a movement to tell that she was at sea.

Gladstone is a small fishing town with an excellent harbor and a fine pastoral setting. A large meat-packing house brings in the overseas vessels for cargoes to England. The town is chiefly remarkable for its unique lighthouse keeper, a woman affectionately and widely known as "The Captain." She is old and bent and incredibly wrinkled, and has as fine a command of sulphurous language as has her father, a shellback skipper of the "eighties" must have possessed. She wears an enormous pair of gum sea boots and drinks vast quantities of whisky and beer, and some say that she can spit in a seagull's eye at twenty yards in a strong wind. The town is rightly proud of her.

Leaving Gladstone, we passed through "The Narrows" to Rockhampton, which we wanted to visit because Rex, who had once been there, described the town and its ladies in glowing terms.

On arriving at Rockhampton, my first action was to dispatch an acidulous telegram to the Sydney agent who sold us our engine. It had never ceased to give trouble since its installation, and I demanded service. His reply stated that he would send a man to Rockhampton in a fortnight to inspect it. We waited the two weeks but it was three before he arrived.

During our enforced stay in that pleasant town of forty thousand souls, the *Sirocco* achieved much unsought notoriety as a result of my incarceration for riotous behavior in Greek Joe's, a restaurant run as a blind for that eminent Australian game, two-up. The entire responsibility for this is to be laid at the door of two journalists on the staff of a local paper. In Greek Joe's, one of the journalists, who had once been a professional boxer, got into a brawl with a notorious bruiser known as Kid Lozatti and received such brutal treatment that, forgetting my cherished role as spectator, I plunged into the fray. The other journalist and I were both arrested. A fine of four pounds each was inflicted, which, needless to say, we were unable to pay.

"In that case, seven days," said the magistrate.

The Dook arrived as we were being marched off to the cell and caused a mild sensation and some laughter in court by offering his personal note of hand for the amount.

Thus incarcerated, my friend and I languished for two days before I raised the money to pay our fines.

An agreeable surprise awaited me at the Rockhampton bank. Before leaving New Guinea, I had deposited a parcel of gold dust weighing about thirty ounces at the bank there and had been advanced what was estimated to be the approximate value in cash. Investigating every conceivable means of raising some money in Rockhampton, I had remembered it and sent for any small amount that might remain to my credit in New Guinea.

Expecting two or three pounds at the most, I could hardly believe it when thirty pounds arrived. It was a joyful moment, and when, the very next day, a further fifty pounds came from Ireland as a birthday gift from my father, our troubles seemed never to have existed.

The eighty pounds seemed a fortune large enough to insure our reaching New Guinea in comfort, without the continual anxiety of wondering where the next meal was coming from—if it was coming. The future looked bright.

The agent's representative arrived from Sydney about this time and overhauled the engine. To test it, we invited the entire cast of that drama of thwarted passion entitled "Married to the Wrong Man" for a picnic upon the river.

I understand the engine behaved exceptionally well.

During the next few days we all lived like princes, feasting richly and drinking deeply, but at last departure could be delayed no longer and the Dook flew the blue peter at the masthead. However, we left Rockhampton under something of a cloud. I had the ill luck to be in Greek Joe's when the place was raided and had escaped another arrest only by taking to my heels.

A breeze fragrant with the scent of flowers and budding trees, hardly strong enough to disturb the clear blue water lying placid as a lake, blew offshore with the first gleamings of dawn. In the night we had made good way under power and sail and now stood off Port Clinton. Later in the morning the breeze freshened, changing over to the southeast, and with topsail set and no sea to break her way, the *Sirocco* scudded along at eight knots.

In the late afternoon the anchor was let go over a coral reef in five fathoms of crystal-clear water in the lee of Percy Island, fifty yards from a white beach with a fringe of graceful coconut trees. While we stowed all gear and got things shipshape, Charlie prepared a meal.

We ate on deck, watching the setting sun paint the sky a dazzling mass of color. The warm evening, the sound of tiny waves rippling along the beach, the grove of coconut trees, looking, in the peculiar bronze light of sunset, like old tapestries, all formed an unforgettably beautiful scene, and the fragrant land breeze completed the enchantment. A little later, when the moon rose, we fell asleep on deck, wrapped in the deep, satisfying slumber that comes from complete weariness.

Next morning we rowed ashore in the dinghy and drank the milk of many green coconuts for breakfast, taking a dozen back on board for future use. Then, keeping a careful lookout for sharks, we dived and swam in the inviting blue waters near the beach.

None of us wanted to leave Percy Island. It is one of the loveliest islands I have ever seen. It was fascinating to study the swarming marine life left in the little reef pools at low tide. I never tired of swimming over the reef with a pair of pearl-diving goggles, examining the brilliantly colored marine growths and the many strange, shimmeringly toned fish.

Turtles abounded. It was the egg-laying season and we would find the females in the early morning ponderously waddling back to the water after a night spent laying a clutch of two hundred or more round white eggs like golf balls.

Turtle riding is a lot of fun. The statement of de Rougemount, in his chronicles, that the coastal waters of Austra-

lia were inhabited by great turtles half the size of a ship's
boat, on the backs of which the aborigines rode for sport,
was hailed with laughter as the journalism of a sensationalist. But we had many a race.

You get on the female's back and hold her at front and
rear. She puts down her head and starts for the waters of
the lagoon. On the beach the going is easy, but once your
mount enters the water, it is a different matter. At first you
find you have to let go and rise to the surface as soon as she
dives, but after a while you learn the knack of holding your
steed's head up in a certain way so that she is unable to
dive, and then comes the real fun of turtle riding. The excit-
ed animals swim about on the surface of the lagoon, trying
to unseat you, and you can steer in any direction you wish.

After several days of this idyllic existence we pushed on
to Cumberland Island, the commencement of the beautiful
Whitsunday Island group. We anchored every night in the
reef, as the many hidden and uncharted reefs made navigation difficult even during the day.

In these dangerous waters, the Dook showed his mettle
as a navigator. He sweated nearly as much over his charts
as I did over the engine and steered us safely through the
reefs with only one or two keel scrapings.

Occasionally we passed over coral reefs, visible through
eight or ten fathoms of pellucid water. Where the reefs had
less water covering them, many more hues than you see in a
peacock's tail gleamed from the depths. While the *Sirocco*
threaded her way through narrow passages, we lay for
hours on the deck gazing in quiet rapture at the little island
pyramids that rose from the sea. Farther out, stretching as
far as the eye could see, a long booming line of cottony
white breakers marked the outer wall of the Great Barrier
Reef, unique natural wonder of the world.

The southeast trades made sailing a delight in these waters. We soon came to Dent Island and the ship was hove to
while Charlie and I went ashore to try to obtain some much-
needed tobacco from the lighthouse keeper. There were
only two men on the island. The life task of these individ-
uals was to keep their light burning night and day. At six-

month intervals the lighthouse tender would call at the island with supplies, making the one exciting incident in the monotonous routine of their lives.

There being no anchorage off Dent Island, our arrival was something of a sensation. The two hermits' first question was whether we could spare them a little tobacco, as the supply ship was overdue and they had been without a smoke for two weeks.

Even before we reached their quarters, it was apparent there was a strong hostility between those two. As though their dreary loneliness were not enough, they hated each other bitterly and we soon discovered that no unnecessary word ever passed between them. They had been living like that for two years and the situation was so strained that we got under way again as soon as possible.

The course some distance northwards of Dent Island was safe and well charted, with none of those outcrops of living coral that make most parts of the barrier waters such a nightmare to navigators.

A subtropical climate and a delightful situation and harbor make Townsville one of the most attractive ports on the Australian coast. The town itself is well planned, with long avenues of tropical palms and shrubs running down the center of the main street, giving a bright and pleasing air to the business section.

On the outskirts of the town, overlooking the bay, a great shaggy bluff rises like a fortress sheer into the sky. Inside the river mouth, a number of launches and small ketches lay at moorings, the latter mainly engaged in the bêche-de-mer and Trochus-shell fishing industry.

In reaching Townsville, we had completed nearly half our journey. It was five months since we had left Sydney on a voyage planned for about two months. However, we were now quite reckless of time.

Cairns was to be the next port of call. Here we were to pick up two drums of a special fuel oil ordered from Sydney, but we had some slight difficulty in persuading the agent to hand them over to us. He had some impractical notion about our paying cash for them, but I finally persuaded him to charge them to our account. Not that we had one, of course, but that was a chance the agent had to take.

Charlie left the ship here to visit Forsythe, his one-time partner in the ownership of the *Sirocco,* who was living on Hinchinbrook Island a few miles north. We arranged to pick him up on our way through the Hinchinbrook Passage to Cairns.

Leaving Townsville, we dropped anchor the same night in the lee of Hinchinbrook Island, and the following morning entered the passage.

Inside, it was as beautiful as the journey through the Whitsundays. The passage was narrower and deeper, however; at times we might almost have been in the smaller fjords of Norway. The bows sliced into water lying placid as a mirror. The echoed throb of the engine resounded with a muffled boom from the steep green hills on both sides, and the many emerald-like islets, thick with tropical fruit trees and palms, nestling about larger islands made this passage a veritable trip through Paradise.

In the afternoon we hove to in a small bay at the far end of the main island. Charlie and Forsythe came out in a dinghy to meet us and lead the way to an anchorage.

Timing our arrival at Cairns for daylight the following morning, we left Forsythe's anchorage at midnight. We sailed slowly out of the bay, steering by the beam of a powerful torch, with Forsythe piloting us to the mouth of the passage. Wishing us luck, he jumped into his dinghy and was instantly swallowed up by the dark astern as the *Sirocco* slipped silently forward, heeling over slightly to a gentle breeze blowing from the southeast.

Still following the Queensland coast, we were now heading northwest, with the southeast trade blowing dead astern. The mainsheet was out to its fullest extent, the knot at the end fast in the block, while the headsails forward flapped uselessly on the stays. But the *Sirocco* loved a stern wind and we were making better than eight knots as we turned the long lines of beacons marking the narrow channel into the lovely little harbor of Cairns. In a day or so we made for Cooktown, one hundred miles farther north. It was the last port of call on the Australian coast before the severe test of the voyage across the Coral Sea to New Guinea. We would have to stop to take aboard provisions, water, et cetera, and try to put the *Sirocco* in her best shape to meet any of the dread cyclones for which the Coral Sea is notorious.

On the way we called in at Restoration Island out of pure curiosity. I wanted to see the island which had once been the salvation of Bligh and his men of the *Bounty* a month after they had been turned adrift in their twenty-three-foot boat near Tahiti.

The island has a high hill with forest to the water's edge and one beautiful sheltered sandy beach, without doubt the one on which Bligh and his starving men landed.

We swam in the lagoon and then lay on the beach trying to recapture in imagination the feelings of those men as they saw the aborigines in all their war paint, shouting and waving their spears only a short distance away, and the dread misgivings in each heart as they launched their tiny boat once more and sailed off to what must have seemed certain death.

We left Restoration in the late afternoon, in time to reach Cooktown early next morning. Almost immediately we had a number of curious visitors; they were rather more welcome than the usual type, however. In prodigious numbers goats ambled onto the pier and stared down at us. It was a sign from above. Meat was scarce and had obviously been sent down to us by heaven in our need.

With unerring aim Charlie swung a lasso. A fine young billy thudded onto the deck with a loud and startled bleat. He was tied up and spirited below into the galley.

For the next couple of days we worked hard to get the *Sirocco* in shape for the Coral Sea crossing, calking the decks and topsides, resplicing the running gear, getting the sea anchors ready, et cetera, until she was as seaworthy as she would ever be.

At four the next morning the alarm rang and sent a shiver of anticipation down my spine. We tumbled out in the dark and on deck found a fresh southeasterly blowing. A good sign, this, and soon we had it aft of the beam, heeling us over as we headed for Cook's Passage, sixty miles away. This is the opening to the Great Barrier Reef through which that prince of navigators, Captain Cook, sailed his gallant little *Endeavour* over a century and a half ago. We could see the passage in the distance, with lines of heavy combers breaking on both sides of the reef, just as Cook must have seen it in 1770.

As we approached the outer barrier, the southeasterly had freshened so much, with a fast-rising sea, that we decided to anchor at Lizard Island, only a few miles from Cook's Passage, and wait for the weather to improve.

As we left Lizard Island, from my position high up in the crosstrees I could follow the breaking combers on the Great Barrier Reef, stretching away north and south as far as the eye could see.

Ahead a rolling swell was coming in through the passage leading to the Coral Sea, a great blue expanse stretching away to the horizon.

As I looked down at the tiny little splinter of a boat below me, I wondered when we would see land again—if we were lucky enough to see it!

By night we had logged good time in spite of the seas. Provided she had sailing wind, the *Sirocco* was never troubled by a hard sea; we were the ones who were troubled— she just dived through the waves like a porpoise and anyone who had to go on deck for a moment was soaked to the skin.

The waves were mounting all the time and as the hours went by I didn't at all like the looks of the sky. The sun was no longer to be seen and black clouds were racing up from the northeast. Then a bilge sounding disclosed the alarming fact that we were making water faster than we should have been. It was even beginning to seep through the cabin floor, making the ship very sluggish and necessitating a watch of hard pumping.

After that the ship handled a little more easily. By this time, it was well on into the night and we were all feeling pretty miserable. I had crawled through the engine room to the cabin to lie down, but with all the hatches closed tight, it was, as usual, filled with sickly oil fumes from the engine. There was another and stronger odor mingling with the smell of oil, but I didn't take the trouble to investigate its cause.

That night and the succeeding ones, the four of us were huddled together like sheep in the tiny wheelhouse aft. It was the only fairly dry spot on board, and if we managed to snatch an hour's uninterrupted sleep, we were lucky. Every now and then some part of the running gear or a halyard would snap. Then the two off watch would have to get out to splice it up. Once the main backstay wore through. While it was being repaired we trembled in fear that the mast might go. No one went on deck without a rope first being tied around his middle.

Since leaving Lizard Island we had had only some biscuits to eat and were feeling the need of something hot. My face was covered with a thick layer of hardened salt and my mouth tasted ghastly.

Charlie and Rex went below and managed to get the stove warm enough to make some hot chocolate, a noble feat, for by this time the strong smell I had noticed the previous day was quite overwhelming and made the cabin and galley uninhabitable for more than a few minutes at a time. One would hold the pot while the other one came up to be sick and every few minutes a sea would force its way through the forward hatch and put the stove out. We drank the cocoa scalding hot and immediately life assumed a more cheerful aspect.

In the late noon it was blowing half a gale, with seas running so high that we were shipping every second one green. The ship was leaking so badly now that our situation was critical. Water was pouring in through the counter like a faucet. It looked as though the old ship might go to pieces any minute, although any possible sail had been eased off to relieve the strain on her timbers.

We had only the vaguest notion of our position. With the ship standing on beam ends as she had been doing, it had been impossible to take an observation. Even now she was still leaking badly and the constant pumping had worn us out. With no food except biscuits and a few apples, I was feeling so weak that my half-hour turn at the bilge pump left me ready to drop. It was the same with the others.

That day passed, and another. At the point of exhaustion we struggled through the third night, pumping continuously, dimly hearing the thud, smash and crash of the angry waves and the constant creaking of the working timbers.

Morning broke, still gray and cloudy, and found us looking anxiously out to starboard for a sight of land. I knew we should be fetching the southwestern promontory of the Gulf of Papua. I also knew—only too well—that if we missed it, we should be lost. Beyond lay the Arafura Sea and we had no chart of it!

Another night of driving before that fierce, howling gale, with no knowledge of the reef-studded waters ahead, would mean certain disaster and equally certain death.

We had reached that semi-lethargic state of exhaustion when nothing matters much—the storm seemed to have been screaming around us forever, although each hour, as it passed, seemed an age.

Then, dimly—only a glimpse at first—land was sighted far over on the starboard. It was salvation. We just pointed at it without even trying to speak.

Then began the perilous business of bearing in to reach it. Each time we got beam on, in an attempt to wear ship, the seas would crash over us again and again. Slowly, very slowly, the land grew more distinct as we played touch and run with the gale. We would run before a sea, then quickly swing the ship's nose landwards in its trough and try to run before the next sea caught us.

It was late afternoon before we knew for certain we would make the shore before dark. At dusk the anchor was let go off a sandy cover dotted with coconut palms. Exhausted, completely worn out, we dropped to sleep in the wheelhouse there and then. We were not even sure this land was New Guinea and we didn't care much. It was land—that was enough. We were safe from the storm.

As I dropped off to sleep, I remember thinking that it

would be unfortunate if, after all our trials, a bunch of Papuans were to come out during the night and collect our heads as trophies as is still their playful little custom in some parts of the vast island.

The morning was well advanced when I roused myself and came on deck. The first thing I saw was two large canoes circling slowly some distance off. We hailed them and they approached within ten yards. There the crews of men, women and children backed water and sat staring at us silently. They made no reply when we spoke to them, but sat with paddles in hand as though ready to fly back whence they had come.

They had great mops of fuzzy dark brown hair and all were naked except for loincloths made of what appeared to be the soft bark of a tree. The men were fierce-looking, with long, thin pieces of bone, about four or five inches in length, stuck through their nostrils.

I tried them out in the Motuan language, of which I had a smattering, and also in pidgin English, but none of them seemed to understand. After a lot of persuasion and coaxing they finally brought their canoes alongside. We were soon doing a brisk trade.

I took a revolver and we made a short visit to the shore. They seemed friendly enough, but I had heard many tales about deserted ships being found in the Papuan Gulf with their crews in excellent health apart from the fact that their heads were missing. Close to the beach there was a village of about fifty thatched dwellings, all built on wooden piles nestling close under a cliff and surrounded by a plantation of coconut palms.

We bought a young pig, arranged for it to be roasted, and decided to anchor offshore meanwhile and get the ship in shape. When the mainhatch was slid back, the smell which had been bottled up inside for days rose in an overpowering cloud that nearly knocked me down. Tying a handkerchief over my nose, I went below and finally located the cause—a bucket of fish in the last stages of decay which we had dynamited at Lizard Island and forgotten.

The news of our arrival must have spread rapidly, the

tourists flocked in from all sides to have a look at us. Among these came one Inamotu, a cheerful savage who spoke good pidgin English. He had a wide grin, a plausible manner and a full and complete knowledge of everything under the sun. He announced at once with becoming modesty that there was no better pilot in the entire world than himself, and with these few words he hired himself and took complete charge of the situation.

We found him a great help. We had many articles on board which made good trade: fishhooks, a few odd knives, some wet matches which soon dried out in the sun, and a few old hats. With these, Inamotu was able to buy native foods much cheaper than we could. Naturally, he pocketed a small commission of two or three hundred percent but even at that we found we still saved on the deal.

At the end of three days the storm had nearly blown itself out. It was settling down to a steady southerly now, so we left the village, taking Inamotu as pilot. Again the wind was right on our bow and blew without cessation as we fought our way against it along the coast toward Port Moresby.

We were only a couple of days from Port Moresby, near the village of Bukausip, when tragedy struck. Today, long after the events occurred, the details of that ghastly day are as vivid in my mind as if they had happened yesterday.

As the *Sirocco* lay anchored in Bukausip Bay, the wind came up with the swift fury of a hurricane. We were ashore at the time but had seen it coming, looming up from the horizon until the whole sky was like one great black cloud. The wind caught us while we were rowing out to the *Sirocco* half a mile offshore. Rex and I were at the oars and it took all our combined strength to keep the dinghy from being blown back before we could get a rope fast to the ship.

On board, I immediately got the other anchor out and the engine started. The gale rose so quickly that its fury was on us before we were aware of it. In spite of the twin anchors and the engine full ahead we were dragging slowly and surely towards the reef.

Then the wind seemed to come from all directions all at once. The ship began to swing in a circle, slowly at first but soon so fast that the anchor chains were twisted. A cyclone!

"Gobu!" shouted Inamotu. "Gobu! Gobu!"

We worked like demons, trying to clear the twisting anchor chains. It was useless; they were hopelessly gnarled together.

"Get sail on her!"

We jumped to the halyards and managed to set one headsail. Then what I had feared happened. The twisted chains snapped, one within a few seconds of the other.

We were being driven fast onto the reef.

The engine was useless against the force of the gale, but within a few yards of the jagged coral the jib filled with wind and we swung off to safety. I wish now that we would have piled up on those rocks. The ship would have been lost, but that would have been nothing to what afterwards happened,

Again we found ourselves running before a gale—a gale which had not yet reached its full force, but still blew us along under headsails like a paper ship.

Inamotu was at the helm when there came a sudden sharp scrape on the bottom. I rushed to the side and saw the reef, dark and ominous under us, as the ship struck for the second time—running far up on it as the shock snapped the topmast off like a match and brought the broken spar crashing down on the deck.

I knew at once it was the *Sirocco*'s death blow. Sickeningly, the bottom was torn out of her as she ground over the reef to lie at length heeled far over.

"Coral niggerhead!" shouted Rex. "Sticking right through her! Half full of water!"

"Get the dinghy into the water!" I yelled back, and clambered below to see the great jagged piece of coral protruding through her bilge.

Stuffing a revolver and the ship's papers into my pocket, I clawed my way on deck again. The dinghy had just been slid into the water on the lee side. I saw a great wave take it up, then crash it back against the ship's side, smashing in its bow like an eggshell. It still floated, but I knew it would never hold five of us. And we were five or more miles from land!

"Dook, get the ax! I'll cut the mast down, then you, Charlie and Rex take the dinghy. Inamotu and I will try to swim the mast ashore!"

But events did not work out that way. Just then the boat heeled farther over, the heavy boom swung across the deck and I caught its full impact in the middle of my back. Only dimly do I remember hitting the water.

I revived to find myself with Rex and Charlie being blown ashore in the dinghy. The oars were lost but Charlie was keeping the boat stern on to the seas with one of the seats. I looked back but of the *Sirocco* there was no sight; she had either broken up or sunk. I tried to sit up but found myself partially paralyzed on the left side as a result of the blow from the boom.

"The Dook?" I asked.

"The last I saw of him he'd just cut down the mast," said Charlie. "He dived in and helped us haul you into the dinghy. You were unconscious. Then Inamotu pulled him back to the *Sirocco* with a rope and they started cutting the mast down."

We never saw him again.

The dinghy was blown ashore onto a beach and we were lucky enough to find a village nearby. I immediately sent for the chief and asked that one of his large seagoing canoes put out to save the two men. The chief shook his head and said that it was impossible in such a sea. I produced my revolver, shoved it hard into the pit of his stomach and said the canoe was going in any sort of sea.

But it was no use. All the men of the village tried time and time again to launch it but each time the sea and wind drove the ten strong paddlers back, until finally the outrigger broke. We tried the only other canoe, but the same thing happened. No canoe could live in such a sea. Fires were lighted all along the beach and we watched throughout the night. Before dawn, Inamotu was washed up, drowned. I worked on him for an hour, but the poor fellow was beyond all help.

In the morning the gale had subsided enough to allow the two repaired canoes to be launched and we began a far and wide search until dark forced us to give up and return, hearts heavy with grief.

We never even found the Dook's body. The *Sirocco's* bones and his scattered over a coral reef in the South Seas, as are the bones of many a gallant ship and fine man, though never a finer man than he.

In the peace and quiet of port, old sailors spin their yarns, telling tales of the southern seas. How once they sailed into the still, blue lagoon, beached their boat on the gleaming sand, and walked beneath the coconut palms and lovely tropic vines to the native village.

But always, ever present behind the brightness of this picture, there lay a gloomy shadow—the shadow of the coral. To the ancient mariners it was no thing of beauty. It was a horror and a nightmare, worse dreaded than the iceberg or the fog of the northern seas.

Today the lure of the beautiful, treacherous coral seas still extracts a heavy price from those who seek adventure. We found it so.

EDITOR'S NOTE: *Beam Ends* met with very respectable reviews and a good public response. It was far from a best seller; Flynn was not that renowned in 1937 and a nonfiction account of a sailing trip would find only a limited market anyway. Critics noted that it was well written and Flynn was pleased with the reaction. However, there were a few Australians who were not pleased, and wrote letters saying that this and that was not true, particularly as it pertained to their own experiences with the author. The light-hearted author dealt with them in his usual manner, either by completely ignoring their letters or by sending an autographed portrait. *Beam Ends* has a factual basis but it is obviously juiced up with some dramatic elaboration, mostly in the beginning and end. His claim that he did not know how he acquired the boat is poppycock—it was bought for him by his mother—and the climax, in which the old *Sirocco* sinks after a violent storm is sheer invention. Presumably Flynn had forgotten that he gave an account of the vessel's activities in his column for the *Sydney Bulletin* a couple of years after he sold her. As for his friend Trelawney Adams—"Dook"—he would continue to be involved with Flynn in various New Guinea experiences and he would live for more than thirty years beyond his invented demise in *Beam Ends*.

PART THREE

Showdown

ERROL FLYNN'S SECOND book was published in 1946 (Sheridan House, New York). He gave it the rather vague title of *Showdown*, which probably did little to capture the imagination of the public. The book met with little response from either the public or the critics. The fact that he was a celebrated Hollywood personality no doubt helped sell a number of copies but it also worked against him on the more serious level. How could such a hedonistic movie star be capable of writing anything worth reading? Already the image was undermining whatever hopes Flynn had of being taken as a man of artistic, intellectual substance.

Showdown is a novel but it is clearly autobiographical—almost as much so as *Beam Ends* or *My Wicked, Wicked Ways,* both of which may be regarded as autobiographies with many of the earmarks of novels. All three books blend facts with fiction. The main character of *Showdown* is a handsome young Irishman named Shamus O'Thames, who adventures around New Guinea in exactly the same years that Flynn was there. His experiences as a rather romantic-minded drifter are quite like those of the author. He lives by his wits and bluffs his way. And it is in those sections of *Showdown* where Flynn talks directly about Shamus that the book most comes alive and reveals not only a talent for writing but some interesting insights into the mind of the author and into the lifestyle of that corner of the world some fifty years ago.

Shamus O'Thames is the product of a good British background, with some of his education received in the higher levels of English academe, and he has a fascination with the beauty of women. His manners are courtly, even a little Chesterfieldian, and his notions of gallantry and idealism are Byronic. He is very much the individual, certainly not a part of the mainstream of life, and perhaps a bit of a lost soul. In short, Shamus sounds a lot like young Errol. So do some of his adventures:

AT RABAUL HE jumped ship and, with a few pounds in his pocket, set out to satisfy his appetite for the South Seas in an attempt to swallow all of Melanesia at a sitting. Six years had passed since then. He had stoked on tramp steamers from the Bismarck Archipelago to the New Hebrides. He had bought wood carvings on Iwa to sell to government recruits at Port Moresby, had joined a gold-hunting party on Woodlark, and netted ten pounds for his share of their scant find made before natives drove them off; he had handled the broad wooden clubs and carved and painted ebony shields of the Trobriands and learned there how to use the gall of a certain fish to poison arrowheads. He had solved the mysterious question of the "bush telegraph" by teaching himself to read the signals pounded on drums, which can send a message to distant natives on New Guinea almost as fast as modern telegraph. On Goodenough Island he had learned, at the cost of a month's lameness, how natives discourage those who would track them by placing tiny foot spears in their trails. Along the Gulf of Papua he had avoided losing his head to the Kuku Kuku only by lying almost motionless in a spot in the jungle for two days. He had learned from natives how to spend incredibly long minutes submerged and how to kill fish, not with a fishing line, but under water. Along the Fly River he had seen a native commit suicide by climbing to the top of a coconut tree and flinging himself, head downwards, to the ground. At Wedau, he had watched nursing women fish by leaning over a stream and milking their breasts into the water, then quietly scooping up with a hand net the little fish that rose to the cloudy bait. He felt he had seen something of that which he had sought.

Especially fitted for nothing but ready for anything, he had found his chance to make a stake when on Goodenough

Island he had been unexpectedly offered the opportunity to run a coconut plantation. He had just landed there broke on a tramp schooner when he encountered a worried-looking white man named Endersby. Over a drink the plantation owner confided that he'd been having trouble keeping a white superintendent. He paid good wages, but he had a tough bunch of natives, and one after another his overseers would leave. He looked at Shamus's lean toughness. Did Shamus know anything about running a plantation?

The look which spread over Shamus's face indicated how inept the question had been. Running a plantation! Why, off and on, it was all he'd been doing for the past ten years, he assured Mr. Endersby blandly, although actually the most he knew was looking at one from a distance. The job was his on the spot. But as Mr. Endersby left the bar, Shamus lagged behind long enough to whisper to the friendly Irish bartender, "How do you run a copra plantation?" The bartender winked at him slowly. "You don't. You bloody well ask the boss boy everything you don't know and let him run the show for you."

The friendly tip saved Shamus's skin. Faced with a row of twenty tall Kanakas ready to work the next morning, Shamus had calmed the sudden panic which had swept through him by gripping his walking stick very tightly and leaning on it with seeming nonchalance, had given them a quick, hardboiled pep talk about what he would expect of them, and then had called the boss boy out of line for a conference. After asking the tall intelligent Kanaka a few routine questions and hoping he wasn't betraying his ignorance, he had told him to carry on with the men. It had been simple, really. He spent most of his time swaggering about the plantation with his walking stick, which gave him an air of authority, looking wise and tough. He quickly picked up just enough knowledge to be able occasionally to burst upon them like an avenging justice with a violent command that they correct something which was being done too sketchily. But for the most part he left the technical knowledge to the boss boy and confined himself to keeping them in line with a combination of a cane in his hand which could smart when brought down on a bare back, a gun at his hip which he never had to use, and a restrained friendliness and rigid sense of fair play.

Since there was no opportunity for him to spend a cent he had his stake in a year and, satisfied with the amount, hopped a tramp steamer to Rabaul. There he quickly found what he was looking for—a ship being offered for sale by a Chinese company. After ten hours of haggling over the price, he gave the Chinese owners his year's wages as a down payment, borrowed the rest of the amount which he needed from Burns Philp and Company, and became owner, in name anyway, of the *Maski.*

To the running of a trading schooner, he applied the same principle of bluff as he had to the plantation, by telling the Kanaka bosun to carry on until he could find out for himself. Meanwhile, he trod his own deck with a restrained lordliness, carrying copra for the most part, but taking on whatever profitable commission came his way. For a while he and his ship had served the government station at Port Moresby. He had taken one gold-hunting party against his protests to a region where Shamus knew there had never been any gold found. For several weeks the ship had been the home of a party of naturalists from America.

EDITOR'S NOTE. Shortly after this description of how Shamus acquired the *Maski,* Flynn gives a description of the boat itself:

THE TRADER *Maski* was a very broad-beamed vessel of some ninety-two feet overall, and a shallow draught of merely eight and a half feet. It was a good thing she didn't draw any more. For in the waters she plied, six inches one way or the other often meant the difference between sliding her copper bottom over a coral reef or squatting stuck on it. She was topmast-schooner rigged, carried too little sail, and was powered with an old-fashioned semi-Diesel engine that drove the native mechanics insane. With the exception of the steaming hot foc'sle, rarely used except as a gear and sail locker, her entire below-decks were given over to cargo space. On deck a tarpaulin awning, which had once been white, stretched almost a third of her length, from the stern to the mainmast, with folding sides that could be let down at any angle for shade from the tropical sun.

She was a clumsy sailor, chock-full of clever cockroaches, slow on the helm, but a good sea boat. And at a pinch, or when freight rates were high, she could carry about eighty tons of copra. Besides Shamus, the ship's complement consisted of eight mop-haired Kanakas, a ship's cat named Hercules, and a pet wild pig named Tikis, a freakish runt of a razorback who had never grown much larger than a terrier, but possessed of such an evil and arrogant disposition it was lucky he hadn't.

Aft, under the poop-deck awning, Shamus lived in lofty and remote state, amid the simple accouterments of a South Seas trading lugger's skipper; several canvas chairs surrounded a sizable table, with slats spaced lengthwise to keep dishes from sliding around at sea. With the slats removed it could be used as a chart table. On the starboard side an ancient phonograph stood on a painted packing case. The port side was given over to a stout canvas hammock and two more painted packing cases crudely partitioned into shelves to hold a large assortment of books.

By the railing near the stern stood a weird contraption—a fabulous and unique refrigerator, prima-donnaish and high-strung, operated by two metal balls filled with chemicals, which, when one of them had been heated, produced some sort of reaction which once had made ice, so legend had it. Always unpredictable and skittish, the crew hesitated to approach it—it had once blown the steward clean overboard. Now Shamus used it only for storing things—especially books, which would otherwise have been chewed up by cockroaches.

In a country where phonograph records were not only scarce, but liable to wilt in the moist heat, the *Maski*'s selection was one more of expedience than taste. But certainly it had range. Gilbert and Sullivan predominated, with a number of songs in German, Japanese and Chinese. A couple of others, more or less in the English language, Shamus had discovered among a pile in the Kuo Min Tang hall opposite Ah Chee's in Rabaul. One of these, called "The Mountains Ain't No Place for Bad Men," was now barely audible due to constant use, being a great favorite on board, together with another choice, "The Black Bottom." The strange, unintelligible argot of these two ballads, some primitive affinity in the barbaric rhythm, would hold all hands entranced of an evening under sail.

EDITOR'S NOTE: The plot of *Showdown* centers upon Shamus and his boat being hired by a Hollywood movie producer named Joel Swartz, who needs location footage for his next epic. Shamus at first declines to take Swartz and his small crew into areas he knows to be unhealthy and dangerous but the ebullient producer wins him over. Swartz's party includes his beautiful leading lady, Cleo, whose arrogant manners irritate the old-fashioned Shamus, and an assistant named Jodo, who is mean of spirit and addicted to a variety of drugs. Flynn writes almost contemptuously about Jodo and his habits but it is interesting to note that by the time of writing *Showdown,* the author himself had dabbled, and continued to dabble, with some of the drugs Jodo uses. Be that as it may, Shamus remains unsullied by his seemingly decadent Hollywood passengers and keeps his distance from them. His best way of keeping distance is to hop over the side and mingle with the mysteries of the deep—and whenever he does this, Flynn reveals his obvious love, and knowledge, of doing the same:

BY DAYBREAK the following morning Shamus was astir before anyone. Quietly arousing the crew he gave orders for four large empty water butts to be placed in the longboat in case water could be found ashore, some cheap trade articles, colored calico, bush knives, ax-heads, etc., wherewith to barter for the taro, yams and fruit it might be possible to find. And two loaded guns, a shotgun and a rifle, in the longboat's bow. The Siassi tribes were said to be trustworthy, but he had been long enough in New Guinea not to take chances. Although a careful survey of the beach through binoculars disclosed no signs of life, he knew a thousand pair of eyes could be watching every movement aboard from the dense foliage above the beach and remain unseen.

As yet none of the passengers had appeared on deck, so sending the crew to breakfast he began making certain preparations. A conviction and a desire were prodding strongly at him. He had need to shake off the miasma of indecision which had gripped him the night before. And he knew what would make him feel like himself again.

A curious elation marked his actions as he opened a deck locker and selected certain articles: a pair of Japanese diving goggles made of bone and rubber; next, a thin steel spear, about five feet long, with two murderous-looking barbs at one end. This spear slid through the inside of a short hollow piece of bamboo, long enough only to fit in the hand, to which was attached a heavy sling. By gripping the bamboo in the left hand, the spear, when pulled back to the full length of the rubber sling, made a fine underwater harpoon.

Shamus spat on his goggles, wiped them off with care and adjusted them to his face. Then he wrapped the lava-lava he always wore at night tight around his loins and slid over the ship's side into the warm glass-still water. After a quick look around below the surface for sharks, he began propelling himself softly toward the nearest reef with the undulating body rhythm of a fish. The ordinary methods of swimming would have been too noisy.

The coral was alive with thousands of bright multicolored fish who gazed up at him marble-eyed as he glided noiselessly above them in the clear aquamarine, only enough of his face out of the water so that he could breathe. He paid no attention to them. He was looking systematically through the water, searching carefully down into every rocky cave and inlet below, peering closely into the dark caverns, in and around the kelp beds and monstrous submarine trees of tentacled seaweed.

Fascinated as always by the wondrous teeming world which lies below the surface, he searched on, letting his body eddy and shift with the undulating current, watching the bright sea gardens moving and swaying in slow and graceful rhythm below.

Suddenly his stomach did a violent flip-flop.

The tentacles looked so much bigger, magnified through the diving glasses, and so did the cold evil eyes glaring up at the end of them where they disappeared under the ledge of rock. The octopus drew in slowly and warily as he drifted by overhead and Shamus felt an acid taste in his mouth as his stomach dropped down to normal.

Then he spotted what he was looking for. The big, fat, speckled sea bass was watching him too. Lying still in a small rock grotto, not much more than his head showing, his mouth opening and shutting regularly with the pulsing of his gills, his protruding eyes goggled up, fixed and wary.

Shamus froze his body into perfect stillness and let the current take command of it.

Tensely, man and fish watched each other for a few moments. Then the fish relaxed. Nothing to worry about, he decided, giving his tail a lazy flick. He began edging casually along the rocky sides of the grotto.

Limply, Shamus drifted over and away—any sudden movement of arms and legs now would alarm his prey— studying the topography down below. It wasn't going to be easy. To get in the right position he would have to maneuver with infinite care, taking advantage of the current, to get that rocky promontory down there between the two of them.

He drifted for ten minutes or more, and despite the water's warmth he could feel a chill from the motionless drifting beginning to creep into his bone marrow.

Soon, soon now, he would be in the right spot. Now. Cautiously, unhurriedly, he let the breath out of his body and sank in a slight circle with the current.

As he dropped slowly down beneath the surface the fish became suddenly alert at the sight of this strange invader of his realm. He turned to face it. Shamus could see he wasn't alarmed though—more curious than worried.

Down and down he sank, like an old piece of driftwood, feeling his lungs already beginning to cry for air and fighting the instinct to pop to the surface. He was out of form, he told himself. You have to keep in practice for this, the most thrilling of all chases, one calling for iron control of all the most fundamental human impulses.

Slowly now—slowly and easily—the fish must be watched with the utmost concentration, watched every split second for a sudden dash. But he's still not alarmed—his tail and front fins haven't yet begun to flutter at increased tempo, the sure sign of a fish about to flee an enemy.

Careful ... the least little abrupt movement and he'll be off in a flash and a flurry. Try to keep that clump of seaweed between you and his line of vision. If the current will just help a little, ever so little, the position will be perfect. Make a spot—near the eye, just where the gills end, near the top of the head. Whatever you do, don't be overanxious. Control natural excitement and the reserve oxygen content in lungs will last longer.

Now start drawing your arm back slowly—slowly edge the spear into position. Hold it firmly with your last split second of endurance. Lungs won't explode just yet, although they may feel they are going to.

Aim again and—now! Let him have it! Hard and savage!

Damnation! The spear's point took him too far back in the soft flank of his belly, and pulled out! A great swirl of cloudy sand and blood and Mr. Speckled Bass is bursting through the water like a crazy torpedo.

Shamus was bursting too. One great shove took him to the surface and he gulped air gratefully. Pulling it in deep he began wiping off his goggles. Well, tough luck—the whole hunt must be started over again. But first, better take a look around. The big boy's dash mightn't have taken him too far. Maybe he doesn't feel well. He could easily have darted into one of those dark caverns nearby.

Inhaling a deep but easy breath he drifted again, even more cautiously than before. The fish, if anywhere nearby, would be scared pink now, aware of his mortal danger.

Wait—that little movement down there, under the ledge? A tail fin—or just a piece of kelp waving in the current? He peered into the gloom.

Yes! It's him, all right! Beneath that overhanging ledge of rock. Probably his hideout, where he always runs for refuge from enemies.

Shamus tensed himself, disciplining every muscle in his body to cool coordination. Slowly; don't exhale any bubbles; not one movement faster than the waving of the kelp or coral plants.

Down he dropped. Down, until he could edge over the top of the ledge, brushing the seaweed aside with infinite caution. The fish's hearing underwater, he knew, was much sharper than his own; the slightest scraping sound, and he'd be off again—this time to seek the safety of the open sea.

He readied his spear and hesitated a split second. Well—take a chance; a sudden lunge over the ledge. If the fish fled he would try to lead him.

Gathering his legs under him he gave a hard shove. As he darted through the water so did the fish—at precisely the same instant. But he ran head-on to his fate. The razor-sharp point of the spear took him in the head, behind the eye.

The big fish screamed in his own tongue—an unforgettable sound which you would have to hear to believe. He struggled furiously, the flashing silver of his underbelly twisting and writhing in desperate frenzy.

In the once-still aquamarine both fought desperately amid the rocky grottoes. Lungs bursting, the man strove to reach the surface. The fish tried to rid himself of the steel that was killing him. But there was little chance of it pulling loose this time—the point had bitten into hard bone.

Exerting all his strength, Shamus drew the spear closer to him, forcing the impaled fish overhead. He reached out one hand and felt along the gills. A sudden hard plunge of his fingers and he had a firm grip. Squeezing with all the force left in the hand he felt the sporadic choking. Suddenly he jerked the spear loose and dropped it—it could be recovered later—and seized the gills by both hands, the death hold.

To kill a fish under water is not so easy. Through the goggles his eyes searched along the satiny skin for a certain spot—a little indentation above the fish's eye, his most vulnerable spot. Carefully he drew the fish closer. Then he leaned forward and bit—hard. Like biting into a crisp turnip, he felt his teeth sink through the soft bone, into the brain. Instantly it fell limp in his hands, trembling with little shuddering reflexes.

He began swimming back to the *Maski*, exhausted but happy. The sweet, flaky meat would taste the better for the knowledge that he had hunted it in its native place, on terms that were more than balanced in the hunted's favor.

EDITOR'S NOTE: Following this account of underwater fishing, Flynn returns to the interplay between the characters in his plot, mainly the relationship between Shamus and the actress Cleo. He gradually falls in love with her and finds her to be softer at heart than her slick, protective veneer had led him to believe. Shamus also finds that Joel Swartz is a more substantial fellow than the glib movie producer he was pretending to be. Swartz is in fact on assignment with the U.S. government, in cooperation with Australia. Aside from making a movie he is also photographing the coast and countryside of New Guinea in order to provide the authorities with knowledge of the area, since so little is revealed on existing maps and charts.The official belief is that within a matter of a few years the Japanese will attempt to take over the islands of the South Pacific, including New Guinea, and that they, the Japanese, are already in possession of much better maps and information. But before Shamus, Swartz and the crew are able to make headway with their mission, nature takes over and provides an exciting but tragic incident—a storm which wrecks the boat and costs the lives of Swartz and several of his men. Again, it is the description of the character and power of the ocean which intermittently makes *Showdown* move from a conventional novel into something of more than average interest. Again it is Flynn writing about what he knows and understands:

Excerpt from the official ship's log: "Dec. 23rd, 1930. At sea. Lat. 142. Long. 89. Hazy ahead. No landfall made yet. Cloudy water indicates Ramu River Spill. No wind. Pro-

*ceeding under power. Preparing small Christmas celebra-
tion. Barometer normal.*"

SHAMUS'S LAST NOTATION was unusual. Unless the
daily barometer check gave a markedly abnormal reading,
no comment was called for in the log. But something intan-
gible, the heavy stillness over the water, the warm sultry
morning, the sun, mist-hidden in a thick morning haze,
made him uneasy. Oftentimes strange and nameless things
will trouble the subconscious of those who follow the sea,
even when instruments give assurance to the contrary.

Thin wisps of cloud idled white and foamy along the horizon, drifting and merging with the haze. Overhead, riffled
gray clouds flew along swiftly on the wings of an upper
wind. These peculiar weather conditions had prevailed
since leaving Siassi, three days before.

To add to the depressing atmosphere, the engine, an old-
fashioned, semi-Diesel type, was misbehaving in spite of
careful mothering, the hot-bulb cylinder heads constantly
overheating. As a result, the *Maski,* no sailor in light winds,
was lumbering along at a sparse three, or at best four,
knots.

Shamus closed the log book, sighed, and started forward.
Never had he wished so heartily that a voyage might be finished.

"White water, ho!"

The cry came from the lookout and Shamus quickly
sprang into the ratlines. Skinning aloft to the crosstrees, he
peered ahead and then muttered a soft imprecation. A few
miles ahead four great lines of curling breakers crashed in
toward the shore. The bar across the mouth of the Ramu
was angry.

Visible for many miles, a great reddish-colored wash
comes boiling out to sea from the mouth of the Ramu. It is
mud, scooped up by the tremendous currents that swirl
forth from the belly of this mighty river, fed in turn by a
hundred lesser streams.

Down at the vast mouth, stretching from bank to bank,
there is an enormous mud bar, shallow and treacherous,

with lines of breakers continuously curving over it, sometimes large, sometimes small, depending upon weather conditions.

Shamus studied the prospect and cursed softly again. Across that bar and through those mighty breakers he must take his ship. He had hoped for a still bar—and considering the flat, oily sea and absence of wind there had been no reason to expect otherwise. But something, some submarine upheaval perhaps, the giant river flooding, perhaps the approach of the nameless disturbance he had sensed earlier, made an immediate crossing a dangerous undertaking.

The only alternative was far from comforting—he could heave to and wait for the bar to subside. But with an engine liable to break down at any moment, and possible bad weather—

He slid down the ratlines and poked his head below for a glance at the barometer. What he saw made him jump down the hatch to tap the face of the instruments. No, it hadn't suddenly gone mad. In a mere few hours the black hand had fallen a full quarter of its entire swing! Stormy, it read.

That settled all doubts. Hell or high water, breakers or ripples, the ship must force the bar, and in a hurry, to find a lee from whatever the elements held in store.

Tulare was waiting for him at the top of the hatch.

"Break out heavy line," he barked sharply.

"Already break out, Taubada. And joined." The big native wore a grin of self-satisfaction from having anticipated the unusual command, although his tense manner showed full comprehension of the danger ahead.

"Good—pay it out astern." Shamus gave him a wallop on the shoulder, half shove and half camaraderie in face of the common danger ahead.

He was going to employ an old-time trick, a wrinkle from the days when full-rigged ships traversed the bars of river mouths under sail alone. By dropping his thickest and heaviest line over the stern and letting it stream out to its full length, the weight and drag of the line in the water would have the effect of keeping the vessel stern-on to the following seas, thus lessening the risk of a comber breaking over her broadside. Caught on the crest of one of those giant breakers she would be helpless. Stern and rudder might be lifted high out of the water and all steerage control lost. Then, as she careened forward over the treacherous shallows without the heavy rope dragging astern to keep her headed straight, she might at any moment take a sudden disastrous sheer to port or starboard. Capsize could easily follow.

Anxiously he peered ahead, trying to spot some inundations in the giant waves. There were none. Overhead the sky, heavy-hazed since morning, was not much darker, an ominous stillness in the hot, heavy air. But the gulls still wheeled planing overhead, their raucous, plaintive cries breaking the steady swish of water along the ship's side.

Slightly reassured by the birds' presence, he went aft to see the passengers. They were grouped by the rail, staring with varying expressions at the approaching line of breakers.

Already the ship was rising on a mountainous swell, a bare fifty yards from the first line of breakers.

"Hold ship!"

He ordered the engines to neutral, calculating the exact second to begin his run.

Soon another great wave rose and started to roll forward. It passed beneath the ship, curving in a giant arc, and then pounded in mountainous foam toward the shore.

Then he snapped the quiet order, "Hard ahead!"

Slowly, all too slowly, the little ship gathered momentum. He threw a quick glance astern. By following this first wave as closely as possible he had hoped to outrun the succeeding ones. But now he could see there was no chance. The wave was mounting too fast—catching up. Ah, for a few more revs, one little extra bit of speed.

"Full ahead!"

Opening the laboring engine full up he knew was risking a breakdown. But it was a chance that had to be taken. Tensely he heard the throbbing boom of the motor smother to nothing in the mounting sea astern. There was a limit to steel. It was racing hard, too hard. All right so far, though.

Now the stern began to rise and he gripped the wheel hard, concentrating every faculty. Not daring to look astern, alongside he could feel the gigantic reddish-tinged wave catch up and begin mounting beneath the ship.

She surged up and forward. The reverberating hammer of the driving engine, the flattening beat of wind pressure increasing, a breathless sensation of hopeless, headlong propulsion, and now she was riding the crest, bow way up in the air, planing along like a surf boat hanging perilously suspended upon nothing.

Then came the sickening downward plunge as her eighty tons dropped into the trough with a great wallop. He caught his breath, praying that her keel might not crash aground to shiver into driftwood.

Again came the plunging race forward on the crest of another giant wave, white spray spuming off to both sides. Shamus, the taut lines of his body showing through the white ducks, soaked and clinging to his skin, the spray running in little rivulets down his face, held her bow steady and dead ahead, ready on the instant to anticipate and check her every impulse to take a sheer.

Once a great following sea caught and pooped the vessel, breaking green abaft her quarter and flooding the amidships. But she shook it off and rode bravely on, until at last the lines of combers lay safely astern and she sailed smoothly into the calm waters of the river mouth.

Now Shamus chose his anchorage, hurriedly but with care. The expected weather was obviously approaching from the north; already black, rolling clouds off in that direction filled half the sky.

A little crescent-shaped cove looked fairly snug. It was rocky, with not much room to swing. Patches of reddish sand showed here and there where the shore ran up a sheer cliff on one side and thick jungle on the other. It offered the best and only protection. This was no time to pick and choose.

The anchor splashed into six fathoms of muddy water. Instantly he ordered all awnings and loose gear stripped off, extra gaskets bound on the furled sails, and the spare anchor broken out. Then he conned ship again.

Above, the dark, sullen sky gave as yet no definite sign. But ashore one of Neptune's most vivid warning signals didn't escape him—the gulls. Ruffling their feathers, changing from one leg to another, they huddled in groups on the rocks ashore, squawking with the sharp uneasy note that isn't lost upon a seaman's ears. One at a time they waddled down the rocks and sipped the salt water, seeming to taste of it. Then, straining a neck to the sky, each one voiced the high desolate cry of alarm and warning that only the sea birds voice—and then only when the ocean, their home, is about to erupt.

He felt the subtle change come over the sea's face—a sudden, minute change in wind direction, a cold draught of air, light as a zephyr at first. But from the south! It brought him quickly to his feet, searching the horizon.

Off to the south the smooth waters inside the bar had suddenly burst into white puffs of cotton. Here it came. The expected—but not from the north. A blow out of the south could turn his snug cover into a nasty trap! He would have to get the ship out of there—and quick!

"Stand by anchor! Start up engine!"

Shamus rarely raised his voice, and when he did, only for the purpose of making it carry to a desired point. But now the bellowed command, bringing the crew tumbling out of the foc'sle hatch on the double, held a note that made everyone stare at him in surprise.

The half-cold engine turned over with a weary rumble, coughing and spitting in protest. Anxiously he listened to its broken cadence. If it should desert them now . . .

"Heave up!"

The winch had just started to grind when it hit—the prelude. Little sharp gusts at first, spurting unevenly, followed by a fine chilly spray that bit into the skin. Almost immediately a stiff, cold blast began breezing a high whistle through the topmast shrouds. The ship stiffened hard up against the cable. Now he didn't dare order the anchor up—not in the teeth of a sudden blast of this sort, and a spitting engine.

"Belay there! Now slack off chain!"

Then the rain came. It came in a blinding sheet that obscured the deck and merged with the driven salt spray, drenching and stinging like gravel. Darkness fell as quickly as if a curtain had been drawn over the heavens. The *Maski* heaved and strained against her chain as the mounting waves clawed at her with a giant grip.

As if by the wave of a magic wand, the little cove astern had become a seething caldron. Waves were now sheet spume—topped combers, crashing mountainously ashore and rumbling ever higher up the face of the cliff. In the pounding thunder even the deep boom of the engine was lost in the wave troughs.

He changed his mind suddenly. The ship could not stay alive here. She must be slipped out of the cove at all costs—and in a terrible hurry.

"Heave up!"

The wind seized the shouted words and flung them away, filling up his mouth like a bag. Amplified a hundred times, his voice would never reach up forward.

"Ahead—hard!" he shouted down to the engine room. If the engine possessed enough power to drive her forward against the gale, perhaps he could fight his way out into the wide river mouth. Out there it might be possible to heave to, with the engine running under storm trysail and sea anchor, and ride the storm out.

Suddenly a heavy jolt shook the ship. She had come up sharp against the anchor chain. With the loss of what little headway she carried, she began falling off rapidly.

"Hold that bow up!" thundered Shamus at the helmsman, although he could see the man's every muscle straining as he fought the wheel desperately.

There came a second heavy jolt. From up forward the faint protesting grind of the anchor winch at work fled by, carried in the high shrill of the wind. Tulare, good man, must be acting on his own judgment, heaving up without waiting for orders.

Slowly, fighting her head around foot by foot, the *Maski* came up over the anchor again. Break the anchor out, that was the main concern. Never mind heaving up—the hook could be allowed to drag while he fought his way out to the cove.

The third jolt was so savage it nearly flung him to the deck. A few more of those, the thought flashed through his mind as he clung to the screaming shrouds, and the whole bow would tear out of the boat. But at least the vicious jolt should have broken the anchor free.

He waited. Again the vessel heeled and slid off into the trough. Again she came up against the chain, and again there came the heavy jarring blow. That settled it—the anchor must be fouled, jamming fast in the rocks beneath.

The situation called for no decision now, for no alternatives offered. To try to slip the anchor and run out of the cove would be to court certain disaster, so fierce was the force of the gale. The only course left was to drop his spare hook, hope that the wind wouldn't increase, and if it did, trust in God that together both anchors would hold the ship.

He started forward, leaning far into the howling wind, clawing his way along the rigging. The gale's force flattened the hair straight down on his head, and he could see it snatching wickedly at the tightly furled sails. Thank heaven he had ordered those extra gaskets on—one loose binding and the canvas beneath would tear to shreds in a second.

In the blinding darkness he could barely distinguish the crouching figures of the winch crew struggling with the chain. Ah, Tulare had taken no chances—already he could see the thick manila line of the spare anchor pointing straight down into the boiling water, stretched taut as a bowstring.

As he leaned over to inspect the line, the bow suddenly fell away from under him. The ship hit the bottom of the trough and a heavy sea came crashing green over the foc'sle, submerging and blotting out everything. As she reared up into the air again, sheets of lashing spray followed, driven so hard he was forced to seize the nearest forestay. It was steel cable, twanging now in the gale like the eerie bass notes of a great harp.

"Anchors holding! No drag!"

Tulare was yelling in his ear. Not yet, he thought, but if the gale kept up its present force . . .

"Keep two men on watch—all the time!" he shouted back.

Bracing himself against the foc'sle hatch combing, he began a grim calculation. There was no way of foretelling how long the storm would last. It might blow over in a few hours or blow for days. How long would the anchors hold? That was the point. Whether they held or not, there was absolutely nothing to be done about it—except hope, and pray. The time for an attempt to get the passengers ashore was past. One look into the uproarious darkness astern told him the futility of such a thought. In that maelstrom nothing could live.

He caught a faint rumble from the engine aft, still pounding wearily ahead. Might as well ease it off. Apart from the imminent possibility of a breakdown the meager spurts of headway it gave the boat were causing both anchor lines to jerk and snap. A steady strain would be more effective now.

Then the blow fell.

As the *Maski* dipped her nose deep in the sea, heaving it high up in the air again, there came a curious grating sound. And following, almost lost in the screaming tumult, a relatively inaudible crack.

The anchor chain—instantly he knew it had broken! Knew it even before he felt the ship heel over sharply and veer off to port. He held his breath, waiting, hoping for her to come up against the spare anchor.

Amazingly, the rope line held.

As the *Maski* righted itself, the tough hemp fiber stretched and strained like a giant length of elastic, drawn so taut it seemed a full inch less in thickness; but it held.

In mute suspense he and Tulare tore the drenched cotton shirt off his back and began wraping it around the rope as a chafing pad. The line was stabbing out of the water, stiff as a pole. Suddenly realizing the futility of his action, the big Kanaka let the cloth fly out of his hand and began shaking his head hopelessly.

Only one course remained. Cupping his hands Shamus shouted into the boy's ear. "An ax! Stand by and we'll try to make a run for it. Cut the line when I pass the word!"

Tulare nodded and Shamus started aft. He meant to try to get an extra bit of power out of the engine. Half crawling, half running, the force of the wind fairly blew him down the deck. Beneath the short companionway leading to the poop deck he found a vague form squatting drenched in several inches of washing water. It was Jodo.

"Grab a life belt!" Shamus yelled at him. "Put it on!"

The boy nodded. He was protecting something under his shirt and briefly Shamus caught a surprising glimpse of a ludicrous, bedraggled head—the parrot Hedda.

Hauling himself up on the poop deck, he bumped into Cleo. She was standing huddled against the shrouds, gripping them with both hands. Wide-eyed and pale, she was making a gallant effort to hide her fear.

Before she could utter a word, it happened. Deadened by the wind he heard the sound he had been straining his ears for—a sudden sharp report, like a muffled bullet shot.

As the rope parted, the wind seized the puny *Maski* with fiendish joy. Her head swung off and she started toward the rocks.

Shamus leaped for the girl and tried to drag her farthest away from the crash he knew must follow. But terror had given her a deathlike grip. She was frozen to the shrouds.

The crash came. A giant sea lifted the vessel on high, held her suspended there for a moment, teetering on her beam ends, and hurled her down with a sickening shudder onto the rocks below. Then with wanton and unsatisfied malice it seized and swept her out to sea again.

The arm by which Shamus had been holding on to the shrouds was nearly jerked loose from its socket. Over the side the furious water boiled, pitch dark. A slender chance, but not to take it, to remain on the ship, was certain death.

"Over the side!" he shouted. "Jump!"

In the darkness and the blinding force of the driven spray he could hardly distinguish her—but he heard her sob. Again he tried to pry her hands loose from the rigging. She clung on with a strength that was amazing. He cast a futile look around but could see no sign of a living soul. No time to look further.

There came a moment of high suspense, as if for a brief second the elements, the gods of destruction, held his hand. Then he felt the vessel begin to waver—the receding comber on which she had been carried out was now about to send her crashing down on the rocks a second time.

For an instant the ship hung teetering, poised almost motionless upon its crest. There was only one thing to be done and Shamus did it.

The short hard blow took the girl squarely on the jaw and with a little moan she fell limp into his arms. He struggled to lift her over the rail, then flung himself together with her into the sea.

Striking out in blind desperation, his most vivid recollection was seeing the ship's stern, with its lettered gold legend, MASKI, RABAUL, tower overhead for a brief second. Then she plunged to her end.

The following wash of the same giant wave seized them. Struggling helplessly he felt himself lifted high on its crest, caught a brief flash of jagged rocks far beneath. Then they too were flung headlong into the abyss.

EDITOR'S NOTE: It is interesting that Flynn chose to end the life of the *Maski* in the same way that he ended that of the *Sirocco* in *Beam Ends*—in violent storms and sinkings. He also wipes out Joel Swartz, presumably a character based on his friend Dr. Hermann F. Erben, in the same way that Trelawney Adams exits in the previous book. In actual fact Erben, like Adams, lived a good long life. And just as the *Sirocco* was never wrecked, neither is there any evidence that any ship on which Flynn worked, whether called the *Maski* or not, came to such an end. It seems Flynn had a penchant for dramatic conclusions to his relationships—a tendency that would have needed curbing had he continued to write novels. In *Showdown* the wrecking of the *Maski* occurs about two-thirds of the way through the book; in the remaining third the survivors of the wreck are washed up on a wild and remote shore, and manage to live through a number of privations, including contact with bloodthirsty savages. The book ends with Shamus and Cleo, now pregnant, pledging their love and their future together. The plotlines and characters are fairly well realized but they are not the strong points of *Showdown*. It is when the author recalls, with a keen eye, his recollections of life in New Guinea and its waters that the book takes on value.

The failure of *Showdown* to make much impresson on the literary world was a severe disappointment for Flynn. It more or less killed his hopes of becoming a writer. This need not have been the case. He had simply not worked hard enough. Nine years had passed since *Beam Ends,* and whatever favorable impression that book had made had been long spent. A pity, because had he followed it within a couple of years with a book like *Showdown,* and then another, he might very well have made his mark as a writer. But it was all part of the failure of Flynn as a man; by 1946 the soft, easy, lazy side of him had already gained the upper hand.

PART FOUR

Errol Flynn: Hollywood Reporter

THE FLYNN RESOLVE to write found immediate response among the Hollywood magazines. To have a major star contribute articles was a coup for any of the fan publications, especially one who could actually write with some style. *Screen Guide* was the first to offer him an outlet but then came a better offer from the much more prestigious *Photoplay.* It seems likely that Flynn could have gone on writing for these magazines but after a couple of years his resolve waned. Most of his output occurred in the first three years of his Hollywood stardom, a time when he also wrote a screenplay, *The White Rajah,* which he sold to Warners but which they never used. By 1939 Flynn's willingness to sit at a typewriter appears to have diminished markedly, most probably because there were so many other more enjoyable things to do with his time. After that, writing would be harder and harder for him. It was so much easier to play the fun-loving scamp.

The articles here presented span a little more than a dozen years and they chart a definite course in his life. The first piece, "My Plea for Privacy," is almost naive in its attitudes; the last, "I Do What I Like," has a slightly bitter tone. Clearly much has happened to the writer in these dozen years. Most of the pieces are of ephemeral value, albeit amusing. Perhaps Flynn's best talent was, as Noël Coward put it, a talent to amuse. Of particular interest is "What Really Happened to Me in Spain," although the title is misleading. Probably less happened than he claimed and certainly less than the newspaper accounts of April 1937, which had him injured by shellfire and, at one point, even killed in combat. Warner Bros. had tried to dissuade their errant knight from taking a close look at the Spanish Civil War but they had learned by then that if Flynn wanted to do something, he would do it. Revolutions seemed to have a very strong attraction for Flynn. Antiestablishmentism was a vital part of his nature.

"Let's Hunt for Treasure" represents Flynn at his "tall tale" best. It is unlikely that many of the adventures in this colorful piece actually happened. And "It Shouldn't Happen to an Actor" is possibly his best-written Hollywood piece. It dealt with his dog Arno, an animal closer to his heart than most humans. All in all, these articles show some flair as a reporter, especially one with a leaning toward humor, and they reveal a man who could very likely have made his living as a journeyman writer—had he not been so busy having a whale of a time as a movie star.

My Plea for Privacy

HAS A PERFECTLY strange girl ever come up to you while you were hard at work and asked with bated breath, "Do you wear silk shorts?"

No?

Then you've no idea what it is to work in Hollywood. Mind you, you might work here for a long time before anyone expresses even a mild curiosity over your nether garments but once they do you are headed for the bracket of fame in Celluloidia. Believe me, the first time strangers begin to take an active interest in your underwear, your domestic habits, your technique with a toothbrush and other intimacies that rightly concern only you and your Maker, you can look yourself in the glass and mutter with conviction, "You've arrived, old boy, you've arrived. Now heaven help you! Your life is no longer your own!"

When I was asked to take a few brief words out of the dictionary and apply them to the mysteries of Hollywood, I found myself unable to reply with the proper degree of *hauteur,* "Why, my dear fellow, kind of you, I'm sure, but I'm rather too busy—my new picture, you know!" That, I understand, is the correct response, but frankly I have been waiting too long for just such an opportunity to pass it up. I jumped at it. You see, there's quite a bit of unrelated nonsense about this strange and admittedly fascinating city

Screen Guide, 1937.

and I'd like to get some of it off my chest. Besides, chest-clearing is a lot more fun in public. It annoys so many people. So here goes!

Did you know that in this business where the color of an actor's sock suspenders is often a matter of note, that we also play a game called "Policy?" It's rather like the old game of "Secrets," or "Guess What?" Let me illustrate: on the way over here from England I met a most intriguing girl. We actively disliked each other at first sight but suffice to say that a few months later we hopped off and got married.

Her name, of course, was Lili Damita.

We were all set up about it and thought the clan and the whole world ought to rally 'round and marvel with us. The first dash of icy water was when I was informed in sepulchral stage whispers that I shouldn't mention a word of it— " . . . bad policy, you know!" I didn't take to it very kindly. "You mind your so-and-so business!" I remember saying among other things. There was quite a bit of headshaking over this. "That young guy is getting hard to handle" was the least of it.

But anyway, the rumors started going their appointed rounds. They didn't bother me in the least, probably because I never heard them. But women have a different outlook on such things and they *did* bother Lili.

Over the connubial coffee and cakes of the morning, we'd note in this paper or that Miss Holly Woode's gossip column, featuring a charming little item to this effect, "Guess what young Irish actor with an Irish name whose first initial is 'E' and who married a young French actress whose maiden name begins with 'D' was seen last night chasing her down Hollywood Boulevard with a baseball bat? It looks to me as though they were 'pff-fft!' or, at least, washed up— but the gory captain denies everything. Can you guess whom we mean?"

Suddenly it dawned upon us—it was bad policy to be openly married, but a swell idea to be "pff-fft!" It puts you in an awful spot. You are told over and over again that the public expects you to be romantic and to be interesting to them, yet you are uncomfortably aware that you're not being honest with them and that you're cheapening yourself too.

The last time it happened, I'd just finished a particularly hard job with another picture coming right up. Lili and I had hopped into the car and trailer and lit out for the Klamath River country for some fishing. Lili had never been camping before and, as we were going to do all our own cooking, I asked her to stock up the trailer with edibles. I admit I was a little surprised to find the very small larder stocked almost exclusively with caviar and pâté de fois gras, but I just contented myself with ordering a few cans of beans—and Lili went with me. Now, when a man takes his wife camping with him, caviar and all, that's love and marriage at a high point.

So we ultimately found ourselves carefully hidden away in the depths of the mountains, utterly remote from Hollywood and tremendously glad of it. We could play like any other couple on a vacation, not worry about studios, costumes, stills, interviews, or appearances. For example, I like to be clean shaven, but for two days I didn't shave at all just to prove to myself that I didn't have to. So right in the middle of it all a gentle old soul who thought he was doing us a favor rode his nag into camp. He'd come better than twenty miles on horseback just to deliver a telegram— thought it might be important, he explained, as he got around a fresh-killed salmon and some coffee. Well, minus the names, here's the wire—judge for yourself how we felt about it:

> *DEAR ERROL STOP JUST HEARD YOU AND DAMITA WERE EN ROUTE TO RENO NEVADA FOR A DIVORCE STOP WILL RUN STORY FOR MORNING EDITIONS STOP WIRE MORE DETAILS STOP I HAVE ALWAYS BEEN A PAL ERROL SO LET ME HAVE THIS EXCLUSIVE STOP WIRE CAUSE OF SPLIT AT ONCE STOP YOURS FAITHFULLY JOE DOAKES.*

I've always wondered what was meant by "Yours faithfully." Faithful to what? And if he was giving himself away, I didn't want him.

Another chap actually rumored, on the strength of an alleged, to use a good newspaper term that covers a multitude of baseless speculations, anonymous letter, that I had "gone Hollywood and high-hat, was treating the extras badly, and was being a general louse on a location trip."

Those are two examples of the really serious side of Hollywood hokum, but in a sense they are not nearly so inexplicable as the standardized technique of the sob-sisters and their cousins, the gush-girls. I'm not altogether blaming them because they must have a market for that type of stuff somewhere or they wouldn't write it. But I still don't like it!

Most men would be downright embarrassed to ask the questions they do of any other man or woman. Mind you, I've lived a varied sort of life, plenty of it necessarily on the roughish side, and I'm by no means a shrinking soul under most conditions. But I was nonplussed shortly after my arrival by one of the first interviewers. She was a lady, but by the black beard of Allah, she scared me to death. She had a curiosity that could only be described as lethal and she was determined to make me sound like either a hopeless idiot or a lecherous Lothario. Everything I said sounded different from the way I meant it when she'd impale me with a piercing glance and nod grimly with a cocked eyebrow.

"You're Irish, aren't you, Mr. Flynn?" she shot at me.

When I agreed cautiously she looked as though she caught me at something and jabbed a pencil at me. I tried to smile engagingly.

"All right, then," she snapped, "what do you think of American women? Could you love one of them?" I realized that this poor woman was giving me her imitation of how she thought a dynamic newspaperwoman should act—masterful, incisive, nothing escaping that quick mind which she hoped would make editors comment, "Get Sadie Glutz— there's a gal who always gets her story!"

"Madam," I answered, "I'm new in this country. Tell me, what do *you* think of American women? Moreover, what do you think of American men? And how about the English, French, and Lascars while you're at it?"

"Why, why, I'm not sure. They're very nice, I suppose. . . ."

"Madam, exactly! I suppose so, too. Now suppose we save some time. We read the magazines and such even down in the Islands, so let me help you with a short-cut or two. I brush my teeth twice a day, except when afflicted with what my wife refers to as a 'hanging-over.' Under such circumstances, I might keep at it all day, but ordinarily twice is enough and is usually accomplished with an eliptical motion bearing upwards and to the left. I am clear-eyed sometimes and at other times not. You might go on to say that I impressed you as fearless—there's your title, 'Fearless Flynn'—but, between ourselves, I'm frequently scared stiff, especially of such things as rumors that can never be traced. As to my private life—well, there's precious little of it left, but according to what I read in the newspapers, I am a master of such minor arts as boxing, fencing, wrestling, jiu-jitsu, horsemanship, hunting, fishing, sailing, swimming, golf, tennis, chess, trap-shooting and jacks. I get up early in the morning and after dashing through Beethoven's *Etude in B Minor* I casually practice each and every one of the above sports, sometimes doing a little Indian club work with my disengaged hand. Sometimes, during my spare time, I work. I think some women are divine and others are awful. I am convinced that a man's Ideal Woman is his private affair and a pretty silly business, to boot. An Ideal Woman would probably catch myself making faces behind her back out of sheer ennui. Further, you might be amazed to know that in a moment of deep insight gained from having read a few scripts, I came to the astounding conclusion that there are four types of women—and four thousand others, too.

"Now, frankly, Miss Glutz, do you care or do you think anyone else cares if I say there are four kinds of women? You know darned well that nobody gives a whoop how many kinds of women I think there are in the world—if there are enough to go around. Anybody that tells you any different should have his head examined."

Miss Glutz was nervously chewing her pencil and muttering, "Most irregular—most irregular!"

Now if anybody ever gets to that extraordinary point where he is really interested in me as a person—I am lucky enough to know three such, my wife and a couple of good pals—it is my quaint conceit that they'd be interested in the same things that I am, and not my reactions to a set of standard questions that sound like an I.Q. test gone mad.

I am terribly interested in a few things that are comparatively normal. I like to write. It fascinates me. I get a tremendous bang out of the mountaintop home Lili and I are building. It has a large and airy sitting room in it that looks out over all of California's valleys and the blue Pacific but it is as remote as Mount Everest. We sit around the fire with a spot of this and that in a tall glass and daydream about the island we want to buy in the South Seas when we're rich enough. Don't you? Ours is down near New Guinea where I've spent a lot of time. The place won't cost much to run, but we do want to have a tremendous stock of books and a good staunch schooner for trips. That's what we want most of the money for—trips. We'd like to be able to run up to China, down to Australia or across to visit the Brookes in Sarawak.

Now those are a few of the things I like to talk about—in fact, try and stop me! If anyone is interested, I'm grateful—if not, well, they probably have a lot more interesting ideas of their own and certainly would not be interested in all that old fashioned bunkum that has been pushed out of Hollywood via wire, air and mail about such insipidities as favorite breakfast foods and most becoming colors in underwear and hose.

At the moment, I've just looked at my watch and it's six of the clock. They are previewing *The Charge of the Light Brigade* tonight at the studio and I'm going to go and see it. I mentioned a while back that I get scared frequently. I am now. They say it's a good picture but you always get scared just before it's shown the first time to an audience, especially when that audience pays your weekly check.

I don't have to, but I'm going. In company with some five

hundred other people, I put all I know into that picture to make it good. We sweated and we swore and we got on each other's nerves, but we all wanted it to be good.

Another thing I'm looking forward to is getting some reactions to this article. I'm going to get some very dirty looks in certain quarters. You're not supposed to say what you think in this business.

Night in Town

FOUR YEARS AGO I quit New Guinea, the most savage, the least known and, in all respects, the wildest country on the earth's surface. In spite of two years in Hollywood movies, I haven't had a really exciting moment since; hadn't had, that is, until a certain night in New York a couple of weeks ago.

I happened to be sitting moodily at the bar of one of the currently popular night clubs, asking myself why I was there. For hours previously I had been at a table with a party of well-meaning friends who, accoustomed to the din, the smoke, and the general impression of Bedlam, were under the delusion that I also was having a whale of a time. Finally, during a reshuffle at the table, I managed to creep over to the comparative peace of the bar, and there, with my customary grace, knocked a gentleman's drink right into his lap. We mopped him up together, bought each other drinks, and began a discussion that bade fair to go on through the years without interruption.

Sid Livingston was a writer—a bit damp at the moment, but still a writer. Several drinks later he had told me all about the fundamentals of acting, and I had given him a brief summary—say an hour or two—on the secret of writing. By this time we knew most of each other's pasts, and we were calling each other "my dear old boy."

Collier's, April 24, 1937.

"My dear old boy," I complained, "cities are damned dull—this city in particular. It's very boring, and all a lot of sham and fiction. Artificial, my boy, that's the word for it!"

"You're wrong," answered Sid. "Just because you've been in the movies don't get the idea there's no reality here."

Stung to the quick, I retorted. "I wasn't thinking of Hollywood, I was thinking of New Guinea. Now there's a place where men are—"

"Yeah, I know—head-hunters," he interrupted. "So you think they're tough, do you? Okay, my pampered pet! How strong is your stomach?"

"Strong as yours, my blasé city dweller," I replied haughtily.

"Okay, we'll see! Let's go."

Mystified, I followed him out into the night. Neither of us had paid the check, so you can see for yourself that our adventure started off suspiciously.

Sid settled his bulk in the tonneau of a cab and grunted, "Centre Street."

Centre Street. Police Headquarters. The Mop and Pail Brigade swapping worn marble steps; a broken old man polishing a bronze plaque; dead men's names, "Killed in Action"; hollow, echoing halls. Upstairs, the radio room with blue-shirted men taking endless calls by phone; low, monotonous voices. Others going on the air: "Car 637, Car 637, Hotel A—Hotel A—Signal 32." Cops like a 32. Anything can happen. A man can go up a grade or stop a bullet, or both; three minutes are allowed for a report or they send another car.

Downstairs, Missing Persons' Bureau, with white-collared dicks checking endless pictures with the Unidentified Dead reports; jewelry and dentures taken from corpses litter filing cabinets. A redheaded boy from Minnesota grinning in a corner; hitchhiked from home to see the world; landed grinning and unconcerned in Centre Street. "Whadda I care? The bulls'll send me home; the old man'll whip the stuffing outta me and next time I'll head west.... You're a movie actor." A flat statement, eyes ruminative, sizing me up. " 'At's a soft racket. Lousy with hot mammas, hunh? Yeah.

Next time I'll head west." The lieutenant told me he was fifteen.

Outside a siren screamed, diminished. A laconic announcement—homicide. Somewhere in the city a violent death. It's routine; guys always getting bumped off; sometimes it's women, sometimes business, sometimes madness. They're bad—the nuts—you know, screwballs. Blast hell out of a platoon of cops; remember the crazy spigotty in '34? Got four men before he took up aviation. "Taking up aviation" is jumping out the window.

Radio Car 701. Long, black, powerful, it idles through the street; the tonneau is an arsenal, shotguns, pistols, submachine guns, blackjacks. The tear-gas bombs roll against your feet as the car careens around corners. You flinch at first but later on you kick them aside; they're just a pesky nuisance, unless you're a G-man. Jimmy at WPEG busts through the speaker: "Car 701, Car 701, Lenox Avenue at 117th Street, Lenox Avenue at 117th Street, a stabbing, a stabbing, Signal 32."

The car lurches ahead, the driver hunched over the wheel. The siren howls in savage glee. The sergeant up front leans out the side window, staring intently, calling off the street numbers as they flash by; the car is going too fast for the driver to watch the slots that speed makes of streets. "Eighty-ninth—Ninetieth—hospital coming up—Ninety-first—Ninety-second." The siren moans impatiently past the sick, shrieks again as their numbers are left behind. The traffic light turns red. I wait, braced, for a locked-wheel stop, but the radio car swings wide to the left, caroms around a vast green thing, a bus full of startled people, darts ahead like a broken-field runner for a touchdown—but nobody runs interference for you at eighty-five in city traffic. The man beside me smoking a calm cigarette grins. "Don't worry. He's a swell driver, only two crack-ups this year."

"Crack-ups? Behind this screeching siren?"

"Sure. Part of the racket."

The siren. God bless it! It clears a jagged swath blocks ahead. Blocks passed in the snap of a finger, left trembling in our wake. A taxi materializes from a side street, dead ahead—dead is right—it's too late for brakes. A sickening veer. Two wheels leave the ground. An infinitesimal second, and it's behind us.

"The damned fool!"

"Nice work, Joe. Another coat of paint—and zowie!"

Lenox Avenue. Pocket pool and fried fish. Somber people, quick to flash knives or grinning teeth. Splendiferous clothes brushing the rags from which they sprang. Ragged pickaninnies clogging under street lamps. Black, silk-clad Shirley Temples hurrying past with leopard-coated mothers.

A sudden scuffle in a side street; a scream; a flow of torrid oaths; the silent gleam of steel; a ragged, bent body falls, another totters away in a horrid mimicry of flight. Running men, the distant scream of the siren, two blood-red lights racing up the Avnyuh—cops. The crowd by the drugstore stands unmoved, grinning. A few generations of towns don't wipe out racial traits. Death is a casual matter. A dusky delivery boy dashes into the drugstore to shout a warning to his boss; carvings mean immediate first-aid business to Harlem pharmacies—and no pay, but they'd wreck the joint if they didn't get it.

The cops drag in a lump of flesh and flannel, brown flesh and gray flannel, both impartially sprayed and clotted with red. The lump groans as it drops on a stool. Its head rolls back. The clerk stares a moment, returns the bandages to the dusty shelves. He doesn't need bandages. A cop is trying to write a report under the single yellowed bulb with a stub of a pencil. His lips move in unconscious sympathy with his labored fingers. Another crosses the counter. "Pack of gum, buddy. That dinge is sure lucky; the shiv missed his pipes by a spider web."

A vast woman barges in, scattering cops and onlookers. "Zeke, you's been cuttin' again! Zeke, you's a damn fool; you never wuz any good at cuttin' 'cause you alluz git cut fust." She turns to the grinning men. "Loses his haid! Gets a picayune nick in his black hide as wouldn't hurt a fly and goes plum crazy fo' true. 'Zeke,' I says, 'Zeke, refrain fum cuttin' an' de Lawd will be musseful,' but he don't lissen at nobody when his body's passion is hot on him. You be taking him in de wagon?" The sergeant figures a wagon trip is a cinch for Zeke. Zeke nods woefully. The ambulance clangs up. Cops start shoving people along. A fistfight starts farther up the street. Laughing gaily, they run to this minor diversion. Nothing more we can do here.

A call comes through: trouble in an alley off Delancey Street. Out of our territory, but what the hell? We roll. More info comes in on the way. Trouble in Nick's flop joint. The driver yawns as we swing into the express highway.

Nick's, a converted stable, tiers of bunks, foul stench, broken men, some young, most old, stained graybeards, rheumy frightened eyes, gnarled dirty hands clutching dirty blankets. A broken toilet burbling somewhere, a bald light bulb illuminating things better left in the dark. Nick mad and blustering, shouting foul names at his guests—mostly beggars; two bits buy a mug of java, a butt and a bunk; it's a classy joint.

A young punk caught slipping his hand under an old man's pillow for a greasy buck. Old men rising in wrath, brownish teeth bared, clinging desperately to a tissue of gum; old, clutching hands, cracking voices gibbering vengeance. The punk helplessly outnumbered. He could have killed ten of them with his bare hands, but there were a hundred of them. He lay in the alley, sobbing terribly, all for a lousy buck. A short shrift from the cops. Sympathy for what? He'd robbed a broken grandfather; send him to Bellevue and kick him to hell out.

Conversation on Fifth Avenue. A friendly dick comes to our car. "How's Eddie? They locate that slug yet?" "Doing swell—only the one slug left now and it's working up to the surface. Yeah, you can feel the damn thing with your finger near his neck. It'll be up far enough to snick off like a wart in a couple of days. Lucky break; got a first-grade detective's pay out of it—$250 a year more." "Lucky, hell! Collins, his sidekick, is the lucky one. He jumped from third grade to first! In less'n two weeks he runs smack into three stickups, shoots it out twice, gets a conviction in the other and is boosted to top pay. Thirty-two hundred a year and him only on the force for eight months. Some guys is just naturally lucky like that."

The radio whistle interrupts. Another 32, nearby this time. A big cooperative apartment house on Fifth commands a subtle change of approach from "the Boys." Their voices are hushed and they tread lightly through the heavily carpeted halls. A stolid Swede elevator boy glances at the badges. "Are you expected?" "Naw! Just stopped by for a bit of gossip, pal! C'mon, step on it!"

The apartment door is opened almost before the lift stops. A pale and nervous butler. "Right this way, gentlemen." Glimpses of gloriously furnished rooms, dim, decorous lights, a magnificent Corot in the library. Two chattering maids peeking out from the butler's pantry. A personal maid rushes by. *"Henri! l'esprit d'ammonia pour Madame— vite!"*

A man's bedroom farther down the hall, cork-walled; low lights; a faint smell of leather; evening clothes tossed on a chair; fine, white silk pajamas folded on the open bed. A locked bathroom door, silence. "In there, gentlemen."

The sergeant looks nervously at the cheval glass in the door, hopes it won't shatter. Solid shoulders against wood; grunts; the door gives. A copper catapults through, almost falls.

There he is, a big man, slumped in a tub of water. The water is cold now. His lips are bluish. Heart attack. We lift him clear, wet and horribly limp. Henri standing doubtful in the background with a huge Turkish towel, the perfect gentleman's gentleman even unto death. Thought they existed only at the movies. I choke back a desire to laugh.

Madame walks into the bedroom, pale, eyes incredibly bright, a mighty and gallant effort at composure before strangers. A single glance at her husband in the bed. "The doctor is coming right over. Is he—?"

"Yes'm. 'Fraid he is."

"I see. Thank you for coming."

She bites her lips. The French maid starts to sob hysterically, drops the small vial of spirits of ammonia. "Marie,

control yourself. Henri, see that the gentlemen have everything they want; it is cold tonight. You must excuse me
now."

As we pass her room I hear deep-throated sobs. Henri offers us Scotch and soda at the door. Somehow we don't
want any just now.

I am glad the attention whistle is shrilling when we get to
the car. A shooting in a nearby hospital. Might be anything:
gang reprisals or madness. Two cars already there when we
arrive. Young Tom Collins the first one there, already in
charge. A low-voiced conference in the super's office.

Now Collins hurries out, face inscrutable. Two harness
bulls follow him to the elevator. Time for a cigarette. In a
moment he comes in again pulling a frightened little boy by
an ear with one hand, holding an air rifle in the other. Little
Hymie had a new present and the lighted windows of the
hospital were irresistible. Twelve armed cops and three
rolling fortresses—against one little boy with an air rifle.
We gravely discuss the possibilities of a life sentence and
let him go. Little Hymie is warned to eschew windows in
the future.

A man-on-roof call in the West Seventies, either a Peeping Tom or an illegal entry, it's an even-money bet. No sirens this time. A quiet sneak-up. Three houses away we
find a new rope tied to an iron pipe. It is taut, pulled over
the rear edge of the roof. We deploy around the suspect
area, peek over. Twenty feet below a black blob is discernible, swaying on the rope. This is no Peeping Tom. Three
powerful lights cut the darkness. "Hey, you! You're covered!
Come on up out of there!—Well, I'll be damned!"

We had to haul him up. A loop of his own rope had
caught him round the neck as he tried to escape. Strangled,
the fingers of one hand still wedged between throat and
rope. He'd been fighting for squeaking trickles of air. Well,
anyway, he was dead. Warm, but definitely D.O.A.—Dead
On Arrival.

As they carted him away, Sid Livingston turned to me
and grinned. "How's your stomach now, my bored young
friend?"

I formed an instant, though momentary, dislike for Mr. Livingston.

"Personally," he continued, "I want a drink."

I was taught never to argue with my host. I agreed heartily. There was something strangely friendly about the night club as we pulled up at a leisurely speed in the taxi. You don't think New York taxis have a leisurely speed? Try the death car—or take my word for it that New York taxis merely crawl along. In fact, they practically browse at the curb.

At the table sat a group of well-meaning friends. They were under the impression that I was having a whale of a time. I was. I drew great refreshing draughts of cigarette-laden air into my grateful lungs. I cast an appreciative glance at the deafening orchestra that had to be loud to conquer the strident voices of all those lovely people.

With a contented sigh, I crossed to the bar and stood for a round with Sid. I even paid up with the bar man for the round we'd walked boredly out on. That proves I was glad to be back.

Outside, dimly perceptible over the cacophony of the orchestra, we heard the shrill banshee wail of a distant siren.

Somewhere in the great city someone else had met a violent end.

What Really Happened to Me in Spain

I AM QUITE DEAD.

I am quite a bit surprised about it, too. Struck me all of a heap, so to speak, when I found out about it. For three weeks I've had to argue with people—try to prove that I'm not some new kind of a zombie. The best authorities between Madrid and Hollywood have all concurred that I'm not. I don't exist. I got killed. And, what's more, they seem to have a cheated look when I show up and start talking.

When I crossed back into France from Spain, a little roly-poly French reporter gazed at me indignantly.

"Mais M'sieur est mort! I have written so! All over the world M'sieur is dead and now M'sieur returns alive!"

He was really quite wrought up about it and somehow I felt I owed him an apology. I suppose I really should have been dead, but when you get right down to it, I just didn't feel like leaving this vale of tear-gas bombs at the moment—the last few weeks having been so crammed with action and excitement. The events leading up to my extremely sad death were more than a bit exciting in themselves.

When Jack Warner said I could have eight weeks off, I left so fast he couldn't change his mind, grab a phone and have me back for portrait stills. Somehow, I couldn't imagine the publicity department following me into the front-line

Photoplay, July 1937. Copyright: *Photoplay.*

trenches of a nice healthy war. It makes publicity men and producers very nervous to be shot at. So I picked on Spain for a few weeks' rest and quiet.

Arriving in Spain, I felt I was right back in "The Charge of the Light Brigade." After having passed through better than fifty "committees," I arrived at the famous old Gran Via Hotel in Madrid. "Committees," incidentally, are small patrols of men, armed to the teeth, who examine your credentials while their rifle muzzles probe at your fifth rib. You may have the right papers, but they always look at you as though you stole them.

I was glad of the comparative peace of the hotel and immediately took a nice, cheap room on the third floor with a lovely view.

At nine-thirty the next morning, I found out why it was so cheap. If you've spent the last twenty hours riding over shell-pitted roads at eighty mph, you rather like to lie abed for a while the next morning, so I was in no mood for levity when awakened by a sibilant whooshing, followed by a loud crash. I muttered something about somebody please let the dogs out and I tried to get back to sleep. At that moment, there came another loud whoosh-bang, and I was suddenly uncomfortably aware that I wasn't back in Hollywood, so it couldn't be the dogs.

I opened a tentative eye and peered through the window. A few yards away, bathed in the morning sunlight stood the huge Telephone Building. But something was wrong with it. It had holes in it. Large, gaping holes. And from one of them, dust, bricks and debris were at that moment still falling. I was pondering this unusual phenomenon when, directly overhead, another whooshing sound approached, banged off, and there, before my eyes, was still another brand new hole in the Telephone Company's lovely building.

I rose and left my bed rapidly.

In fact, I didn't even wait for the elevator. My pal, Doctor Erben, and I swooped down three flights of stairs with an ease that would drive a trapeze artist to an early, brooding grave. Arriving in the lobby, we wrapped ourselves in bathrobes and dignity and approached the clerk.

"Buenos días," he smiled. "I trust that you have slept well and are over your fatigue. The accommodations are excellent but, of course, the service—" he shrugged—"La guerra!"

We agreed that the service was a bit hampered by the good old guerra and that the view was indeed excellent. The clerk expressed polite interest when we informed him that the view had three spanking new holes in it. He glanced at his watch.

"Ah, yes, to be sure! Nine forty five. It is that way every morning. The enemy warm up their guns with three shells at the Telephone Building every morning. You may return to your rooms now in complete safety. There will be no more bombardment until tomorrow morning at the same hour— excepting, of course, strays. But they won't be intentional."

Erben cleared his throat and mentioned something about quieter rooms anyway. They could be had, but they cost three times as much. They were in the cellar and the view was very bad. We hastened to assure him that we would readily sacrifice the view of the sorely wounded Telefonica and in a few moments were installed in the crowded but capacious cellars of the Gran Via Hotel along with dozens of war correspondents, soldiers and Government officials. Off duty, they used the common rooms of the basement for quiet drinks, billiards and a rousing game of dominoes at the table near the furnace. They turned out to be a grand bunch of guys who took life easily and very, very lightly. In their business, they have to!

With their help, it was only a few hours before we had our salvo-conductos (safe conduct passes) in order and an armed guide and car driver assigned to us. It is really a strange thing to see an embattled city, under bombardment half the time, continuing its business more or less as usual. The men on the streetcars, going to and from their regular work, don't even look up from their daily papers as the shells howl overhead. It wasn't long before we felt much the same way, hardly even turning to look when a twelve-incher split the air. One thing that I never did get over, though, was the chilling and deadly staccato bark of the machine guns.

But all the guns and bombs in Spain frightened me only half as much as Pedro. Pedro was a dark, sleepy-eyed little Spaniard who wore an outsized revolver at the ready even when he went to bed. He piloted us around Madrid and the front sectors with unquenchable ardor. He had a habit of driving at 120 kilometers an hour over bad roads and turning around to the back seat for a friendly chat at the same time. When I add that he had the Spanish habit of talking with his hands, you'll see what I mean.

He must have had an extra eye in the back of his head. I would see a large shell hole dead ahead but would be ashamed to mention it. I'd done that so often before. I'd sit there and feel myself going pale with horror as we roared on towards it, without any slacking in speed. Just as disaster seemed inevitable, Pedro would take a casual glance at the road, see the hole and, with one hand, swerve expertly around it on two wheels and return to the conversation—all without batting an eye. Once, coming back from the Guadalajara front, we heard a plane approaching, looked out and saw a huge trimotored bomber swooping down over the road. Pedro stepped on it!

If we'd thought we'd been traveling before, we then found out how Pedro could really dynamite along when he put his mind to it. He kept the car careening from side to side to make a more difficult target for the machine-gunners above. Just as I was about to feel I'd rather be bombed than drive on like this, Pedro jammed on his brakes. The car immediately turned around twice in its tracks like a top. We wrenched open the doors and dove headlong into a ditch. A few seconds later, the plane roared overhead, a single burst of machine-gun fire cutting a neat dotted line down the length of the automobile. A few minutes later, that same plane dropped hell and fury on an airdrome near Albacete.

Back at the hotel, we really felt the need of a few Malagas with the boys. It was then that we heard tell of one of the war's most fascinating scenes—the front lines at night.

We'd been up and all through the University City front in the daytime. The passes were devilishly difficult to wrangle and we were told that night passes were frankly impossible. We had, however, our night and day passes for the Madrid front proper and, when I caught an answering gleam in Erben's eye, I knew that sooner or later Erben and Flynn would be watching the fireworks at night on the front.

If I'd known what was in store for us then, I have an idea that at least one Irish actor would have gone to his grave without ever having seen the fascinating horror and repellent beauty of spouts of flame belching into a velvet night while the drums of war resounded in a crashing, menacing crescendo.

As soon as darkness fell, we started. Once outside the hotel, we were stopped every block or two by a "committee" who suspiciously examined our passes. There are no lights in Madrid at night and you make your way by the aid of extremely dim flashlights. One bright enough to really see by would land its owner in jail at the first corner. The black silence of the city at night is enough to make your hair stand on end. Very occasionally a dim, firefly-like glow slowly moving down a street will warn you of another pedestrian. Hurriedly, silently, you pass, holding your breath. Suddenly out of nowhere, you hear a swift movement, the metallic triple-click of a carbine and a barked command— *"Alto!"* Believe me, you *alto.* It isn't healthy to even twitch an eyelid after that blunt order to halt.

A lot of those "committees" think it saves time to ask the questions afterwards. Slowly, your heart in your mouth, you make your way through the bitterly cold streets. It seemed forever and a day before we reached the limit of the patrols, crawled past the picket line and into the depopulated area just behind the front, where night passes don't do you any good.

At that point, it was necessary to slide along, cautiously flattened against walls, ducking into cavernous doorways, squirming over loose piles of incredible filth and debris, guided only by the increasing volume of sound from the firing lines. It must have taken us a full hour to cover a distance of not more than five or six hundred yards—and every yard is indelibly in my memory. Scared? Of course I was! But I wouldn't have missed it for a million, cash in hand. However, the real kick lay ahead.

About the time when I was beginning to think that the rest of my life would be spent flat on my belly crawling, scrambling, running and dodging through impenetrable blackness, a blackness so dense it made you feel almost dizzy, we came to a corner.

"The Rosales!" whispered Erben.

Once the gayest and proudest plaza of all Madrid, the Rosales is now a shambles of gutted buildings. In the place of music, song and laughter, all you hear there now in the line of music is the tenor of machine guns and the bass of heavy artillery.

It was impossible to go any farther. Although the lines were dead ahead, most of the actual combat was going on about a quarter of a mile down to our right. From where we stood, we could look obliquely along the lines, get a full view of the fighting. Both in sound and vision, the whole scene was a little like a symphony coming up from lulls into arpeggios and rising into earth-shaking fortissimos. It was staggering and a bit bewildering to realize that human beings were down there trying to kill and maim men they'd never seen, had nothing against—blindly killing under orders for a cause they hardly understood, if anyone does understand those things at all.

There is no cover across the wide Rosales, and a few hundred yards away a machine gunner sent blasts of flame and lead whipping across every few seconds. A little further along was the concealed emplacement of large caliber guns firing at minute intervals. Concealed, that is, by day. By night the Rosales is lit up for fifty yards as the orange flash jumps from the muzzle. Almost immediately, from across the valley a couple of kilometers away, would come the answering flash from the opposing artillery position. Nearly a full second would elapse after we saw the flash before hearing the dull boom and then the whine of the shell as it hurtled overhead into the heart of the city.

Erben and I took shelter, such as it was, around the corner of a ruined building, only half of which was left standing. That particular spot had once been heavily contested and blasted into debris, but as far as we knew, no shells had landed there for about two weeks. Therefore, we felt as safe as possible that close to the lines.

We weren't.

Erben had brought along his camera to take some night shots and was just closing up the equipment, preparatory to starting the long squirm back to a drink and a cigarette. I took a last look at the lines. Across the valley, I saw the now familiar flash, waited for the boom and the whine.

It came. But this time the whine sounded different. Closer it came. Closer! Paralyzed, I suddenly knew that this one wasn't headed into town. Erben opened his mouth to yell, but no sound issued. The whine became an incredible shriek. . . .

I'll never know whether some spontaneous muscular convulsion or the concussion of the shell itself threw us flat, but whatever the agency, it is to that that we owe our lives. We landed on the ground, nearly unconscious. The shattered wreck of the wall at our backs was a tottery shield, but it worked. In the split second before I lost consciousness, I heard the sickening sound of shrapnel smacking up against the brick with a sound like fifty eggs cracking on a footpath.

When I came to, someone had, I was sure, inserted a singularly unpleasant and painful baseball between my skull and scalp. There were lights all around and I couldn't quite make out if the pearly gates now had neon signs instead of pearls, or if it were actually the cubicle in the basement of the Gran Via that we had inhabited for a couple of weeks. I was about to make some angry remark to Erben, to stop him from swimming about the ceiling that way, when he lit of his own volition, grinned and asked me how I felt. I told him. I can't tell you—not in print, anyway.

All that had happened, fortunately, was that a large chunk of plaster had been jarred loose from the building by the concussion of the shell. It had dropped like a large sombrero on top of my crown from a height of twenty or thirty feet and laid me out for about four hours. I still get head-aches, and I'll be much more careful about walking under ladders in the future.

As I started to feel a little more alive, I began to be faintly and modestly proud of my war wounds until my Spanish confreres gazed dispassionately at them in the bar and passed them off as mere scratches. Scratch, indeed! It was my head and it hurt like hell!

It wasn't until I got to Paris that someone of the French press told me I had been dead for some days. Naturally, I appreciated the notion and then rushed around to send off much-alive wires to the parents in Ireland and telephone my small French pal in London.

She was so relieved at learning the Master's person was all in one piece, she ran me up a telephone bill which looked in French francs like Einstein's Theory! By the way, she got a telegram during that period which she insists on having framed. She says it will serve me as a reminder any time I begin to get the urge to return to the wars.

It's a strange feeling to read a sympathetic little note writ-ten about yourself to someone else.

It starts:

"In this hour of your sadness we want you to know how we feel for you over the loss of Errol. We feel sure that his death will not ... "

Try reading one of those sometime when you're feeling warlike!

Personally, I'm settling down to long years of peace!

Young Man About Hollywood

THE WEST SIDE Tennis Club is the most remarkable club in Hollywood for two reasons. It is on the west side of town and people do play tennis there.

Most Hollywood clubs have little or nothing to do with their names. The very sight of clover in the Clover Club would fill the natives with superstitious awe and, personally, would put me on the water wagon for life. The fundamental purpose of a club out here seems to be to serve as a place where the inmates and members can get together and talk about the inmates and members of the club across the street. A club has one other important social advantage. When guests start breaking crockery and spilling drinks on the rugs, no one worries but the club manager, and he's paid to worry about such things.

It is an accepted fact that gossip is the primary product of our clubs. The members can take a tiny tidbit, mull over it, pull it about, add a touch here and there until it becomes a truly amazing thing. But at the West Side we are proud of our record. Forty percent of the membership plays tennis and it has been reliably rumored around that the other sixty can recognize a tennis racket if they come upon it after ten in the morning. In my opinion that compares very favorably with the Santa Monica Swimming Club and its neighbor, The Beach Club, only ten percent of whose memberships ever get wet externally.

The West Side has another distinct advantage. It is hid-

Photoplay, August, 1937. Copyright: *Photoplay.*

den away in the nether regions between Los Angeles and the sea, far from the haunts of the autograph hunters. If it weren't so far from the usual tracks, there wouldn't be room to drink, much less play tennis, on the club grounds, for the simple reason that we have more celebrities there over weekends than any other acre west of Times Square.

The gossipers and box-hoppers seem to find something inexpressibly soothing on a hot summer day in dragging their tall drinks out on the veranda and watching two grown men run themselves into a ragged sweat after a small white ball. Their heads wag from side to side rhythmically like a mass formation of cobras under the influence of a powerful Oriental narcotic. But, no matter how much the heads sway, there is no diminution in chatter.

Swaying or not, that gallery is really something to see. It makes the average premiere turnout look slim and unimpressive, especially if you prefer your female figure in shorts and such instead of sables and ermine.

Frank Shields and I were playing off a match in the men's singles one day. We met at the net for the usual handshake and kidding. Frank glanced over the gallery and back. We looked at each other and grinned, both with the same thought—that it would be far more fitting if we took a couple of chairs out on the court and watched the gallery, rather than the other way round. And a great deal more entertaining it would have been, too.

Strewn around the boxes and veranda was what I would conservatively estimate to be better than fifty million dollars worth of actress, leading men and so-called brains.

Michael Bartlett could be seen leaping gracefully from box to box. Kay Francis was doing something languid to a cigarette. Connie Bennett was looking for Gilbert Roland and Gary Cooper was chewing a piece of grass from the lawn while Rocky talked about the women's doubles to Paulette Goddard and Dolores Del Rio. Nigel "Willy" Bruce was snorting around trying to find someone to whom he could tell a story about the guardsman and the charwoman. Cesar "Butch" Romero was looking menacingly around the veranda wondering about a gin rickey while Myrna Loy

was asking Arthur Hornblow to help her focus a Leica camera so she could take a picture of Hymie Fink taking a picture of Bill Ulman taking a picture of Humphrey Bogart who was taking a picture of an airplane and doing a bad job of it, judging from the way his eye was squinted. Gloria Stuart and Maggie Sullavan were talking to each other about babies while Liz Pierson sat by knitting a sweater. That sweater, incidentally, is commonly believed to be a prop. She's been at it for two years. Somewhere, further down the line, was a green Tyrolean hat with Douglas Fairbanks sitting under it talking to Lady Ashley about Wimbledon. Sally Eilers and Glenda Farrell were trying to find some shady seats, while Harry Joe Brown and Freddie March were chatting with Keith Gledhill. Somewhere down front was a New York society editor, looking frustrated as she sat in the middle of a ring of broken pencils. I laughed then. She was so obviously going mad, trying to get all the names and addresses and couples straight and down on paper.

But I'm not laughing now.

I know how that industrious young lady felt. When I agreed to do a series of articles on this cockeyed town for *Photoplay*, I thought it would be, if not easy, at least not a very difficult job of reporting. But stand alongside a merry-go-round with the steam calliope sounding off in your ear and try reporting what it's all about sometime and you'll see what I mean.

The only things that are worth reporting anywhere are the unusual things and, in this town, the unusual is an everyday occurrence. The unusual thing at the West Side is that the membership is almost one hundred percent picture people, so there's a tacit understanding that it is the one place where you can come in unarmed and let down your back hair without landing in a gossip column the next morning. You can even speak to a girl you haven't got under long-term contract.

The girls seem to like it because they don't have to be dressed and coiffed like a Schiaparelli fashion show. Kay Francis drops in with her hair knotted in a bandanna and wearing an old coat that she's gotten used to and likes be-

cause it's comfortable. The men who have reputations for being "snappy dressers, on and off," come around for the serious business of tennis dressed comfortably and not like a page out of *Esquire.* The reason for that may be that if you actually dressed on the court in such a flamboyant style, your opponent would probably be blinded, which is not considered sporting.

On top of that, we are developing a brand of tennis out here that bids fair to being the best on the West Coast. Frank Shields and I had the pleasure of playing, and being beaten by, the ranking aces of Japan—the Davis Cup winners—a few weeks ago. My own opponent, Mr. Nakano, played a game of tennis that for sheer steadiness and powerful, flat forehand drives was a wonderful thing to watch.

After beating me 6–3, 6–3, he met me at the net and I had another taste of Oriental "face-saving." He grinned, stuck out his hand, complimented me on my game and added, "The loss wasn't entirely your fault, Mr. Flynn. You may blame it on Their Majesties' Coronation Ball last night." Matter of fact, I'd been thinking much the same thing. The endurance was ebbing a bit that day, due to the fervor with which a bunch of us had gotten together to celebrate the big show in London.

David Niven, who is keeping bachelor's quarters with me, broke a record of some years' standing that afternoon by refusing to meet a dazzling blonde visiting town from Dallas. Instead, he sat mournfully watching the tennis in a ringside box, cheering the Japanese, me and the King with fine impartiality. I was really touched by it all until he met me at the showers and muttered something about, "A splendid game, old man, splendid! Best cricketing I've seen since I left England!"

In a town where nearly everyone, regardless of sex, does something to earn a living, the big days are almost always Sundays. To give you an idea of how the routine goes, I called Cedric Gibbons last Sunday and arranged to meet him and his wife, Dolores Del Rio, at the club for lunch. Somewhere along the line, they picked up Gary and Rocky Cooper and brought them along. We picked up Paulette

Goddard, who was Cedric's partner in the mixed doubles. The usual crowd was milling about. Archie Mayo was loudly declaiming to Humphrey Bogart that the best-written script he's ever worked from was *The Black Legion.* The rest of my gang went on down to the courts to sprawl on the lawn and watch Paulette and Cedric work out while I wandered into the locker room.

I was peacefully wriggling my toes when the door burst open and in popped "Tubby" Griffin, the president of the club. He doesn't like to be called "Tubby" any more than he likes to be kidded about his slow-motion service. I started the nickname myself and he has been searching for revenge ever since. By the look in his eye, he'd found it. He was literally quivering in an effort to be nonchalant.

"Oh, hello, Errol—you here?"

I admitted that the last time I had looked in a mirror, I had indeed been there.

"Did you bring Arno along today?" he inquired with the bland innocence of a Capone wielding a gun. Then he snickered. Immediately I examined him closely. When "Tubby" snickers, something is afoot and the nation is in peril. Skulduggery.

You see, Arno is my favorite dog. He's a good-natured tramp, a schnauzer with the mind of a clown and the heart of a wolf. If pressed, he'd fight and lick four times his weight in wildcats.

Now, there's a strict rule in the club that no dogs are allowed on the premises, but Arno is no respecter of minor regulations. Matter of fact, he's even got me feeling that way. So Arno has been the privileged canine of the lot, wandering free and clear about the club, much to the envy of the other dog owners. What's the use of being on the Board of Governors, I always say, if you can't rate a special privilege?

But to continue—I left "Tubby" snickering. He paused long enough to cock an ear. I followed suit. We sat cocking ears at one another. In the distance, a faint roar could be heard—the noise of the madding crowd.

"Exhibition match?" I queried.

"Uh-huh! It's Arno!" and he went off into mirthful howls. I felt a bit shaken. No telling what my child was up to, but I was sure it must be bad. Gathering my pants about me, I sallied forth.

The grandstand and the veranda were in an uproar. Bets were made hysterically. Johnny Weissmuller and Hal Roach were holding each other up. Helen Flint and Mary Carlisle were all but weeping. Everyone was staring down on the broad expanse of sward before the courts. And there stood Arno. Not his old insouciant self, not the Arno of confidence and boisterous good nature, but a harried and puzzled pooch. He was being attacked and couldn't find the attacker. The lawn was naked of man or beast, but something was definitely chivying at his tail.

Two smallish birds, known as butcher birds, were indulging in a bit of ground strafing that would have made Richthofen's Flying Circus look like amateurs. They'd circle above my poor hound, waiting for the proper moment, and then one would drop over into a power dive straight at his rump. The bird would zing down, jab with its beak, haul out a couple of hairs and fly off, leaving Arno mortified and worried. While the first bird flew back to the nest to deposit the haul, the second one would kick over its joy stick and drop to the attack. No matter which way Arno ran, his rear was in danger and the betting odds had mounted to eight to three in favor of the birds, with no sign of diminishing.

I covered one bet with "Tubby," more out of loyalty than hope, and started cheering Arno lustily. Tennis was forgotten. It was a titanic, elemental war. "Tubby" had bet that they'd both get him again, but Arno suddenly got sense. He sacrificed dignity for security, turned to face the grandstand and sat on his vulnerability, snapping waspishly every time a bird came near. I felt that I'd won the bet when the birds retired to map out a campaign on an Angora cat a block away, but "Tubby" swore that it was no contest and that the birds had won by default.

I really enjoyed tossing "Tubby" into the swimming pool. He made an immense splash and then Arno and I went into the clubhouse to mend our shredded dignities.

Inside, I found Frank Morgan and Pat O'Brien in a deep argument. Morgan had lost a bet on the recent encounter, but was holding forth in favor of the birds. He was about to write to the War Department with a recommendation for a training school for butcher birds in time of war. Expanding the theory, he was sure that they could be trained to speed after enemy airplanes and harry the backs of the pilots' necks, thereby destroying their morale. I left.

Lunch with the Coopers and the Bing Crosbys followed on the open veranda while we all listened to Bing expound on the beauties of his new race track at Del Mar, which opens this month. He was drawing a picture on the table-cloth explaining about the new type of photographic finish device they're using and we were kidding him about it.

"It must be good," he wailed. "A guy by the name of Lorenzo de' Medici del Riccio invented it! With a name like that you can't go wrong!"

Just then, Myron Selznick, the agent, came by and solemnly announced that the part of Scarlett O'Hara in *Gone With the Wind* had at last been filled. The producers had decided to wait until Shirley Temple grew up.

After spoiling our lunch, he went on in search of new victims while Crosby went to sleep and Cooper ruminatively chewed blades of grass. I played a few sets with Paul Lukas who, incidentally, plays a very fast and hard game, and then flopped into the swimming pool, vaguely hoping to find "Tubby's" body floating around in it. Instead of that, I found Eadie Adams' body gliding around, which was a pleasant surprise. She was wearing one of those rubber outfits. Something awkward must have happened to it, because she got down at the deep end and started bleating to Paula Stone. With firm determination and precision, Paula and her female cohorts cleared the pool and surrounding walks of all the men while Eadie made a dash to the locker rooms.

It was all very unfair, I thought, running us out like that! Anyway, we had fun diving in the pool later trying to find out what Eadie had lost, if anything. The answer remains as inscrutable a mystery as the Sphinx.

Sunday is a pretty dull day at best in Hollywood, so the club starts crowding up early and you can wander from group to group listening to the talk about last night's parties.

Pleasantly recuperated from Saturday, in a gentle glow from the workout, you sit around gabbing unimportantly over cool drinks until the Buffet Supper is announced. This is the really big event of the week, aside from periodic dances. For one dollar per person, you can eat more of the best food in the ensuing hours than I've ever seen anywhere before. While you're stowing it away, some energetic lad will wander over to the piano in the big living room and start playing something like "The Trail of the Lonesome Pine" until there are a dozen or more hanging around him and singing.

I recall one particular night it was really swell. Jeanette MacDonald started improvising a song and held everybody spellbound, especially Gene Raymond. Later on, Jack Haley got into the groove and began heating one up and in a couple of minutes half the club was clustered around in a bit of close harmony.

After Buffett Supper that night, bridge games sprang up and gorgeous pals sat around sadly in need of rouge and powder on their sunburned faces. In a far corner was another mob that didn't have to work the next day and wanted us all to know it enviously. They were working up a bit of mild whoopee. To give you an idea of what I mean by mild whoopee, let me tell you what happened.

I'd been working like the devil and had played a lot of tennis that afternoon and had eaten a sizable dinner. The result was that I got sleepy, but, perversely, I didn't want to go home. I went into the locker room and lay down on a rubbing pad for a minute. The minute lasted three hours!

It was after twelve when I hauled myself up, cursing myself bitterly for being such an idiot. As I stalked up the stairs, I heard a piano banging away at something, then a crash and a lot of silly giggling. I looked into the huge living room. It was empty except for Ann Sothern, "Butch" Romero, Betty Furness and a half dozen others. These "sophisticated" celebrities were having a wild party—a real wild party. They were playing "Musical Chairs" and "Going to Jerusalem" and loving it!

That's why the West Side Tennis Club really is the favorite club in town. You know everyone there and they know you and there is no one to impress or to be impressed by.

At the West Side, comedians don't have to be funny and tragedians can tell old jokes; athletes can take sprawling naps and writers can play a hard game. Beauties can come out in the open with their hair in curlers. But Western stars are positively not allowed to ride their trusty mounts into the clubhouse—that's about the only thing that is forbidden.

You can be yourself.

Hollywood Women,
Heaven Preserve Them!

EVERY MAN HAS his ideal woman.

So have I.

She's slim, tall and graceful. Her figure is divine and she's definitely what you'd call the athletic type. I suppose you'd call her a blonde. She loves speed but when I'm weary and want to relax, she idles along with me, her head high and proud as they make them in the sunlight. Her name? The *Cheerio*—and the finest fifty-two-foot yawl-rigged lady in the Santa Monica Yacht Basin. She has a magnificient disposition and is never hard to handle, though occasionally she might toss a few gallons of water at you in a sportive mood. But her most important attribute, in my opinion, is her knowledge of men. She knows, for example, that men have a roving eye and sometimes wander far from the home harbors. Does she mind? Not at all! You haul her hull out of the water, undress her, put her to bed and there she stays without a whimper until you get back.

She's quite a contrast, by and large, to Hollywood women—even women in general—who are prone to be quite annoyed when you dry-dock them, even for their own good. That seems to be especially true out here where the career bug bites them if they don't watch out.

For some strange reason, you seem to run into a number of ladies of an unusual type in California. They are definitely predatory. They don't wait for the men to cluster round—they go out openly and, with bow, arrow, or the weapon

Photoplay, September, 1937. Copyright: *Photoplay*.

best suited to their personalities, proceed to pick off a male.

It's more than a bit startling. One has been more or less brought up to believe that man is the hunter and woman the coy little rabbit who prolongs the chase long enough to ascertain the serious intent of the pursuer.

In Hollywood, there is a whole tribe of Dianas who never heard of a closed season. They'll even knock a man off when he's roosting. The male players in this town, who have a reputation of having a way with the ladies, haven't a way at all—they merely like to be caught. You can see them perched on fence rails in every club in town, ruffling their plumage and emitting low calls calculated to attract the attention of the blasé huntresses.

You can imagine the huntresses chatting as they glance over the well-marked coveys.

"Look," the young featured actress will murmur, "there's a big buck! Shall I drop him?"

"Don't be silly!" will comment the seasoned star. "He's not prime meat yet—only a six-month contract! Now look over there—there's as fine a head as I have seen in many a day, plus a long-term contract. I'll kill that one myself!"

"No, please don't kill him—just wound him. He's got a doe and three fawns at home—and anyway, they're not going to take up his next option."

And the silly part of it is that that particular buck was dying to be killed, I know. He told me.

One thing that is certain—careers breed a different type of women, even if the career is not their own. In most of the communities in which I have lived, women have had a totally different sort of life. That may account for it to a degree. In an average small town, in the islands or in a great city, most women have certain definite responsibilities attached to their homes. Even if they have something else to do in the nature of a career, that career is mostly spoken of in quotes. Their primary interest is domestic—or am I getting profound? I really have no right to carry on this way, I suppose, but even actors do have their serious moments.

In Hollywood, everything is on a different scale. People make ten times the money—when they have a job—that they'd make on the same job in any other part of the world. It seems to be a corollary of making money that you spend it, and the Hollywood wives are no more of an exception than any others.

The first thing they do is to relieve themselves of most women's normal responsibilities by the employment of superlative servants. I am, of course, speaking of the vast majority of Hollywood women—the wives, not the actresses. These poor souls find themselves in the unenviable spot of having days upon days on their hands and nothing to do with them. Nothing, that is, that doesn't soon pall on them and become monotonous.

Their husbands work. They work in a very exacting business, a business that takes well nigh twenty-four hours a day. Frequently, they are away from home on ten minute's notice for days and weeks at a time. Even in their homes there is no discussion of anything other than business. Perhaps a fascinating business, but still something foreign to the home circle.

More as a result of sheer boredom than anything else, many of these women start playing the field. They become predatory. Word goes out among the boys that "so-and-so's wife is on the loose," and many of the boys immediately pop up on a convenient fence where they provide suitable targets. These women of whom I speak are not necessarily bad in the accepted sense of the word, but it goes without saying that the woman who has no particular responsibility toward her home, no particular job to do in the outside world of affairs, is either going to go mad with ennui or is going to find greener pastures.

But Hollywood wives are a subject more suited to the piercing mind of a Dorothy Dix than they are to me. I like many of them—am sorry for most of them.

Fortunately, all the women in Hollywood are not married. If they were, it would be the unattached stag that I'd be sorry for. I'd let the women take care of themselves without sympathy from anyone. It would serve them right!

Strangely enough, the so-called "career-girls" who pop out at you from behind every bush are the worst menace in the town, if it is indeed menace and not a Moslem's idea of Heaven. Most of these lassies have read in various sensational magazines that *there is only one way to get ahead in Hollywood.*

Now, I'd hate to take the bread, to say nothing of the butter, out of the mouths of the sob sisters, but that remark is strictly poppycock. The brutal truth of the matter is that the most consistent of the roués—yes, we have them here, too—are more than a bit bored by this distinctly amateurish approach. They've been braced for a job by experts and feel that the girl who parades her sex in an all too personal manner is merely advertising her inexperience.

Don't misunderstand me. Hollywood is not all sweetness and light any more than is your own home town. The fact that the fundamental business of this town is to parade glamour and beauty and whatever else goes with it on the screen doesn't mean that it is a sexy town. One might parallel that thought with the statement that a town whose primary business was bathing suits and ladies' undergarments was necessarily a sex-mad community because the advertisements for such garments were usually in a distinctly— shall we say, attractive?—key.

So many girls arrive out here with mediocre accomplishments, a driving ambition and no particular brains. Most of them don't really want a career. They want the adulation and the luxuries that go with success, but none of the fighting, tearing, sundering heartaches that are a part of all attainment.

It was once said by a very grand director, Henry Hathaway, that "a person with a real desire for a career is something of a masochist, someone who enjoys the miseries of suffering for a purpose more than he enjoys the completion of the struggle." In other words, these people only want the theater as a means to an end. They want to be celebrities. Having an inferiority complex, they want to be stared at. If their own achievements do not qualify them for attention, then they must shine in the reflected glory of their companions.

There is still another type of woman that inhabits Hollywood. Maybe the Greeks didn't have a word for this type, but we have. They're celebrity-chasers.

In one respect, they are quite closely akin to the predatory Dianas I first mentioned. Anything for a laugh, so to speak. They don't care if the man they snare is a low comic, a broken-down character man, a lead or a star. If his face is familiar, their imaginations will do the rest. Mark you, I don't mean to imply that these girls are just the neophytes of Hollywood, or the tourists, or that the chasing is limited to their sex. In this respect, many men are just as bad. The celebrity-chaser is like any other kind of collector, with one important exception. Their collections comprise only human beings and that is hardly cricket. It is not playing the game of human relations because, like collectors of inanimate objects, they discard the erstwhile famous as callously as a stamp the day that person becomes passé, or less rare.

As a result of a series of incidents, coincidences, breaks and a lot of hard work, I have a good job. I have a job that happens to be in the public eye—I hope I'm not a sty in yours—and as a result of that job and my own personal experience, I feel that I can say that I can spot an insincere person a mile away. By that, I mean people whose primary interest in me is simply because I'm on the crest of the wave.

I have been a seaman all my life. I've seen a lot of waves and I've never seen one that didn't break sooner or later. That applies to Hollywood as well as every sea I've ever sailed. Personally, I have no desire to go on exhibition for any Hollywood hostess because I have a job.

The mistake all our charming huntresses make is that they only flatter a man's vanity—the surest way of bagging him—in a most limited way. He'd have to be a complete idiot in so many cases not to realize it was a name and a bank account the *jeunes filles* were really after.

The most successful women in the gentle art of sniping are the ones who are hard to get, the ones who make a man feel as though he had never really extended himself before. A girl who makes a man feel that he is pretty good, but has a long, long way to go before she would even be interested in aiming at him, is a clever young lady. She puts the man on his mettle and makes him lead to her. If it's marriage she's after, she'll be building for her own happiness if she continues to make the man take that same initiative long after the padre tells them it's legal.

It seems to me, thinking this all over, that I've at best just brushed the surface on the parlous question of women in Hollywood. Maybe it would be a good idea if you and I understood each other right here and now. I'm just as big a sucker for Mr. Kipling's "rag and a bone and a hank of hair" as the next man.

I perch myself on a handy fence and I see a gorgeous creation in the offing. I say to myself, "Here comes a career hunter—or a celebrity-chaser—or a woman with ideas, and . . . oh, boy! she's looking my way!" And do I love it!

See?

Hollywood Morals, If Any!

FROM WHAT I HEAR this must have been quite a town in the days before the Law of Publicity was brought west of Pasadena.

In those days men could pick fights and their women were glad to pick them up afterwards. Not only that, but I understand that they even had sex out here in the old days—great gobs of it—and in their own naive way, they thought it was all pretty swell—grand climate, buxom wenches, two-fisted men and an easy living.

If a man wanted to get wall-eyed, by golly, he got wall-eyed and the citizenry lined Hollywood Boulevard in cheering thousands as he rolled home in a colorful if not pious manner.

The ladies (bless 'em!) seemed to feel that the salubrious subtropics of Southern California offered a perfect setup for Beatrice Crimshaw's settings of South Sea love.

But I wouldn't know anything about that. It was all long before my day in Hollywood and I resent it just a little. By the time I had arrived, full of the legends of high jinks in Movieland, the missionaries had moved in and told Hollywood it was all wrong. Mr. Hays called the girls in and begged them to please, for heaven's sake—forget about this sex business for a while.

Well, the first thing people knew, the Sweetness-and-Light Era had hit Hollywood with a bang. On top of that, they found out that they couldn't stay on the screen and

Photoplay, October, 1937. Copyright: *Photoplay.*

earn their living unless their moral and home life was at least a cut better than Caesar's wife. After all, she was above suspicion, which was a lot more than you could say for the lads and lassies who first populated the studios. Maybe they were wrong—at least, the papers seemed to think so.

While all that was going on out here, I was rambling blissfully through the Islands among a race of people who hadn't been taught that it was more blessed to be able to read and write than it was to enjoy life. The climate was warm and the girls really believed in getting a thorough suntan and a reasonable collection of husbands. The average price for a wife ran about three pigs per mate and everybody was thoroughly content with the whole setup.

But, before I left the Islands, I had seen the workings of civilization and tourist boats on these innocent people. I had seen cotton dresses with long sleeves slip over the astonished bronze bodies and I had seen the creation of jails to take care of the boys who liked a fight before breakfast—and all this to make the Islands safe for the easily shocked eyes of Mr. and Mrs. Tourist.

Much the same sort of thing hit Hollywood. It wasn't missionaries equipped with Mother Hubbards so much as it was a sensational press that sent its circulation up by printing things that were only partially true and using salacious composographs to prove it, so that everybody started thinking that Hollywood must be worse, if anything, than they said.

Pretty soon the Hays Office stepped up waving a bunch of pictures of young ladies clad in scanties, panties, and smiles. Quite lovely, too, I might add. But it seems as though that was very bad for the young of the nation. Anyway, the Hays Office said, this will never do—why, it's practically the same as sex and we've just found out how bad *that* is!

Today the moral code is strict to the last detail.

The upshot of it was that everybody agreed that if the papers must have leg art, let them have it, but you can't pose the pictures so any of the inside of the lady's thigh shows

During the making of *Virginia City* on location in 1940, Flynn confers with Michael Curtiz, the director of many of his best films. Neither man had much liking for the other. Curtiz considered Flynn a handsome puppet and little else, and the actor looked upon Curtiz as an exceedingly tough, humorless taskmaster. They did three more films together, and then Flynn refused to work with Curtiz ever again. *(Rick Dodd Collection)*

Flynn and Olivia de Havilland while away their time between takes on the shooting of the final scene in *They Died with Their Boots On*. It would be their last working day together. The scene, Custer's farewell to his wife, is a particularly poignant one. Says De Havilland, "Errol was quite intuitive. I think he knew it would be the last time we would work together." *(Rick Dodd Collection)*

The turning point in the life of Errol Flynn — his trial for statutory rape. On November 2, 1942, he appeared with his attorneys Jerry Giesler (left) and Robert Ford at the preliminary hearing in Los Angeles City Hall. *(Robert Matzen Collection)*

Flynn's trial stretched through three weeks of January 1943. Well covered by the press and well attended by the public, it did nothing to diminish his popularity. Each time he left the courtroom, women were lined up for his autograph.

In 1945 Flynn indulged his great love of the sea by buying himself a 120-foot schooner, which he named *Zaca*. It was his retreat and frequently his home for the rest of his life. *(Rick Dodd Collection)*

On board the Zaca in 1946. With Flynn are his second wife, Nora Eddington, his painter friend John Decker, and his father, Professor Theodore Thomson Flynn. *(Rick Dodd Collection)*

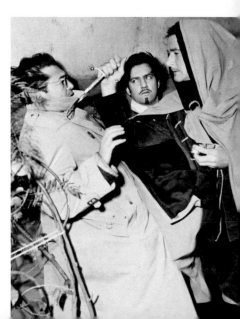

While making *Adventures of Don Juan*, director Vincent Sherman demonstrates to Raymond Burr how he should react when Flynn attacks him. *(Neal Stannard Collection)*

By the age of forty, the handsome face was beginning to show the signs of a lot of living. And he did nothing to preserve his looks.

In 1949 Flynn made his first film away from Warners. He joined Greer Garson at MGM to appear in *That Forsyte Woman*. His portrayal of Soames brought good critical notices, but the public showed little interest, and back he went to swashbuckling, a decision that did nothing to halt his spiritual decline.

In 1953 Flynn paid a happy revisit to the Northampton Repertory Theatre. The company gave its most celebrated alumnus a gala reception, even though none of the members could match his drinking. *(Rick Dodd Collection)*

Flynn's production of *William Tell* in Switzerland in 1953 might have been a triumph, but his backers deserted him, and barely a half hour of the film was completed. With him on the set: Antonella Lualdi, Aldo Fabrizi, and director Jack Cardiff.

With Dorothy Malone in *Too Much, Too Soon*. Flynn's portrayal of his hero John Barrymore was possibly more pitifully accurate than he realized.

With daughter Arnella, born in Rome in December 1953, and his third wife, Patrice Wymore. *(Rick Dodd Collection)*

At the Paris premiere of *The Roots of Heaven*, with Trevor Howard, Juliette Greco, and producer Darryl F. Zanuck, the man who had revived Flynn's career. It was a short-lived revival, and there would be no more major films. *(Rick Dodd Collection)*

In late 1958 Flynn moved around Cuba, collecting material for a series of newspaper articles on Castro and the revolution, in addition to filming shots for his drama-documentary *Cuban Rebel Girls,* the last and the worst of his movies.

Flynn's final work as a performer took place in the first week of October 1959, when he was a guest on *The Red Skelton Show*. With him at the rehearsal are Skelton and Beverly Aadland, who had been his companion for the previous two years. *(Courtesy of CBS)*

On October 9 Flynn arrived at Vancouver, B.C., airport. He borrowed a bowler hat to pose jauntily for newspaper shots. Five days later he succumbed to a heart attack, and the erratic adventures of Errol Flynn came to an abrupt end. *(The Vancouver Province)*

on the plate. If I may hazard a comment, that is like splitting a leg between Nor' and Nor'-East. But maybe I'm wrong. Maybe that's morals.

The ex-convict trying to go straight had nothing on Hollywood. In both cases, their reputations were against them. And the silly part of it is that Hollywood had never been so terribly bad. In every town there are a few bad eggs, but why damn the whole place for that? The major difference between Hollywood and anyplace else turned out to be that in Hollywood the mildest misdemeanor, which would be forgotten anyplace else, was instantly magnified and publicized into a tremendous scandal.

Since I've been here, for example, there have been half a dozen incidents of a more or less unsavory nature, incidents, however, that can and do happen in every other town in the world almost daily. The real difficulty is that a sensational press broadcasts the marital difficulties, say, of an actor and actress throughout the world, not because the difficulties are interesting in themselves to anyone other than the people involved, but because the victims are, in a sense, popular.

Men without number have been sued, rightly or wrongly, for alleged misdemeanors involving ladies in their pasts. No one pays any attention to it. But let that be a member of the theatrical profession and the same indiscretion, true or false, makes international news.

The result is that Hollywood is the most morals-conscious town that I have ever been in on any of the six continents and innumerable islands. Where else in the world are man and wife forced to consider a projected stag fishing trip as a matter of vital importance? It is no exaggeration to say that if a male star wants to go hunting in the High Sierras and his wife wants to visit relations, they must consult with a round dozen of studio employees for weeks in advance. If they don't it is almost sure to be rumored that they are pff-ft! Everything else that happens in their private lives is proportionately exaggerated.

Hollywood has been forced, therefore, to adopt a new

and passing strange sort of moral code. Of course, being Hollywood, they built the moral code like a studio set—all front and rather undressed-looking behind.

I remember when I first came out here. I wanted to take a woman friend of mine out dancing one night. I asked a pal where to go and he began naming a lot of little hideaways. I told him that I was fresh from Ireland and had heard about the wild life in Southern California and was fairly champing at the bit to get at it. Gravely he shook his head. "You've got a lot to learn, my boy. If you go out to one of the big spots you'll get your name linked with hers and—well, don't you see?"

I didn't. I still don't. As near as I can get it, everything is all right in Hollywood provided no gossip columnist sees you and if you are sure Hymie Fink won't pop out at you from behind a bush with his trusty Leica. The cardinal sin of Hollywood is to be caught.

They even have it in all the standard form contracts—a long paragraph about moral turpitude. It's not that anything is ever done here that isn't done in your own home town, but in a normal community, if you step out of line a little bit when the family isn't looking, you're not apt to trip over five photographers and seven reporters who will then run like mad to the nearest newspaper yelling, "Looky, looky, looky what I saw!"

Along with the morals came a code of everyday actions that would make the compiled Mosaic Laws look like child's play. Emily Post, for example, wrote with considerable authority that when that awful moment occurs and divorced husband meets divorced wife they should positively not start throwing hors d'oeuvres at each other, but should bow formally, like complete strangers, and move on, surrounded in a cloud of dignity.

Try that in Hollywood! The silence of the grave would fall upon every party in town and people would have to start learning to wigwag at each other. The rule out here is to greet each other with a wild show of laughing enthusiasm and slap the "ex-" on the back, after having first made sure that there is no knife in the hand. In other words, "We're the best of friends but, for the sake of our careers, we just had to separate." It's just as well that they did formulate that idea because, otherwise, Hollywood hostesses would have to start giving their dinner parties in relays.

Another thing that is considered very bad form is to make dates with your producer's wife. This is important, but like all other generalities, it has its exceptions. If the lady in question is winsome and has shown a predisposition in your favor—and if the producer in question is out of town, or is dating your own wife on the side—then the rule may be discreetly suspended. On the other hand, if the said producer is known to be jealous and is well entrenched in his job, it is considered the worst taste imaginable to dally around in his swimming pool in his absence. Still again, if the gentleman's wife is not lovely, winsome, and so forth— well, what's the use? After all, a code is a code so you might as well follow it sometimes. . . .

I have noticed that people all over the world have a tendency to cock an eyebrow or two at Hollywood when the subject of matrimony is mentioned. Suppose, for the sake of argument, that there is a difference in that grand old custom when it is applied to the life of this unusual community; very well—why shouldn't there be? Acting is a peculiarly difficult manner of earning a living if you are lucky enough to be within the first five hundred of the profession. It places demands on marriage that sometimes cannot be withstood and divorce follows. Immediately there are protests from utter strangers, squawking about the awful example being set to the nation. These Paul Prys don't seem to realize that in most cases, if they closed the divorce courts, they would lower the marriage rates in Hollywood appallingly. Hardly a moral goal, that! The alternative in a professional marriage would mean that one or the other would have to give up a career—which is neither fair to the individual nor to the profession they love.

Players, of necessity, are a more than averagely self-centered group of people. They have to be, for they draw upon their own confidence and ability to spend long periods in profound self-analysis in order to articulate later on the screen the emotions and authentic actions required of them. While they are working they cannot spend the time upon domestic management that is sometimes necessary.

On top of that, many a leading lady has met and fallen in love with an actor, only to find, after marriage, that what she had fondly hoped was the love of her life turned out to be a guy as stage-struck as any amateur fan waiting in the theater alley for an autograph. Don't think that professionals are not so susceptible to their comrades' charm and acts as the public in general. We are, but we also have more opportunity to be subsequently disillusioned.

There are, of course, many contributing factors, such as that terribly obvious and much discussed status when the wife is knocking over three times as large a weekly stipend as the husband. That used to be a far greater hazard in Hollywood than it is now. I personally know of several happy families out here where both people work, and the husband, professionally, is paid in a scale far below his wife's. The girls themselves seem to realize the psychological jeopardy this condition imposes upon their private lives and, consequently, make ample allowances for the matters of petty but important pride in the bosoms of their men, both in courtship and in marriage. Still, it's a hazard.

In many communities a man wouldn't live long if he made love to the wives and sweethearts of four other men in one day. He couldn't live any longer here if it weren't for the fact that the professional lovemaking for the screen isn't much different than boxing or anything else. Half the men I know sweep Sadie Glutz, the big European svelte-and-sex girl from Prague, into their arms before the camera and start thinking about their wives. In other words, they give nothing that means anything from the depths of their own private hearts. Most players' wives and husbands realize that, and nothing much is thought about adolescent jealousies.

Any time that you hear that Hollywood is immoral and a den of iniquity just tell your informant for me that he doesn't know what he is talking about. One thing he should always remember. Glamour is its own best protection. You really can't lose your head over a girl when somebody is always standing by on the sidelines telling you not to rumple her hairdo and lipstick, and, for heaven's sake, not to throw a shadow on her nose, no matter how passionately you kiss her.

Hollywood's Not-So-Ancient Mariners

WITH SOME PEOPLE it's horses; others like cars and others still go for postage stamps. Personally, I'm one of the men who gets a bit weak in the knees at either the sight of a slim-hulled yacht or a ditto mermaid.

I haven't seen any of the latter since I went on the water wagon.

I have seen one of the former, however—the *Cheerio II*—and I promptly bought her. A new life began and it was then that I learned of a new side of Hollywood—the side where driftwood is substituted for dance floors, where kelp beds take the place of feather beds and blondes. That sounds swell. I wish it were true.

Perhaps you'll think me naive, but I had assumed that these chaps who are forever playing parts before the mast knew something about sailing. For the most part they are very convincing in their pictures as they stride the poop deck and bawl their orders at chantey-singing seamen. Then when I heard that some of these same men owned their own boats in private life and occasionally could be heard discussing the relative merits of certain types of sail, I began to feel a certain brotherly emotion surging in the bosom.

It didn't surge there very long before it became the surge of nausea and, with it, came the realization that the best seaman in the bunch and the man who should be Commodore of the Hollywood fleet was Popeye, the Sailorman.

Photoplay, January 1938. Copyright: *Photoplay.*

At a party you can always spot a pair of these boat-owners by the wary look in their eyes as they talk shop. Like a couple of fencers they feint around with tentatively salty language, obviously quoting from some nautical magazine and praying to high heaven that their vis-à-vis hasn't read the same one.

Don't get the idea that there aren't a few—a very few—real yachtsmen in Hollywood. There are, but they are hard to find because they don't talk yachting, they practice it—which means you'll only find them beating up the channel, running down the coast or, clad in dirty white dungarees, over the side with a bucket of white lead. But where you won't find them is in the Trocadero Bar getting a good coat of Mazda Tan, or giving an indecent exposure of their minds every time they open their mouths when the talk turns to the subject of yachting.

It's really quite a sight to see one of the newly-rich subway cowboys, or even just a cowboy for that matter, putting off in the club tender for his boat. His boat, mind you! He's the Master. He comes down to the float nattily attired in studio photographers, peaked cap, whites and pea jacket, with the smell of salt still in his hair from his morning sitz bath.

All he knows, or wants to know, about a boat is how many she'll sleep. To him a boat is like a floating crap game—a party in a new place every night. I rather imagine to the latent male it is identified with the sea only when a charming lady or two happens to be along to admire his masculine stoicism when the boat ships a sea.

Perhaps I'm a little touchy on the subject of overdressed dry-land seamen with more money than courage, but I've had to make my living from the sea and, believe me, she's no lightweight mistress to work for. That was before I began to learn about pleasure yachting, Hollywood version.

That was in the days of the *Sirocco,* not the *Cheerio II.* The *Cheerio II* is the loveliest yawl you'll ever come across—fast, graceful, and tender. She has quite a bit of freeboard, but when she starts running, close-reefed, with rails under—well, she's marvelous! I've wanted to own a boat like that ever since the days when I used to sail small cargo ships of my own in the Southern Seas. I did have some grand serviceable, commercial boats—the *Maski,* for instance, God bless her!—but they were all of a different breed. Steady, good-natured, almost maternal. I left the *Maski* draped shamelessly over a coral bar off the New Guinea coast. Beaten, bedraggled, hopelessly stove-in, she waggled her masts at me in farewell, for all the world like a drunken old harridan ordering another "Gin-and-it."

But Hollywood sailing is another game entirely—a game, not a vocation. It's a lot of fun too, and a lot of laughs if you can keep your sense of humor up.

Nearly all the Hollywood fleet have Oley Olsens on board to do their sailing for them—and nearly all the Oley Olsens are quaint old gentlemen who have a nodding acquaintance with the sea and a line of salty dialect that would make a Maine fisherman think he was in a foreign country. I think most of them come from Central Casting, but for some arcane reason, these gentlemen all say they have been skippers of ocean liners and have just mislaid their papers.

In their gnarled old hands is placed the fate of the fleet's newest mariner. But the responsibility doesn't weigh heavily on them. They know that the new owner will never want to go much farther than Catalina anyway. And, too, they have found out that they can ride the devil out of Hollywood people and make them like it, on the theory that the more the owner is put in his place, the greater will be his respect for his Oley.

There is a grand legend told around the harbor about Mike Boylan and his Oley. Mike had just taken delivery on his boat and planned to leave San Pedro at noon for a weekend's fishing off Catalina. They got underway shortly after five. This particular Oley Olsen seemed to have great difficulty in starting the auxiliary—so much so that Mike finally did it for him. Then, clear of the breakwater, they had a worse time upping sail. By the time the mainsail was up and the jib made fast, it was quite dark. But that didn't bother Oley. He'd raise the island by dead reckoning, no fear. Four hours, maybe six; depended on currents and winds.

Somewhere around two in the morning Boylan began to have his doubts. There wasn't a light anywhere. He questioned Oley rather harshly. Oley was hurt. After all, didn't Mr. Boylan have faith in him? One thing led to another and relations became strained. Just then they raised some lights off to starboard and Oley began to crow. There was Avalon, right on the nose! Mike was humbled. He begged Oley's pardon. They had a drink and turned in as soon as they'd dropped anchor. When Mike got up there was no Oley in sight. He'd disappeared. When Mike turned shorewards, he understood why. They were snugly under the lee of the San Pedro breakwater—after seven hours' cruise in a circle!

A typical weekend map of the Southern California coastline would drive my old pals in the islands mad with the sight of beautiful women, luxurious craft, and bad seamanship. But, good or bad, it's fun, so what difference does it make? Dotting the coves and bays from Santa Cruz Island on the north to the Todos Santos group off Ensenada, Mexico, you will see enough actors floating in brine and Scotch to stock a dozen studios. And that's not all you'll find.

I was coming down the Santa Barbara channel not long ago, minding my own business and at peace with the world, when I heard the approaching roar of a high-powered speedboat. She quickly overhauled us and cut by to port much closer than she need be. I cussed out the girl and two men aboard her fluently as her deep wake set the *Cheerio* to rolling heavily and I heard the rattle of crockery from below.

In a few minutes the motor of the speedboat ahead began to sputter and pop, then die out entirely. Half a mile ahead she lay wallowing in the trough with signs of considerable confusion. As the *Cheerio* loafed along in the light following breeze, the skipper came aft. Did I want to put over? The people on the powerboat seemed to be in difficulties, were signaling for assistance. Personally, I felt that it served them right, but the first law of the sea is never to pass a boat in distress.

Grumbling to myself, I put her over. We dropped the mainsail and came alongside with just the jib for steerageway. One look at the passengers convinced me that any three people as serene as they were, powerless in a running sea, must be either insane or incredibly stupid. One chap hailed us, wanted the loan of a monkey wrench. The skipper heaved him a line and disgustedly went below for the tools.

At that moment the girl jumped nimbly aboard the *Cheerio,* whipped out an autograph book and, before I realized what had happened, had my autograph and was over the side again. Laughing boisterously at their little joke, they cast off, kicked the motor into a roar and were gone as the skipper perspired up from the forepeak with the wrench. Our comments as we hoisted the mainsail again and got laboriously underway do not belong in the hallowed pages of *Photoplay.*

Farther south we raised Catalina and through the binoculars spotted a pair of boats that made the Honolulu race last year. Tom Reed, the MGM writer-producer, master of the *Paisano,* and director John Ford, aboard his hundred-and-ten-foot ketch, the *Araner,* were racing around Catalina Island—which is a good day's sail for any man. At the isthmus we found Jimmy Cagney entertaining a gang on the *Martha.* Jimmy admits he's no seaman, never raises a sail on the *Martha* and gets deathly ill in the slightest swell. But, paradoxically, he loves the *Martha* and spends his spare time aboard.

However, he hasn't fallen to the level of producer Harry Cohn of Columbia, The Gem of the Breakwater. Cohn owns a luxurious cruiser that he keeps permanently moored in the yacht basin with complete telephone connections to the shore. Never takes it out, but will tell you that yachting is his favorite recreation and pastime.

You'll hear loads of legends and folklore about this basinful of Hollywood seamen. You'll hear about Preston Foster trying to bag a whale with a rifle off Catalina and how the annoyed mammal then set about the serious business of turning the *Zoa III* into the *Zoa IV* and the race Foster had to make harbor; you'll hear about the time Dick Arlen took Gary Cooper and Jack Oakie for a fishing trip on the *Joby R.* and Oakie arrived in what might be the Esquire's idea of a Patagonian Rear Admiral's Coronation uniform and how the two enraged, dungareed players dumped him overside and towed him around the harbor; you'll hear how Jack Moss, Gary's three-hundred-pound manager fell in after a yellowtail and, despite his indignant denials, had to be hauled back aboard with the power winch.

You'll hear how Chaplin's skipper spends half his time in search of quiet coves in which to drop anchor for days at a time while Paulette and the owner are resting with their pals; and you'll hear how Barrymore's *Infanta* got lost in a fog and followed the riding lights of a tugboat halfway to San Francisco one night under the impression that the light was the beacon at the Isthmus; you'll hear of the game of tag played in the harbor between a drunken Japanese fisherman, Ronald Colman's *Dragoon* and Spence Tracy's ketch, the *Carrie B.,* when the fisherman, full of saki and the joy of a newborn son, tried to ram first the *Dragoon* and then the *Carrie B.* and so on—just as a gag for over an hour while the players had to indulge in fast maneuverings to save their vessels. Yes, you'll hear loads of legends around the Santa Monica Yacht Basin—and lots more that couldn't be printed, besides.

Farther south, toward the marlin waters of the Islas Coronados, is still another anchorage in the lee of the aristocratic old Hotel del Coronado, but there is an achorage of seamen, not Hollywoodians. Matter of fact, the Hollywood crowd is none too welcome down there unless they've come for sport fishing instead of the usual weekend binge on the bounding main. It's a lovely little spot and I, for one, get quite a lift of threading my way through the armada of Navy ships moored in the roadstead.

It was an early dawn like that when I was putting out for the Coronados recently with Dolores Del Rio and her husband, Cedric Gibbons, and Lili.

Dolores and Damita weren't being fashion plates that dawn; they were in ducks and had decided to go barefooted as long as Cedric and I did. I must admit they looked a bit odd with the red nail polish on their seamanly bare feet, but we were really having fun and looking forward to dinner in a cove I knew on Santa Magdalena Island.

On the way down, in addition to plenty of yellowtail, we caught a hundred-and-ninety-eight-pounder, using live flying fish for bait. While the skipper started dishing up the dinner of yellowtail, we took a quick dip in the cove, got into the speedboat and ran across the Bay to buy some Mexican wine from the San Tomás vineyards.

That was very nearly the last time the skipper saw any of us. We started up the main street in our swimming trunks and were immediately surrounded by a wildly gesticulating crowd of khaki-clad *soldados* who seemed to be very angry about something and were moving us off in the general direction of the bastille. Neither Cedric nor I was quite sure what to do about it as we didn't feel like tying into the whole Mexican army at that point, especially with our wives in the party.

Of course, in the stress and strain we had both forgotten that Dolores, as well as being a beautiful girl, happens to have been the reigning beauty of Mexico. She waited calmly while we men tried to assert ourselves and find out the meaning of this outrage. Then she quietly spoke a word or two to the sergeant who instantly became all smiles, bows and fluent cordiality and started leading us in the opposite direction. On the way down the street she whispered to me that we had been under arrest for appearing on the public streets of a Sunday insufficiently clad, but that she had saved the day by telling him that our clothes had blown overboard while we were swimming and that we had come into town to re-outfit.

Fifteen minutes later we were hurrying out of town feeling extremely conspicuous in four ill-assorted bathrobes that looked and smelled faintly like secondhand horse blankets. We also had the wine and the best wishes of the policeman—whose brother, strangely enough, ran the town clothing store!

Ensenada, the Land of Tamales and Tequila

THE FACT THAT Ensenada is fast becoming the most popular resort of the West Coast, especially among that crazy gang of rather pleasant idiots known as the "picture people," is the truth.

Of course you will always have your lads and lassies going to Arrowhead in the mountains and Palm Springs in the desert, there to be photographed and to be made much of, but we are speaking now of the so-called hideaway groups.

Mexico is thoroughly delightful and the people more so. Naturally, that doesn't mean the border towns. They are no more Mexican than they are typical small towns of the United States. It is not until you penetrate nearly a hundred miles below the border that you find the real, the genuine people of Mexico.

Not long ago Dick Powell and Joan Blondell were a-wearying of onyx swimming pools, crystal goblets and orchid-bedizened premieres. They wanted a rest, far from photographers flashing light bulbs, far away from police escorts. They wanted to be just people.

We met at lunch in the Studio commissary and they asked me if I knew how they could manage it. I'd just come back from Ensenada so, of course, that was my answer.

"Now, wait," said Dick Powell. "Are you sure it's safe? I mean bandits—Pancho Villa and all that."

"Mexico safe? Don't be silly! You run a bigger chance of being held up in any city in the United States than you do

Photoplay, February, 1938. Copyright: *Photoplay*.

down there. The Mexicans are quite sensitive about it now-adays—so sensitive that one of the few crimes calling for capital punishment is any form of banditry—and they mean it!"

"How about kidnapping?"

"Hasn't been a real case in a dozen years—which is more than you can say for California!" I answered. "Go on—you'll love it. They'll turn the town upside down—and when Mexicans really start paying homage to the honored guest, it is something to see. If you're not careful, they'll start having an annual Ricardo Powell Day!"

So the Powells took the stars off their dressing-room doors and packed them in with the toothbrushes and cold cream and started for a week in old May'-hico. They were both new to the country—and to its tongue—and so, when they saw the big sign by the Aduana Station just outside of Ensenada that read both "Alto" and "Stop," they stopped—in both languages. That proved they were greenhorns.

The *soldado* on duty leapt to his feet, stood at attention, saluted, and rattled on brightly in his mother tongue.

"Bienvenidos gran Señor y Señora!" This remark was followed by a garrulous and colorful flow of incomprehensible—to the Powells—Spanish.

"Well!" commented Mr. Powell to Mrs. Powell at the conclusion of it.

The *soldado* showed his teeth, bowed graciously and jumped on the running board, a display of activity reserved for matters of international importance only. Barking important commands to pedestrians and sleeping dogs, he piloted the startled Powells down Avenida Ruiz as though it were a torturous channel, and thence over the bridge to the famous La Playa.

The hotel was in a state. People were darting about in barely suppressed excitement. Red, white, and green bunting festooned every available cornice; flowers were banked in profusion throughout the lobby; a stringed orchestra was tuning up in the patio.

The Powells were touched.

At the desk of the hotel, they were welcomed by a gentleman of beaming countenance and a warm handshake.

"Bienvenidos a La Playa Ensenada! This is indeed an auspicious occasion! Your rooms are ready. Guerrero! José! Conduct the Señor y Señora!"

Well, this was sure pretty swell, thought the Powells; turning the town out was right! Not many places where foreign picture stars were treated with such naive courtesy. Quite humanly, the Powells began to develop a hidden affection for Mexico and its quaint people.

Throughout the dinner that night they were even more impressed by the feeling that at any moment the curtain was going to be raised at some climactic act, amateurish perhaps, but sincere. After a couple of champagnes, Dick and Joan were at the point of giving the simple little town a new library.

After dinner they went out on the balcony to gaze at the glorious moonlit bay and the Todos Santos Islands that had inspired Robert Louis Stevenson to write *Treasure Island.*

Almost as if their appearance were a cue, a loud (and exceptionally military) town band struck up a march and, with torches and flags, started down the road that stretches between the little town and the hotel grounds.

Joan was ready to cry, she was so moved.

A little group of *soldados* down on the wharf started firing a salute on the town cannon—slowly, sweating enthusiastically and making a great noise. Twenty-one guns! "Gosh . . . !" gushed Dick. "Twenty-one guns! The tops! You know they shouldn't have done that. That's—that's for royalty!"

Just then the torchlight procession took a sharp turn off the road and marched bravely out along the pier where the *soldados* were proudly puffing from their labors. They drew up to attention, facing the bay, where, barely discernible as it approached on the dark water, a small tender was putting in from a battle cruiser, screened from view by the point.

Vociferous in the impressive stillness after the music and gunfire came the massed voices of the 200 inhabitants and 2,000 dogs of Ensenada giving vent to three hearty cheers for the Governor of Baja California who had just arrived for an official visit!

It is reliably stated that Mr. and Mrs. Powell repaired quickly to the bar, there to meditate and take stock.

The presiding genius of Ensenada is Arturo Barreda. Officially, he runs the hotel; actually, he is known far and wide as *El Rey de toda Ensenada.** Son of a Sonora *haciendado,* heir to a two-hundred-thousand-acre rancho, he is a man to be reckoned with. In him is a strange combination of the blood of the Conquistadores and modern Mexico. On duty he has the natural suavity of a Continental diplomat; off duty he is a caballero on the loose. The well-banked fires in his eyes break into flame and Ensenada sits back in watchful admiration to see what Arturo will do next—he usually does it.

One of Arturo's best friends is Jimmy Dunn—and Dunn has the same love of Mexico that you will find in anyone who has lived there and known the people intimately. Together they have bought three hundred acres just south of Ensenada upon which they plan to build a ranch. They will grow horses and cattle (from Arturo's Sonora estate), beans (indigenous), and dudes (imported). They will also lease certain choice lots to a few Hollywoodians who like the country for something other than a place in which to get cockeyed, so that they too, may build.

One of the first of these lots went to Grace Moore and her husband Valentín Parera. Between pictures it has been the wont of the songstress to hie herself and husband down to the Ensenada Bay in a trailer and pitch camp among the tacos and frijoles. She and your humble correspondent, along with several others, would long since be property owners in Baja California were it not for the fact that Mexico has passed laws forbidding the owning of property by foreigners. And for very good reason, when you consider the land and mineral-grabbing propensities of certain of our wealthier men.

When the screen's "favorite wife" decided to find out for

*"The King of all Ensenada."

herself what all this marriage business was really like and stepped into the bonds of holy wedlock, she did it in Ensenada. In case you have ever married Myrna Loy in the dark of a theater, you probably felt a certain jealousy toward producer Arthur Hornblow when it was announced that they had up and done it.

You would have been even more jealous had you been in Ensenada when it happened. They had a whale of a time. No one recognized them, but all of Ensenada knew that here was a young couple about to be married. That's all a Mexican needs to know to declare a national holiday. They immediately gave their undivided attention to the job in hand, with all the critical friendliness of intimates.

The Hornblows were married by the *Alcalde* [mayor] in an office that can be likened only to the bottom of an elevator shaft, so high is the ceiling, so constricted the floor space. In sonorous Spanish the *Alcalde* intoned the lovely ceremony, pausing appropriately for the wholly superfluous official interpreter's interjections.

There would be a flow of liquid Spanish and a pause. The interpreter would glance over the *Alcalde's* shoulder, gauge the place by the *Alcalde's* thumb and comment briskly. "Do you take this guy to be your husband?" More lingual beauty followed the response. "Do you want to marry this lady, huh?"

And then the *Alcalde* really got in the groove. He gave it the works and the bridal party was quite affected—only to come back to earth as the bored interpreter hurried away to his work, calling from the door, "He says it's all right now!"

But that's not the end of it. No indeed! Meanwhile Arturo had snapped across the street to the *carniceria* for the sack of rice—and the owner refused to be paid when he learned that it was for a wedding, not eating. Not only that, he, himself, seized a sack and followed Arturo back across the street, tossing the grain about like a flower girl on a binge.

That, of course, called for drinks at the old El Rancho Grande bar. But were the newlyweds permitted to buy? I should say not! In Mexico? Don't be silly! Practically every town official stood for at least one round, and Javier, the proprietor, became so touched by it all that he wanted to give the Hornblows the bar as a wedding present.

Now, lest you think that I, myself, am on a tequila binge as I write this, let me point out that Mexico is not the Islander's idea of heaven—all free drinks, food and affection. Not at all! At least, not quite at all. It depends upon the individual.

Many superior Nordics barge into Mexico as if on a slumming expedition and take no pains to conceal the fact that they believe the proper spelling of the word "Mexican" is g-r-e-a-s-e-r and should be prefaced with such adjectives as "lousy," "dirty," or "filthy."

They can hardly contain themselves when they arrive south of the line. They disdainfully and angrily stride about the streets like strange curs looking for a fight, and they usually get it—on the same basis that an intoxicated Mexican would get it in Portland, Maine, if he adopted the same attitude.

The people that really get the typical reception Mexico has to offer friends are the people who come down to Mexico because they like it—and, strangely enough, large sections of the Hollywood crowd fall into that category. Reserves drop. They are in a foreign and friendly land where no one is an undercover man for columnists. They are taken at their face value.

If they go on a gentle binge, no one will call from the studios the next day reminding them of the youth of America and clause four in the contract, concerning moral turpitude.

A certain very well-known leading man, who will remain nameless, due to the aforementioned clause, went on what is colloquially known as "un rondo." And, believe me, it must have been a rondo grande! They say that all Ensenada lined the streets in cheering thousands when he finally agreed to return to the hotel. After the last bar had reluctantly closed due to exhaustion and the serious depletion of its wares, the actor was overwhelmed with gratitude for his *buenos amigos.*

He must do something for them!

In the dawn's early light he spied the slightly soiled statue of "El Libertador" in the plaza. Now, no one knows who "El Libertador" is, other than that he came from Mexico City with a bill for 20,000 pesos; but he does cut a lovely figure. He'd be lovelier, however, if an old family of crows hadn't been using him as a pied-à-terre these many years.

This thought occurred to the swashbuckling actor, and he instantly and imperiously demanded large quantities of soap and water.

Eager to comply with the slightest wish of a guest, the townspeople added a painter's spatula to the order and proceeded to stand about the plaza in open admiration of such industry, as the man whose profile has chiseled a million female hearts chiseled the accumulated dirt from the face of "El Libertador."

To the simple Mexicans, such a person is veritably un hombre y medio—a man and a half. He is vastly respected for his prowess as an imbiber of spirits.

Let it be clearly understood, however, that to gain the heart of our southern neighbors you do not have to be able to absorb two quarts of tequila on a quiet evening at home—but you do have to be sociable.

But all visits to Mexico don't end that way, though most of them have their unusual twists. George Brent and Constance Worth flew down there for their ill-fated nuptials. They landed in the big field just out of town, and sundry natives gleefully ran over to welcome them and inspect the ship.

When they learned that it was a marriage party, they went mad with joy—as usual. While the party was filling out the sundry blanks pertaining to holy wedlock, the word spread and all roads led to the airport.

The Brents returned to the ship for the northward flight to find it completely unairworthy due to festooning from wing tip to wing tip and prop to tail with the old familiar red, white, and green crepe paper.

Surrounding the bedecked craft was a crowd of admiring Mexicans of all ages who hailed the bride and groom with delight and rice. Brent was in something of a dilemma. He couldn't strip the paper off the ship without hurting their feelings. His Spanish wasn't up to an explanation. He couldn't wait until dark, not having night-flying instruments. Every abortive attempt at suggesting the fun was over was met with loud and noncomprehending "Huzzahs!"

Brent knew when he was licked.

He shrugged, got into the ship, gave it the gun. With crepe paper shredding all over the field in the slip stream, he took off like a tattered wizard of old, amid the frenzied acclaim of the multitude.

The ship was badly off balance, despite the fact that Brent could find nothing wrong with the controls or surfaces. Considerably worried, they flew on and Brent trimmed her down to compensate for the invisible obstacle. He was soon rather appalled to find the ship acting in an even more erratic manner. As far as he could see, the ship was clear of festoons, but every time he'd trim her down she'd whop off center again.

It was a nervy trip back to Burbank.

When they set her down at United Airport they found out the cause. An outraged mechanic came yelling across the field after them, demanding that they take care of their own so-and-so livestock. This was an airport, not a ranch, said he! It seems that a Mexican, in the transports of matrimonial glee, had presented the Brents with their first wedding present, which was stowed well away in the tail of the ship for safekeeping.

It was a very much alive ninety pounds of extremely indignant pig, thrashing about in the rear assembly of the fuselage!

The Seamy Side of Hollywood

WHY IS IT that the only things one ever reads about this town are the prop stories—the stories of glitter and glamour and money and fine gestures and beautiful people?

I've been here two years and some months now and I'm frank to admit that for a long time I was hemmed into thinking the same thing. One never sees headless bodies lying in the streets nor does one smell the stench of disease or abject poverty. Of course, there are poor people here as well as everywhere else, but not in the same sense; they don't eat offal as they do in China, nor live in actual sewers. After a while, thanks to the Chamber of Commerce and the Best Feet Forward Boys, one begins to believe that Hollywood is as much of an ideal spot as the illusions created here.

Did you ever get bored with perfection? Did you ever go to a party as a child and see a lovely, prissy little girl who was so darned perfect you yearned to smack her in the face and smear mud on her frock? If you've never felt that primeval urge within you, please don't read any more of this—because, after two years of scintillating perfection, I got bored stiff one evening recently, and decided to go backstage and see if the town of Hollywood, itself, wasn't just a huge stage setting, behind the perfection of which might lurk the denizens of darkness.

Photoplay, April, 1938. Copyright: *Photoplay.*

I had two companions during the evening. One, Captain Steed, then in charge of the Homicide Squad of the Los Angeles Police Department, I'll never forget. With the looks and attitude of living of a YMCA boys' counselor, smooth, gentle and calm, he holds a job that is one of the most dangerous in the city. He has the well-earned reputation of being able to break down the most confirmed killers.

My other companion was a gentleman named Pat. Pat drives an ambulance and spends eight hours a day in a welter of gore. In his spare time he paints lovely water-color landscapes.

The three of us had dinner in what passes for Chinatown in Los Angeles. Why they call it Chinatown is a mystery. The young Chinese there speak far better English than most assistant directors and at least two millionaire producers I've met; and, as a general rule, the food they serve, if presented piping hot to a mandarin in Shanghai, would be considered an excellent example of the American table d'hôte.

Just as we had reached the coffee and cigarette stage, a telephone call came through. A Chinese had been stabbed at a nearby address; no details.

We threw a bill on the table and ran for the car. The driver got the call over the radio so the motor was on and we were under way before the door slammed.

Black little alleys flashed by with frightened, disembodied faces peering out. Brilliant neon signs flashed ads of Chinese-American whoopee, mostly enjoyed by Filipinos.

We rounded a corner on screaming tires and saw a freight train bearing down on us with loud clanging and whistling. Now a Chevrolet is a substantial car, but I doubt if its most avid booster would advise you to tangle one with a freight train. After all, bulk is still bulk.

I'm not just clear as to what happened next, but we squeezed by in a fine flurry of sirens and locomotive blasts. I looked at my companions. They were smoking calmly and discussing the forthcoming World Series.

A moment later and we pulled up in front of a narrow doorway before which milled a crowd of Chinese, Japanese, Filipinos and Negroes, to say nothing of a few miscellaneous types, all trying to maul and shriek past a harried patrolman.

Upstairs lay a twisted little body. A Eurasian, he seemed to be; nattily dressed; room heavy with scent, crowded with stills from dozens of films. Everything was quite neat and orderly, but his head wasn't where it belonged. It was about three feet away from the rest of him, looking quite surprised.

A fat lady who'd forced her way up with us looked, gagged, fainted dead away. Somebody moved her out into the hall so the ambulance men could get in, but there wasn't anything they could do just then. Mr. Kong was quite defunct.

He had been some sort of a local picture agent who had had the bad taste to collect for jobs in advance. When the jobs failed to materialize, one of his clients had become annoyed and called on him with a snickersnee.

On the way back to headquarters, I learned that that is one of the favorite local rackets.

Not calling on agents with snickersnees, but being a phony agent. The whole town is riddled with them, despite the sincere efforts of the Hays Office and the Better Business Bureau. Obviously a cheap form of chiseling, you'd be surprised at how much of a toll the racket extracts annually from gullible would-be actors and actresses.

But the seamy side of Hollywood is not limited to agents, though that is quite a field in itself. As a matter of fact, the incident I've just described was merely a prelude to the evening's real events. From downtown Los Angeles we wandered out toward the mountains of Hollywood and Beverly Hills, just jogging along, listening to radio calls and waiting for something to happen in a district near us.

I came to the conclusion then that a policeman's life is one long series of prowlers and drunks—and most of them imaginary. As far as the prowlers are concerned, the story of the old maid and the burglar is as good an illustration as any. A lot of these nervous ladies apparently just want someone to talk to because the prowlers usually evaporate without leaving a single corporeal sign.

The men were telling me the inside story of one of the most amusing of Hollywood's extortion cases. A certain prominent producer—forgive me for not mentioning names, but someday I may have to work for him—received, with his soft boiled eggs of a morning, a pointed note from an amateur extortionist and crank. He was demanding ten thousand dollars on pain of kidnapping the producer's wife, but was obviously a novice in that he signed his name and address to the note. The producer was no whit ruffled. Instead, he called in his secretary and dictated a polite reply to the effect that he didn't have the ten thousand, but was very much interested in the extortionist's proposition. That ended that.

The radio suddenly shrilled into action. A disturbance in a swank apartment house near one of the major studios. Investigate. That was all. . . .

The lurch of the car nearly snapped my head off. Behind red lights and sirens we wailed down the Boulevard, through stop signals and past frightened pedestrians. The manager of the apartments met us on the sidewalk, literally wringing his hands and bleating, "No publicity, gentlemen, please! No publicity!"

To which the sergeant replied, brushing him aside, "What do you think we are—advance agents for a circus?"

The Negro elevator operator was much more helpful. "The lady in 4-B, she done it ag'in, gempmun, on'y this time she sho got the miseries for true!"

The lady in 4-B was a pathetic sight. She was, we learned later, nineteen, the daughter of a substantial Midwestern family, who had married against her family's wishes. When her shiftless husband disappeared, she had too much pride to go back home, tried to crack into pictures with more looks than ability. When we got to her flat, she was lying across her bed, practically nude, and retching horribly. Attempted poisoning went on the books while Pat, the ambulance man, was using the Lafarge on her, pumping from her tortured stomach the patent antiseptic she had used.

On the dresser was a polite little note from Central Casting informing her that it was impossible to register any more extra talent and that, since there were fifteen thousand already enrolled ahead of her, she would have to wait her turn.

The pathos of such cases is not so great here as elsewhere. It is not that Hollywood is hard-hearted, but, after all, I suppose there are a lot more suicides in Movietown than in the average community.

Unlike most cities, according to police records, women suicides predominate in Hollywood. Blasted careers and unscrupulous men who use a girl's ambition for their own ends seem to be the primary motives for such tragedies.

The next hour was rather dullish as far as action went. We drove over to the Brown Derby on Vine Street and had a badly needed cup of steaming black coffee. The driver remained in the car, waiting for calls that never seemed to come.

I learned to my amazement that Hollywood is the locale of more attempted extortion cases per annum than any other city in the United States. This particular brand of criminal seems to feel that we who have attained a modicum of success on the screen are natural-born suckers; that all they have to do is say, "Boo! The bogeyman'll get you if you don't watch out!" and we'll immediately part with large quantities of our hard-earned funds.

Fortunately a man by the name of Blaney Mathews started a squad in the District Attorney's office some years ago known as the Special Investigation Detail. So far they have a perfect record—1,098 successful cases at the time Mathews took up other duties.

The men were praising Mae West and Clark Gable for their courage in fighting such cases out, regardless of the publicity, when the driver raced in for us.

"Something hot out in Beverly Hills—a shooting. Local men are on it—do you want to cover it?"

We did—emphatically!

I've never known that Sunset Boulevard could unroll so fast. At times we were hitting eighty and eighty-five—down past the Clover Club, the Troc, Lamaze, the Cock and Bull. I had an insane desire to giggle as I caught a flash of a huge sign down near the bridle path—*NEW GUIDE TO MOVIE STARS' HOMES.* I don't know why it was so amusing just then, except that, in moments of the sort, one is rarely normal and, too, perhaps I did have a new guide to some famous home right then—a guide at eighty m.p.h.

We cut south of Sunset onto one of the swankest residential streets in Beverly Hills. Vast mansions on both sides, hidden in royal palms; two houses I recognized as belonging to friends of mine. I wondered what one hostess was gossiping about as we drove past, what she'd say if she knew what was happening a few yards from the scene.

When I saw the house before which an ambulance and police car already stood, I nearly fainted. I'd been there countless times for dinner. The young picture couple who lived there were great personal friends of both Lili's and mine. He was a young director with a great future, she a successful actress.

I sprinted across the lawn in a nightmare. I might have saved myself the trouble. When we got in the house we learned that my friends had leased it and moved out into San Fernando Valley six weeks before, when I had been away on a Mexican fishing trip.

The man who had leased it was a gambler and racetrack follower. He had come home and found his nightclub hostess wife doing a bit of private nightclubbing with a song-and-dance expert. The gambler decided he had been done wrong, took a couple of pot shots at the fleeing couple and apparently missed them. He then took a shot at the petrified Filipino butler. He missed all three and then, either because he had been betrayed or was humiliated at being such a bad marksman, he tried one on himself.

I must say that he was extraordinarily inept at handling firearms, for all he succeeded in doing, after a total of four shots, was to give himself a slight wound in the fleshy part of his shoulder, just to starboard of his armpit. The way the man moaned and groaned when they carried him out to the ambulance, you'd thought he'd been through the three days at Vimy Ridge.*

The next call was unusual, even for Hollywood. A certain well-known character actor whose morals are no better than they absolutely have to be had called on a few girls living in a lovely house up in the hills. There were a couple of other male guests and one thing had led to another and everybody had had a lot of drinks and laughs. The character actor decided that he should give his impersonation of a faun. Apparently he had. Pretty soon they all had started being fauns, frolicking all over the house with veils and bacchanal wreaths and a gay disregard for the furniture, vases and windows.

Unable to contain themselves within four walls, they had started their Spring Dance on the lawn around the goldfish pond. Maybe the neighbors were narrow-minded or maybe they just wanted to sleep—in any event, they had put in a call.

It is presumable that the giddy young people had heard the wailing approach of the siren and, suddenly sobered, had made a mad dash for the house, because the only person we found was a disheveled actor in an extraordinary miscellany of clothes pounding on the front door with anguished fists.

"Lemme in!" he wailed. "Lemme in! I'll be good! Honest, I'll be good. . . ."

He looked around and saw me through the haze, grinned foolishly and turned back to the door. "C'mon! Open up! Y' don't have to hide anymore—it ain't the cops, after all—it's just Errol Flynn!"

I wasn't much flattered because all that answered him was the silence of the tombs. The sergeant tried his hand— or his stentorian voice, rather—but to no avail. Just then the driver came around the house to report that its back door opened on another street and that the birds had flown. If those particular birds want the rest of their wearing ap-

---

*A World War I battle.

parel they may have same by applying to headquarters downtown.

The last call I made that night was the last one I ever want to make in Hollywood.

It came from the manager of a cheap hotel. He was worried. The door of one of the hotel rooms was locked from the inside and no one had seen the woman who occupied the room for four days. Being wise to the law, he called the police to open the door. I, unfortunately, was along.

As we opened the door we saw, from the light from the hall, two fiery little eyes staring, unblinkingly, from under the dressing table.

We switched on the lights. The room was neat; poor but decent. The girl—middle-aged, really, but it's hard even now to realize it—was lying face down, on the bed, watched over by her beloved pet dog.

When I went closer, I was shocked to see that this woman was an actress you have all known and loved for many, many years—as have I.

From now on, I'll let the seamy side take care of itself. Boys and girls, give me glitter, even if it bores me!

Let's Hunt for Treasure

FOR SOME REASON that I've never been able to understand, people are envious of a lucky break. Way down
deep, they sneer at luck—unless they're the ones who have
it. That, of course, makes the whole thing different. For the
same reason, they find it excruciatingly funny when someone else follows his luck and it turns out to be all bad.

I've had my share of both.

There's a small mountain in Alaska named after me. It's
called Flynn's Folly. Yes, I was the goat in that deal. There's
a cove in New Guinea, a tiny little spot where the sea battles with the jungle unceasingly. Its name, translated into
pidgin-English, is Man-Go-Along-Dog. That's me—the natives couldn't pronounce my name. It's another spot where
my luck ran out and provided laughs for the boys in the island bars. There's an abandoned shaft up the Sepic River in
Papua . . . but why go on with the grisly list?

Friends and business associates and relatives have come
to me dozens of times with sad headshakings and asked,
"Look, old boy, why not drop this? It's a harebrained
scheme. You'll lose your shirt!" To which I usually reply
that I'd sooner lose it than wear it out. The tragedy of life is
in its frayed edges and all that they imply. I don't like that.
Right royal robes or sackcloth. One end or the other. Never
mediocrity.

The result is that at heart I'm a treasure hunter. I always
have been, since I was a lad, digging in the garden of a sub-

Photoplay, April, 1939. Copyright: *Photoplay.*

urban villa near Sydney, Australia. I'd heard that the previous owner had been a miser. In all the books I had ever read, misers invariably buried their hoards in the cellar or in the back yard. We had no cellar, so it was the hollyhock beds that were elected to suffer under my youthful but enthusiastic spading.

In one way or another I've been at it ever since.

Nor am I alone in that urge. I think that nine men out of ten have the same instinct, but not all have the opportunity to gratify it. Still others have the chance but are afraid they'll be laughed at if they lose out.

Personally, I don't care. Lest I sound whimsical, let me point out that my treasure-seeking is quite practical. I'm still a little ahead, by and large, even including the more obvious financial failures.

But, most important, I've enjoyed myself doing it.

I even get a laugh out of all the wild stories that have been circulated through the taprooms, mostly untrue, about my so-called adventures. But, if the truth of them is not quite up to the elaborately concocted tales told over a whiskey-and, they were still not run-of-the-mill and were delightfully absorbing while they were going on. Beside them, Hollywood is a very tame place. People out here work very seriously to make a living. I'd never done that before. I'd played to make a living and, I hope, always will. When a job got to be serious and seemed to be jeopardizing my personal liberty, I quit. There was always some treasure, a mine, a jewel, a pearl or trochus shell bed on a forgotten shoal around the corner or across the seas that seemed much more worthwhile than any job whose familiarity was beginning to make it prosaic.

Hollywood was the first place I had ever found that paid enough money to make it worthwhile to endure the banalities of maintaining a permanent anchorage in any harbor. But even with the money and the pleasure of working at a pleasant job, I'd chuck it in a minute if I couldn't have a few months every year in which to get back to that fascinating game of bucking Mesdames Lady Luck and Mother Nature.

One of my really successful treasure hunts was for a mine

up in the wilds of the head-hunting country on the Wau Plateau in Morobe, New Guinea. Before I left there, I'd seen the airplane shorten that long, arduous overland safari; formerly it had taken a traveler eleven days to make it and almost another eleven to recuperate. I made money for myself and three pals. It didn't last long, but then, what's money for?

It was not so long ago that I heard of a mine up in Alaska. The whole situation surrounding it seemed ideal. One of my best friends, Bud Ernst, was at loose ends. He pitched in with me and we began on that delightful stage of treasure hunting accomplished with elaborate maps, one bottle of ink, a pen, one bottle not of ink, pipes, tobacco and an open fire. That's the time when all the participants make at least seven million dollars apiece, find Paradise Lost and meet the beautiful Eurasian princess who invariably will fall madly and excitingly in love with you. It's always you she falls in love with—never the other guy.

Of course, in your heart you know from previous experience that you'll probably lose even the pipes and tobacco, get knifed by a native who never heard of paradise and doesn't want to, and the beautiful Eurasian princess will turn out to be more Asian than Eur- with most of her teeth gone from too little hygiene and too much betel nut. She will also have four angry husbands and a child in every port. But never let those sober reflections dampen your ardor.

Bud and I decided that the Alaskan adventure would have to be experienced by air. Any other route would mean months of overland mushing and neither of us could afford the time. We bought a ship, a used Waco in excellent condition, and proceeded to trim her down and outfit her for the flight. Days were spent in test-hopping her at the airport under all sorts of weather and load conditions; nights were spent arguing and figuring and dreaming. It really looked as though this was the one treasure hunt in the proverbial million.

Then the first blow fell.

The studio wouldn't let me go. I was heartbroken. Bud was the guy who was going to have all the fun—and he did.

The mine flopped at the sneak preview, but Bud, probably feeling I ought to get something for my money, named a mountain to commemorate it. Flynn's Folly.

To my mind, Flynn's only folly that time was to have let a job interfere with all the fun.

But there's always a recompense for everything if you want to see it. Mine came almost before Bud had gotten back to Hollywood. An old ship captain whom I'd known for years and in five of the seven seas wandered into Hollywood. When I first met him, years ago, he'd lost his ticket in some nameless scrape in the islands. We were both working our way back to England aboard a tramp. As kindred souls will, we got to swapping yarns and little by little he told me of one of his cherished ambitions—to unearth a vast and fabled cache of gems and gold buried near Addis Ababa.

We agreed we ought to have a crack at that treasure. We were off Aden when the captain of the tramp we were working on received a radio from the owners. He was to proceed at once to an unscheduled stop at Djibouti, French Somaliland, and there pick up a cargo of rubber. When word of this reached the forecastle, Captain M. and I merely looked at each other. Nothing else was necessary. No discussion of plans. We knew.

We jumped ship in Djibouti (which, incidentally, is no place to jump ship unless you are rich or well-connected), found an amiable French colonial and his wife with whom we stayed until our ship had left port. They turned out to be delightful people and Madame gave us the name and address of her cousin in the capital, some sort of a high-ranking official.

We took the comic train down to Addis Ababa. Obviously, it was beneath our dignity to arrive without baggage or the full accouterments of the lion hunt we were presumably engaged upon at the time. A bored gentleman with more faith in his poker ability than was justified by his belief in two pairs provided a few items of apparel and a few hundred francs, but we were still without baggage. Nor could we interest anyone else in taking a chance at the gaming table with us.

In Addis Ababa we were met by the Frenchman, cousin of our late hostess. Captain M. and I both exclaimed angrily over the deporable state of the laws of Somaliland and the thieving proclivities of all baggage agents. We made quite a fuss about the whole thing and, after a few drinks, we made even more of a fuss about it. The result was that we over-played our hands and what looked like a gift from heaven turned into a boomerang.

Word of the sad plight of the two indubitably wealthy Inglisi hunters reached the Foreign Office; from there it traveled to the Prime Minister, Ras Somebody-or-other, and thence, I imagine, to Haile Selassie himself. Now, at that time, the Ethiopians were encouraging tourist trade to the limit. The Conquering Lion of Judah wanted to demonstrate the innate hospitality of his people; so, forthwith, he or his prime minister dispatched two emissaries to the pub in which we were discussing the country with obliging white residents, pumping them as to caravan routes to the south and the possibilities of moving around without a Government escort. Native police, of course, would be a definite handicap in smuggling anything out of the country if we did happen to find something.

At that moment there was a stir in the room. Everyone rose respectfully and the waiters bowed low to the two impressive-looking gentlemen. They crossed to us with majestic austerity, bowed and informed us that henceforth we were the personal guests of His Imperial Majesty, Haile Selassie, Emperor of Abyssinia, Ras of Tigré, Amhara and Shoa, the Conquering Lion of Judah, Defender of the Faith and half a dozen more titles. At the end of the recitation they smiled again, bowed and led us out.

We were taken at once to one of the minor palaces in the capital and there ensconced with full honors, a large staff of servants, bales of fresh clothing, tobacco, wine and food. It looked like what it was—a regal windfall.

But when the next train came in from Djibouti, Ras Tafali, our Escort in Chief, began to look strangely at us and ask embarrassing questions. Later, our French friend told us that the Foreign Office was burning up the wires to Djibouti in an effort to locate our nonexistent baggage. That same day Ras Tafali took us on another tour of inspection of public buildings. This time it was the local bastille—and a more revolting spot I have never seen. It made us wonder uneasily what the score was.

We had been there ten days and were still no closer to sneaking away with a proper little caravan to cover the eighty miles southeast to where we judged the treasure was buried near an old Coptic monastery—and the regal hospitality was beginning to wear a bit thin. Very thin, we felt.

The next Friday, the second train since our arrival came in. Naturally, we felt that we should meet it just to keep up appearances, but our lamentations over the ever-missing baggage seemed false even to us and met with no responsive cluckings from the stony-eyed station agent. By the time we got back to our palace we found it stripped of its finery and of its staff. One man, the gate-keeper, remained. He handed us a note requesting our immediate presence at the Foreign Office.

From the little hill overlooking the town we could see the Foreign Office and ever so many other public buildings.

We could also see the bastille.

We nodded cheerily to the gateman and headed in the general direction of the Foreign Office, turned abruptly off into some back streets, grabbed our French friend in the middle of his siesta, snagged him for the ready cash he had on him in case of emergencies, and sneaked quickly out of town.

We lay in a culvert, damning all buried treasure heartily, until the Djibouti-bound train chuffed past us up the grade. It never made more than fifteen miles an hour, so it was easy to swing on board and lay low on the rear platform until we crossed into French territory.

For all I know, that treasure still lies beneath the ravaged soil of Ethiopia. Personally, it can stay there.

I never saw Captain M. again until a day not so long ago, when he barged into Hollywood. He'd read in a paper about my purchase of the *Sirocco* and my plans to go after the wily sailfish in the Caribbees.

Now, as you have probably gathered already, treasure hunters are essentially optimistic. Captain M. was no exception. He cocked one rheumy eye at me as he stoked his pipe and spoke ever so casually.

"I hear you're getting under way for the Barbados."

I waited.

"Very strange," he muttered, trying to look mysterious. "I'm planning to make a voyage there myself."

I nodded. I knew he needed no prompting.

He lowered his voice appropriately. "I've a map, lad. Chart. Sunken cannon. Treasure. Isle of Pines!" He fairly hissed that at me and then sat back complacently to gauge its effect.

Yes—you guessed it! Captain M. came along.

On this treasure trip the Captain and I fished our way from the Florida mainland to Cat Cay and down through the chain of islands bottling up the Gulf of Mexico.

We found the cove we were looking for near Nuevo Gerona. It was idyllic, a perfect place for our work and we lost no time in digging up our diving equipment out of the hold.

I started diving as soon as the sun was high. I dove for four days trying to find that cannon with its treasure, narrowing down the field of search in concentric circles, limited by the length of my air hose and life line. It seemed to me that during those days every time I came to the surface someone handed me another frantic cable from the studio. My next picture had been moved up on the production schedule and they wanted me back. They wanted me back with almost as much determination as I had to find the cannon first. I was on a hot lead and I knew it. I felt it in every bone. The next dive would be it. . . .

At length I could stall the studio no longer. I had to give up.

And the day after I left, Captain M. went down. In his first dive he lit squarely atop the weed-grown cannon. Intrinsically the value of that treasure was not a great deal—most of it was semiprecious African bracelets, a few of them gold; however, as I write this article my paperweight is a beautifully wrought bit of metal of African workmanship, one bit of loot to serve as a reminder of the Captain's and my second treasure hunt.

Captain M. cabled me the other day from the Isle of Pines. He's gotten hold of another chart. A Chart of Buried Treasure.

So, as soon as I finish production on "Dodge City" . . . well . . . maybe . . .

It'll be worth trying, anyway; treasure hunting always is!

It Shouldn't Happen to an Actor

DID YOU EVER in your life meet up with one of those unique dogs who seemed to have been waiting at a certain spot at a certain time for the particular purpose of meeting you? I suppose I've been lucky, because out of the innumerable dogs in whose life I've been, there were two who looked me right in the eye at our very first meeting and said, "Well! I knew you had to show up soon."

The first one's name was Pikis. I bought him from a Chinese copra trader for two tins of salmon and lost him to an alligator in a river in New Guinea. After that, dogs came and dogs went. Nice enough dogs but never very special. Until the day I looked down to see a gray, ugly beast of a dog, a schnauzer, jumping perpendicularly up and down on a leash held by a black chauffeur.

Glad to see me? He was absolutely out of his mind, although, of course, he had never laid eyes on me until that moment. "You don't happen to want him, do you?" said his owner hopefully. "If I don't get rid of him, the police will shoot him. He's a nuisance."

Thus destiny brought me Arno. Arno was more than a nuisance—he was a one-dog gang. All other dogs hated his guts the moment they saw him. They fought to get at him. Arno never seemed surprised at this. Every dog's hand, he seemed to expect, was raised against him.

This didn't faze him. As he growled back and lifted his

Esquire, May 1942.

leg disdainfully on the nearest object, usually a white-walled tire or a French chaise lounge, there was that note in his voice which said clearly, "Why, you jerk! If you weren't tied up I'd whip the hell out of you." He would then kick up the carpet a few times and circle the dog at a safe distance to see how much madder he could get him. The other dog usually went temporarily insane or strangled himself. Once this practice cost Arno dearly. He miscalculated the strength of an overwrought bull terrier's leash. It snapped and he was beaten to a pulp. The ensuing few days were the only time I ever saw him low in spirit.

He was arrested regularly. The police, acting on neighbors' complaints, were continually on the point of shooting him. But the high point was the day the Beverly Hills dog-catcher rang my doorbell. There was humiliation in his voice. "Please, Mr. Flynn, please. Keep Arno tied up if only on Tuesdays and Thursdays. That's when I make my rounds. He chases my car and gets all the dogs inside to fighting. It looks silly."

It was commonly supposed that Arno was housebroken. But in point of fact the rule struck him as absurd.

He favored curtains in less-used portions of the house. Yawning casually he would get up and stroll off as though suddenly bored with the conversation. A few minutes later he would reappear like a conscientious watchman who had just given the house a thorough check-up. You could never catch him at it. If you followed him he would be innocently looking out the window. It wasn't until the curtains took on a strange multicolored shade at the bottom that the device was discovered.

Among humans, he had hardly a friend. Kindly people who bent down to pet him, a thing which Arno loathed, were met with a look of cold hatred. Muttering to himself, he would then rise and deliberately stalk as far across the room from them as possible. And don't think he wasn't a crashing snob. He drew class distinctions in every human relationship, snubbing the servants and keeping his contacts with them as curt as possible. The only person he ever palled up to a little was a burglar who dropped in for some silver.

All in all, Arno had quite a lot of patience with me, particularly about such failings as practical jokes. His attitude was that if I wanted to be stupid, could he help it? I could go too far, of course, like the time I persuaded him to jump into the front seat of my car and he landed squarely on a live gopher snake I had put there. He hated snakes and his next jump took him fully ten feet away. You could see he didn't think it at all funny.

One day the cook on my boat gave him a big beef bone. He knew he wasn't allowed to eat it on deck so he carried it, mouth watering, down to the boarding ladder, jumped into the water and swam ashore. We were anchored about one or two hundred yards off-shore so I watched him through binoculars. He made a light snack, debated the bone's possibilities and took a look around to see if he was being watched. Next he carefully buried it under a tree. Then he swam back to the boat with the smug look of a guy who had just put over a cagey deal. I waited till he was busy and then rowed ashore, dug up the bone and put a hard-boiled egg in its place.

Next day Arno slipped ashore for another snack. He dug and unearthed the egg. It seemed to surprise him for a second. But he pushed it aside and went on digging. The hole grew enormous as he searched for the bone. Finally he sat down and looked at the egg. He nosed it over a couple of times. Then he got up and circled it. He sat down again, and thought it over. The more he thought about it the more the mystery of it all stunned him. An egg, a hard-boiled egg, appearing as if by magic in the place of his bone. By the look on his face all that day I could tell he was repeating to himself, "An egg! How do you like that. An egg! I'll be a son of a bitch! An egg!"

Friendship with Arno meant you were a cinch to lose most of your friends. There were times when the only answer seemed to be to change my name or leave the country. Like that time at the Coronado Hotel. The Coronado

Hotel is an austere establishment where rich old folks go to play bridge until they die. The waitresses get off weekends to visit their grandchildren. You are kept awake nights by the dull thud of guests dropping dead.

Disaster, ever Arno's sidekick, struck one day in the dining room of that hotel. Eating was always a problem because Arno insisted on eating with me. If you chased him out of the restaurant, he would just come in another door. When the door was shut he would wait for some customers and come in again camouflaged between their legs. On this particular day I had (I thought) double-locked him in my room upstairs.

Now one of the hotel's younger set—a quaint little thing of about seventy—always complained that the dining room was cold, in spite of the temperature being a good eighty. She also maintained it was so dark she couldn't see, though you could take snapshots in there at night and they would have been overexposed.

So she announced she would provide her own lighting. Soon a tall stand-lamp arrived and was installed behind her chair. When lit the first night it was found to contain a 200-watt bulb of such brilliance that it temporarily blinded everyone who looked in her direction.

The waitresses were the ones who suffered most. They would serve her something and turn around to get something else, and everything would immediately go black. They would usually drop whatever they were holding. One of them partially solved the problem by wearing dark glasses.

Of course, nothing much could be done about the heating arrangements. From the heat generated by her lamp, people at adjoining tables already perspired freely throughout meals, but the frail little old lady sat serenely under her 200-watt umbrella and remarked how cold she was. She finally achieved some measure of comfort by coming into meals wearing several silver fox furs.

This was partly the cause of the trouble. One night I was sitting in the dining room over a bottle of wine when a cat passed by the table. I knew this cat slightly. He was a prosperous executive-looking kind of cat and apparently had the exclusive use of the kitchen and dining room. Business was good with him.

Suddenly there was a commotion at the dining room entrance. There was a scraping of chairs; the head waiters began moving around agitatedly. The hair on the back of the business cat shot up as though someone had got by the secretary he didn't want to see. It was Arno. How he got out of the room I don't know. He had just started to give me a brief nod, a sort of double take, when he saw the cat. That was enough! They broke beautifully from the gate without a second's difference in the start. Hugging the rail the cat skidded around several tables three lengths ahead of Arno. At the far turn Arno had shortened and was coming up on the outside. Coming into the stretch it began to look like a photo finish when the cat, taking a desperate gamble, swerved sharply under the frail little old lady's table. Arno, trailing by barely half a length now, saw dangling in front of him the fox fur and—!

It was horrible. The screams of the waitresses, the hoarse shouts of the men, the smash of crockery, rose to a sudden deafening explosion as the 200-watt lamp crashed to the floor and broke shivering into a thousand pieces. Arno had the little old lady's silver fox fur by the throat in a killer's grip.

On dark nights, the sounds still ring in my ears.

All in all, the hotel was very nice about it. After I had paid for the damage the management said I could come and stay there practically any time—alone.

EDITOR'S NOTE: Flynn's 1942 version of the Coronado Hotel in Coronado, California (across the bay from San Diego), does not stand comparison with the hotel today. Perhaps in 1942 it was as quaintly conservative as he suggests, although it is safe to assume he exaggerated that impression in the interest of humor. But the venerable hotel—made familiar to many moviegoers by its use in Billy Wilder's film *Some Like It Hot* (1959)—is today a lively, bustling resort spot, and hardly the kind of place where the elderly go to retire. It seems likely Flynn stayed there for an extended period when he was making *Dive Bomber* in 1941, much of which was filmed at the nearby San Diego Naval Air Station.

Flynn's attachment to his dog Arno is much as he described it in this article. For some years the two were almost inseparable. Sadly, their friendship came to an abrupt end in 1946 when Arno fell overboard from Flynn's ketch *Sirocco* and drowned. The body was washed up a day later and Flynn was called to identify it. He declined to do so, which caused some newspapers to comment that the actor was somewhat heartless and indifferent. Flynn's view was that he had been so fond of the dog that he couldn't bring himself to look at the body.

My First Screen Kiss

I HOPE YOU remember the picture *Captain Blood.* As far as I am concerned, that was a film I shall never forget.

I had looked over the script *before* I met Olivia de Havilland, so I knew there was a love scene of some intensity in the picture. *After* I had met Olivia, I looked forward to the tender passages with the same placid approval as a wolf lavishes on a herd of spring lambs. Yee-ow!

Olivia, her hair gleaming under the lights, was gowned in a velvet affair with a pleasantly low neck in front and a starched, upstanding gold collar encrusted with paste jewels in back. I came to hate that collar with a frustrated and humiliated loathing.

It will not come as a shock to you, I trust, that I felt adequate to manage the love scenes. I am not without a certain—hmm—fame in that respect.

So when the director carefully explained the emotions we were supposed to feel, I restrained from leering. He stressed the care with which I was to take Olivia into my arms. I must not close her too tightly to my eager chest for fear of wrinkling her gown. I must not cast a shadow on her face with my nose. I must be careful to keep my own face in my key light. I must not actually kiss Miss de Havilland until the final take—no genuine and delightful rehearsals, you understand—for fear of smudging her makeup.

"Now—are you ready?" asked the director.

MSP Movies Magazine, 1948.

"I think I'm embarrassed," I said in all sincerity. Certain callous fellows around the set laughed.

I stepped forward, chilled with diffidence. I slid my arms around Livvy's fragile waist. "Darling . . . " I began in a quavering tone.

"That won't do," shouted the director. "You're standing too close to her. Reach out and draw her in, but not too far toward you. Remember those marks on the floor. Let's try it again."

We started over. I held the lady lightly. I cast no shadow. I stepped into my camera marks. I allowed Livvy to remain on hers. With one arm around her waist—without wrinkling the gown—my other arm sought her shoulder.

Promptly, the pearl buttons on my sleeve snagged the gold lace collar.

The wardrobe woman shrieked with pain and it required several moments for interested bystanders to separate our costumes.

The director, his mouth on one side of his face, his eyes glowing with sardonic light, admonished me coldly. "Technique! That's the problem," he said. "Please, Errol, think! Haven't you ever kissed a girl?"

"If we could try once more . . . " I ventured humbly, wondering who had set fire to my neck.

That time it was all right. It must have been because the director yelled, "Cut and print it!" With those happy words ringing in my ears, I realized that I had fallen to man's lowest estate: I had kissed a beautiful girl without remembering one single thing about the taste or the feel of her lips.

Making motion pictures, brother, is a rough business!

I Do What I Like

THIS IS THE LAST article Errol Flynn ever wrote for a Hollywood magazine and it is perhaps the most revealing of all such pieces by him. Its very title sums up the Flynn creed; he did precisely what he liked all his life—and paid the price. Written in 1950 when he was forty-one, the article shows a considerable change of attitude in philosophy from his early devil-may-care days in Hollywood. There is an undercurrent of regret in this piece and some appreciation for what fame has brought him. It indicates a more introspective side to a man everyone thought was a total extrovert:

FRIENDS HAVE BEEN telling me for years that I'm among the luckiest of men. It's always been hard for me to agree with them. I've had my share of troubles, and everything I own today, including whatever freedom and peace of mind I possess, has been bought with an equal share of worry and work.

Of late, however, I begin to realize what they mean. Few people in life are fortunate enough to find a niche for themselves which enables them to live in approximately the way they think the most desirable. Acting, or some other form of artistic endeavor, is the only way I could have earned my living while exercising my yen for travel and adventure. Yet, this freedom has not been without its cost.

For one thing, while I appreciate any attention I may receive in public, I must admit that crowds terrify me and I

Screen Guide, 1950.

hate the feeling I am on exhibit all the time. I want to be one of the crowd, to relax, be myself, instead of being followed and inspected by watchful and often critical eyes wherever I go.

When I first came to Hollywood, I enjoyed whatever fame I had but gradually it began to pall on me and from now on I want more privacy, especially in matters of my personal life. I happen to be a guy who enjoys solitude on occasion and there are times when my idea of heaven is just to be alone and I mean completely alone, with perhaps a book about ships and the sea which have always fascinated me.

The dream of retreat from the world is a common one. Almost everyone has his desert island, his Tahiti, Shangri-La, or whatever you may call it. Perhaps as much as any man, I have attempted to find this personal retreat from civilization. The closest I have ever come to attaining isolation from the world are the times when I am at sea, aboard my ship, the *Zaca.* But even then, there is the wireless, and you must come to port some day.

Take my word for it, no matter where you seek to hide, the world will soon seek you out.

And, when you come to think of it, someone who professes to be an actor cannot very well withdraw from life. Even acting begins with living. If my job as an actor is to interpret life, I must draw my material from primary sources. An actor, like any other artist, must lose himself in the stream of life. Only from life can he draw the knowledge of humans that will enable him to project their foibles, loves and hatreds on the screen.

I think it fortunate that Warner Bros. have allowed me to make mostly historical and outdoor dramas, like my current film. These are much more agreeable to my temperament than the suave dramatics of boudoirs and drawing rooms. Making romantic, historical dramas, I find myself in an atmosphere I love, and it's easier to combat my restlessness.

It's no secret by now that a wild desire to travel is my predominant characteristic. The days of my poverty and vagabondage still come back to me now with a nostalgia that has the force of a blow. It's pleasant to remember I had few worries then and practically no financial responsibilities. I felt rich when I had accumulated $25. No one had invested millions in me and the jobs of hundreds of others were not dependent on me. Yes, it was pleasant to be irresponsible and carefree—but these days there doesn't seem to be any geography left in which one can be irresponsible and carefree.

Naturally restless, however, I frequently find myself rebelling inwardly at the deadly routines of picture making. I get the feeling that life is slipping by me—the time is passing and I am not living fully. When this feeling of restlessness comes over me, I have to remind myself how fortunate I am to be able to earn my living as an actor.

How else could I combine work and travel so successfully. I have just completed a western for Warner Bros. entitled *Rocky Mountain,* in which my co-star is lovely Patrice Wymore. The picture was filmed on location in New Mexico. I learned intimately about a part of the United States I had never visited before. When I say intimately, I know whereof I speak—I'm still trying to scrub particles of New Mexico out of my skin.

It was an enjoyable and interesting experience, however, and by the time you read this, I will be in France, making my first independent production, *The Bargain.** This is truly an exciting project. Much of the action of the picture will be filmed aboard the *Zaca.* The rest will be made in Nice—although the picture actually is laid in eighteenth-century New Orleans!

The reason for this seemingly strange location is that Nice today resembles the old French crown colony of New Orleans much more than does that bustling Louisiana metropolis today.

During the past year I have been to India to film *Kim* for

*Released in 1951 as *The Adventures of Captain Fabian.*

MGM, made a tour of Europe and now am on my way back to Europe for my own picture. What more could someone born with the itch to travel ask from his work?

In the years to come, I intend to work as much and as hard as—perhaps even harder than—I have done in the past. Because of the new freedom I now enjoy, however, I intend to plan my work so that I can combine it with my wanderings. I want to make motion pictures in all the far, exotic places of the world.

Since I first came to Hollywood, my attitude about a number of things has changed considerably. I once looked upon all work with sheer loathing—as a matter of fact, there were those who said I was incurably lazy. Lazy? Sure. But not incurably. Today I look upon work—sincere, honest work—as man's normal function and one of the few worthwhile things he does.

I don't mean to imply that I am ambitious in the accepted sense of the word. I have no desire to excel others—to win an Academy Award, for example. I merely desire to be creative, to leave the world something I have created, whether it be a book, a motion picture, a painting or whatever—that will add to its beauty, knowledge, understanding.

Most of all, however, in the years to come, I desire to achieve freedom—to do what I like, to go where I like, with whom I like; to choose my own friends; to avoid pretense; to maintain my integrity, both as a man and an actor.

PART FIVE

Faith and Cuba

THE SAD THING about the listing of Errol Flynn's work as a writer after he arrived in Hollywood is that it is such an obvious accounting of his attitudes toward his life. In the three years following his 1935 arrival, there was a fairly copious output. Instant fame gave him a flush of confidence about his ambition to write—but then that fame, ever increasing, slowly fostered the more trivial side of his nature. He sat at the typewriter less and less. He girded his literary loins in the mid-1940s and came up with *Showdown,* but its failure to bring him any great credit caused him to retreat again.

Flynn found himself with little or no desire to turn out magazine pieces. He had in mind to write a sequel to *Showdown* and call it *Charlie Bowtie in Hollywood,* which would have chronicled Shamus O'Thames's adventures in the movie capital. But he let that idea drift into limbo. With time he realized that the only likely chance at success in print would be an eventual autobiography, and to that end he kept notes.

Flynn's last notebook, a kind of diary covering the last few years of his life, contains numerous observations not only about his life but about life in general. Much of it is rather philosophical in content and reflects a generally wry and frequently dour impression of people and places. It clearly is not the work of a happy man and reveals a side of him almost totally at variance with the roistering, cheerful image he presented to the world. He often quipped, "I allow myself to be known as a colorful fragment in a drab world," but it was a rather desperate façade. Flynn was not a man who ever went to church or expounded any particular religion, yet there was a yearning for some kind of religious belief. Of all the facets of his nature, this was the one he most kept to himself.

Some of his notes are quite extensive and with little reshaping they could easily have been turned into magazine pieces. But he never submitted any of it. Instead he turned the diary over to Earl Conrad when he and Conrad began work on the autobiography. Only one of the entries is given a title. Written in Rome in 1953, both the title and the contents are surprising for a man who was generally known as a complete hedonist:

Faith?

SOME SAY THAT we shall never know God's purpose, that there is no God nor any purpose, that we humans are like the ants crushed under a boy's foot for the fun of it.

But then there are those who will tell you with firm conviction that never a flea jumped from a dog's back that God didn't know of.

What is Faith? And why are you born with or without it? For certainly from what I have observed in this life, Faith is not a thing you develop. On the contrary, if I have developed anything definite it is a dull smoldering anger at the abysmal mystery of my presence of this earth, with not the least clue to any reason for it; a mystery that probably not even death will solve for me. Why am I alive?

What, then, is Faith? In what? Today, in my early forties I find myself in a state of tortured confusion where my every past action or experience, my daily movements are measured and appraised by one who does not seem to be myself; an alter ego who stands by with detached and contemptuous mien, sneering at the bumbling efforts of a human in search of a soul; a human daily more wrought upon and bewildered by the external questions: "Whence do I come? What am I? Whither do I go?"

Swept by doubt, desperately seeking just one little sign from Heaven—the sign that those of Faith do not demand— I am carried along like duckweed down a Chinese river, feeling yet always denying the existence of a benign Diety, knowing so goddamn well in my heart that I have reached the supreme goal of egoistic existence. For what?

Faith? Why does it elude me? Why cannot I find peace of mind like those I envy? Those who have listened and heard and felt, and having done so, contritely let fall all other barriers and started to believe wholeheartedly in God?

Why am I even unable to begin by renouncing the material things, the transitory and ephemeral? Why, knowing—and knowing, strangely, with humility—my faults, my myriad imperfections, do I go on with outward complacency, yet with growing inward desolation? Why must my mind remain factual, materialist whilst within me I stifle my cry for help and will not yield an iota to the stumbling craving in my soul? Will this rebellion against God never end?

Quos deus vult perdere, prius dementat (Whom the gods wish to destroy, they first make mad). Perhaps this is what is happening to me—or maybe I can seek solace in the thought that I am only going through a male menopause.

So this life is only a preparation for a hereafter? This is still an illogical premise to explain the period of human history in which I have lived. The graveyards of Anzio and ten million of the world's finest men swallowed up, sacrificed upon the most incomprehensible of all mankind's bizarre alters—man's inhumanity to man, war.

Twice, three times that number could probably be accounted for, if Russia and China were included. Was it the Sublime purpose to abbreviate for these millions of souls the preparation for the hereafter in anguish and torture? And now we prepare for the unspeakable horrors of yet another war, with weapons which may well portend mankind's final self-destruction.

So Faith is a word the meaning of which eludes me. I mean Faith in the concept of a benign, all-seeing God. God, in the sense of a creator, yes. God in the sense of a Supreme Being I can believe in. But a God who believes in me, a God who is aware of my soul's existence, who after death will clear up the great mystery of my reason for life in this world, in this God I have no faith, nor can I begin to seek it with a full heart.

Today I see a strange world, more bewildering and paradoxical than anything I have read in history, even the birth of Christianity—one half of mankind grimly devoted to the task of stamping out the idea of God and Religion; the other half apathetic to both. Supine and hypocritical, the professed believers in a Christian God today give lip-service in the various totem-houses, listening in private to their priests denounce the other Christian sects with hatred and malice. In the light of the Church's sordid history, its stubborn refusal to keep pace with modern thought, its failure to satisfy the religious needs of today, perhaps this apathy is understandable.

The world's need for Faith is desperate, more desperate than my own, for I am only one lost individual in a tortured universe, a world weary, shocked and shattered. No philosophy, no fanatical political dogma can stand against a true belief in God.

Faith—I wish I had it.

EDITOR'S NOTE: Errol Flynn's last pieces as a writer were about Cuba and Fidel Castro, and they appeared in the New York *Journal-American* in the first week of February 1959. After finishing work on his autobiography, and presumably feeling elated about being a writer again, he proceeded to Cuba to seek out Castro, whose revolutionary ideals intrigued Flynn. He spent much of the previous December and January on the island and did indeed inveigle his way into the Castro folds. Flynn's political idealism—his interest in politics never went beyond idealism—veered toward the left and he seemed always fascinated with revolutionaries. In going to Cuba he was somewhat reliving his 1937 trip to the Spanish Civil War, and there can be little doubt that the Cuban adventure was an attempt at reviving his heroic image, a kind of "last fling" of Don Quixote Flynn. Later he appeared on U.S. and Canadian television, notably on Jack Paar's show, and told of his experiences. By this time in his life he was beyond raising eyebrows. He was simply a "colorful fragment" and a rather sad reminder of former times. But here is what he wrote about Cuba—reprinted by permission from The Hearst Corporation.

Me and Castro

REPORTS THAT I found myself on the wrong set, in the Cuba situation, have been profoundly exaggerated.

I also discount the report that Batista, when he heard I was with Castro, tossed up his arms and said, "The jig is up, boys, Flynn is with him. Let's get out."

It was said that Batista read into my partisanship toward Castro a fatal turning point of American sympathies, but I think that occurred some time earlier.

I remember the strictly ridiculous instance of having seen the former dictator at his home very bare-skinned in an unruly bath towel. I got a shock. Because you expect to see a bemedaled dictator in all his uniforms, and there he was, with his towel a little too short, and it kept getting loose, and he didn't look like a dictator then at all—and he doesn't now.

Though the cartoonists and the editorialists had their usual circus with what they conceived to be my latest antic, I was actually very close to Fidel Castro for a five-day period, and the fact of the matter is he told me that no American knew either him or his brother Raúl better than I did.

It must be true because nobody else was with him for as long as I was. I saw him intermittently over the five-day period, for long talks, jeep rides, one military action, and I even discussed with him the histrionics of speech delivery.

"Shall I call you comandante, or Señor Castro, or what?" I asked him, when I met him on December 27, at his headquarters in a sugar mill deep in Oriente Province.

"Call me what everybody else calls me," he said, "Fidele." Fidele is a more intimate form of Castro's name, Fidel.

And it was Fidele and Errol from then on.

"Look, sport," I said, speaking in my limited Spanish, "do you mind if I take an occasional draft of the delicious wine of your land (rum) so as to make a revolutionary situation a little more viable?"

He did not object, but as for himself he disliked liquors in any form. I gathered from the way he presented his objections that he was trying to convey the thought that he had an actual allergy to alcohol.

"I have the same thing," I said, "but by dint of great discipline I have managed to overcome it."

That got a good belly laugh out of the comandante, and I followed through by suggesting that it was the rebel in me that had conquered the allergy.

Once we were in a red jeep, ricocheting over the so-called roads in the Santiago area where Fidel led his uprising when I asked him how and why he had extracted from his fellow rebels a pledge not to touch alcohol until the war was won.

Smilingly, the big bearded fellow with the translucent skin—pale, olive, Cuban skin—leaned back from his front seat and said, "I know the Cubans well enough to know that if they fly at the rum bottle they will not have the discipline and self-control which is so necessary to victory."

Nonetheless, I did manage to find a few drops of rum left in a very much squeezed bottle, and I needed the sustenance, for I have the very deuce of a time riding in automobiles. I have a bad back, a few vertebrae not exactly aligned, and auto riding is not my favorite sport.

"How the devil," I asked, "can you be so relaxed in this cement mixer?"

He laughed and explained to me that he had been going up and down these gulleys and mountain roads for years, and it was easy. I wondered how it was that Castro sat on the outside seat; his secretary, aide, and good companion, Celia Sanchez, sat in the center; and his driver occupied the spot behind the wheel. Didn't Castro have any regard for his own personal safety? Seated where he was, he was a bull's-eye for any sniper.

I touched the back of the driver—this was really a steel guy; his shoulder was as hard as a marble table—and I said, "Un poco más despacio, viejo."—"A little slower, sport."

The driver had been carrying Castro about four years, and he didn't slow down for an American visitor. Perhaps my secret fear was that if anybody drilled Castro they would get me. Two fellows were with me, in the rear, one on each side, both with guns cocked, and safeties off. In fact, I wondered several times, when we stopped abruptly at some ditch, whether I wouldn't more likely get it from one of our boys.

This spin with Castro was one of several rides I took into the neighboring towns, visiting liberated places.

"I feel that the citizens will know who you are," he graciously told me, "and it will cheer them to know that someone from the United States, whom they have perhaps seen on the screen, is interested enough to come such a long way to see them."

"Booked!" I said.

Now it chances that I take my revolutions seriously. It may possibly be forgotten that I went to Spain during the Civil War, as a newspaperman assigned personally by the late William Randolph Hearst, and that I was there for a couple of months, that I picked up some injuries, and returned to the States, resuming picture-making for Warner Bros.

Many people say I never got to Cuba at all. There were a few hints from among the more celebrated columnists that I fought out matters at the Nacional Hotel, in Havana, leading the daiquiri brigade in repeated charges.

Joking aside—if it is possible to put aside anything so important—I was deeply interested in the Cuban uprising for the simple reason that I have known the Cubans for more than twenty years. I have made my share of errors in the gambling casinos of the land, I circled the island many times in my yachts and came to know peasant and power with equal familiarity.

Way back in 1936, not long after I made *Captain Blood,* I bought a yacht at Boston. At the time I was married to Lili Damita, known as "the red hot babe of Hollywood"—too hot for me, I might add parenthetically—and with this new toy sailed down the coast. I hit bad weather around Cape Hatteras, went eastward to the Bahamas, then on down to Havana. I pulled in there, intending to stay a day, and I stayed a month or more.

At that time Batista had just come into power, his slogan "down with tyrants, down with crooks and corrupt politicians." He was a dramatic figure, young, a sergeant, and it was my fortune to be present at the rise of the Batista regime, and to be at hand for its fall—to be, in fact, in Castro's quarters when he heard that Batista had fled the land.

I did not make any hurried foray into Cuban rebel territory in the closing hours of the crisis, as some have hinted. I was in Cuba from Thanksgiving Day onward, and neither Castro, Batista nor myself knew that the change of power was so imminent.

The Castro movement had been in progress for five years, and as far as anyone could tell, the struggle might be going on for one or two more years. I chanced to be there on one of my frequent trips to the Caribbean when it became clear to me that a crisis ensued and I made arrangements to visit the camp of Castro himself.

Ever since boyhood I have been drawn—perhaps romantically—to the idea of causes, crusades. And that is because there is, behind the façade of the rompmaster, a young man who still believes in the world. I yet like to see the plain John Does of the world get a break, I am with them and of them. Maybe the making of the motion picture *Robin Hood* rubbed off on me—and when I see a poor land that wants its due, why then, I am willing to lend a hand—even if, as some say, it is only to reach out for a glass.

Now, add to all of these substantial reasons for my being there the fact also that I went there for the hell of it, and you get the complete picture.

I think it a very strange thing that no other Americans, or damned few, had enough interest in the welfare of the Cuban people to identify themselves with the Castro movement.

I only met one other, a young fellow from the Midwest, who shall be nameless. He was fighting with the Castro forces, with little to lose. He was in Cuba, alas, because he had shot and killed an unpleasant father-in-law—with heavy provocation, I might add—and he was there to avoid the U.S. authorities, bearded like the Cubans, and full of valor for Castro and the new idealism. Outside of him and Flynn, the flag of the stars was sadly unrepresented.

My old acquaintance, Ernest Hemingway, apparently made the observation that this was a situation which the Americans would do well to stay out of. Strange. It's all right to be interested in Spain, Korea, Europe—any row anywhere in the world—but steer clear of Cuba.

Why? Aren't the Cubans part of the human race? Isn't it a matter of some concern to us in the States if the Batista regime killed 20,000 Cubans who wouldn't toe the line? Where does legitimate interest begin and where does it end?

Who, officially, draws the line? What is it that determines who should be interested in the freedom movement of one country and not that of another? Not that of Cuba? Let the Cubans have Batista and grow sugar at the same prices.

Believe me, I have as much interest in sugar as anyone else. I have consumed my share of it, in various states and strengths and proofs, but I was with Castro because I knew and believed that he was with and of his own people. I may ultimately be deceived by the figure of Castro—I don't know—nobody does—but the people behind him, and the reasons they had for being behind him, these are eternal.

For weeks I waited in the Hotel Nacional for word to come through that Castro would see me. Mutual friends were trying to arrange such a meeting, and one day, December 23, the message arrived that a certain visitor was in the lobby.

I saw him, I received certain directions, all strictly on a secretive level, and I was told I was to board a four-engine Constellation on Christmas morning at the Havana airport.

I was to go with John MacKay, an American photographer.

The deal set, I dragged an old, beat-up briefcase on which were printed the words "Flynn Enterprises." I stuffed it full of vodka, tangerines, a couple of sweaters, two pairs of undershorts, shaving gear and a precious pack of toilet tissue. I packed too fast and the zipper broke. So I tied a rope around it and went through the whole deal with the briefcase tied up and stuffed into a pillow case.

On Christmas morning we went to the Havana airport.

Two plainclothesmen of the Batista police searched us before the ship took off. They stared hard at the sign "Flynn Enterprises," took stock of my vodka, found no guns, nothing, and we got through.

We flew across Cuba as far as the town of Camagüey. That was about three-quarters of the way to Castro's headquarters in Oriente Province.

We stepped off the plane and walked into the terminal. We stood at the bar—according to instructions—and ordered the national drink, a Cuba libre, and waited for an emissary to make himself known to us.

It wasn't easy. The Flynn face and form were swiftly spotted and the trip into rebel lines, at this stage, tapered down to a grim autographing hassle.

I suppose you could say I went by autograph into the rebel lines. Armed with pens and pencils provided by public and bartender, I signed indiscriminately for a time, Batistans, Castroites, Cuban bobby-soxers.

All the while I was looking out of the corner of my eye for my contact. Where was he or she?

A little later we learned our contact was none other than the traffic manager of the airport himself. He was a young American, Bill Patton, married to a Cuban girl. He announced to me that we were old friends, we had met before—and so we had. Bill had helped me on my last trip to Cuba, when I few my own plane, a single-motored Navion, down there.

He directed us to check in at the Grand Hotel. The following day we would be picked up by Fidel Castro's private pilot in the rebel leader's personal plane. In the interim,

Patton suggested, why not move about Camagüey, talk with the people, sample the sentiment.

Naturally we headed for the nerve center of all communities everywhere—the bars, where sentiments are exchanged, toasts delivered, confidences revealed, politics discussed, and the ways of the world inveighed against. In several of these marketplaces of truth we learned that Camagüey was under siege, that four rebel forces had strongholds commanding all approaches to the town.

The next afternoon, as we sat out of doors at the airport café, we heard the sound of an airplane motor. A red and silver Cessna circled. Informed rebel sympathizers knew the colors of this plane, that it was Castro's.

We had a final meeting with Bill Patton, who got us by the armed sentries on grounds that we were tourists who had chartered a plane to go into the countryside to scout locations for a film we were planning to make. Actually this was in some part true because I originally had thought of seeing Castro with a view of making a film about him and his movement.

Soon we were in the air, with a silent pilot, spinning over the mountain ranges, seeing below the wide rivers, the green fields of a Cuban winter.

The pilot had a gun beside him.

"In here it is fully loaded," he said. "I got this bullet marked. That's for me if they catch me."

"Why?" I asked.

"I'm not going to let the Batistans torture me," he grinned.

I learned later from Castro's own lips that my pilot, whose name I never learned, never had a chance to use his bullet.

In another hour or so we put down on a tiny airstrip near a large farmhouse where I was met by a Captain Luis Perez. He wore a black scarf around his neck. He took it off and handed it to me.

"This is for you," he said, explaining a rebel girl had made scarves bearing the insignia of the Castro movement for each member of his company.

"Commander Castro wishes you to have one of these."

Then we took off on the wildest two-day jeep ride I have ever had.

The engine of the car was an extra large one, giving the machine speed and power so that we went at a breakneck pace, taking the bumps into our spine as gracefully as we could. I was reminded of the rough riding I recently did in Central Africa while making *The Roots of Heaven.* Now we only went over roots.

We stopped at the home of a certain retired army colonel, a Castro sympathizer, and his women folk served us a dinner of steak, rice and fried bananas.

I noticed the old Cuban custom, actually Spanish, that after the women served the men at one table, they dined separately at a table of their own. Cussed luck, I hadn't seen a girl in hours and now the available ones were being kept at more than arm's length.

We resumed the wild ride through the canefield region, through swamps, over small streams, and getting deeper into rebel territory. Every hour or two we had a new man enter the car and stay with us for a relay, guiding us nearer to Castro's quarters, and whenever we stopped we talked with Castro's soldiers.

Once we saw Batista prisoners and we talked with them; apparently they were being well treated by the rebels.

Early on the evening of December 27—a Saturday—we pulled up in front of a big building, a sugar mill called the Central America. The commander, we were told, was inside.

Castro sat on a bed. I couldn't make out his face very well. There was that frame of beard and he was busy; he had his ear cocked to the tiny loudspeaker of a radio receiver. On a table a foot or so away from him there was a Belgian revolver, an ugly-looking weapon.

He paid no attention to us for a time, and I glanced about the room. It was medium-sized, sparsely furnished, with a makeshift look about it. But it looked well lived-in, as if many people came and went in these quarters.

Getting no rise out of Castro himself, I turned to face his secretary, a heroine of the revolt, Celia Sanchez. She was in uniform. So was Castro, so was a third figure, apparently an officer and aide of Castro. They wore regular army tan coverall fatigue outfits, and no army rank was evident. Celia Sanchez wore a pink orchid pinned to her right shoulder. I shook hands with her and looked down at her waist. There was a .32 calibre revolver lashed to her slim figure.

I wasn't so flabbergasted that my Hollywood eye was in any way thrown. I noticed at once that she wasn't built like the usual Cuban, but on a more slender scale. She was beautifully formed, and I put her down as 36-24-35.

That's not a Cuban female dimension. Your Cuban male usually prefers a dimension something like 38-28-40. She had dark, thin black hair, and luminous eyes which darted about steadily, missing nothing, and constantly reverted to Comandante Castro himself.

The broadcast ended, and Castro raised his face, saw us, and stood.

He was about my height: that is, six feet, two inches; he had grace, agility of movement, and a simplicity of manner which I hadn't quite expected. It simply wasn't the imperial thing that I thought I might encounter, the manner of a man who commanded.

My first impression was of his casual quality, that it was underlain by reserves and force. He didn't look like a man who had been burned in the sun. He showed no signs of having lived five-and-one-half years in the jungles, mountains, close to trees, gulleys, and the earth.

His face looked soft. So did his hands. Actually his hands were not soft, everything but that, but they looked soft, almost delicate, with no veins showing. They looked more like the hands of a man who has been behind a desk instead of a machine gun. His grip was very firm, but not overstrong.

He wore glasses and I noticed how, as he opened talk with me, his secretary, Celia, watched out for him most considerately. While he talked, she removed his glasses, but he didn't notice it. She wiped them off and put them back on, attentively, but subtly, not getting in his way.

An interpreter translated for us.

"I suggest," he said, "that you go to the villa of Palma Sorina. That place has just been liberated by the freedom forces, and they will be happy to see you, and you will be able to observe how the Cubans feel after we have taken them out of Batista's hands. "

It was then I asked him what I should call him, and we fell into the Fidele–Errol relationship.

"You have complete freedom to do whatever you wish. Talk to whomever you wish, take all the pictures you want to take. I only want you to see the happy faces of the liberated Cuban citizens."

"Can we take your picture also?"

"Mine. My secretary's. Everybody's. You have complete freedom of the press."

He said something that, interpreted to me, I didn't fully get. But it implied that the freedom he allowed was in sharp contrast to what we knew very well was going on in the Batista camp. We had learned that a couple of American newspapermen had been tossed into a Batista clink.

He wouldn't be able to see much more of me for a day or two, he said. Urgent matters had arisen, but he would spend much time with me very shortly. Until then, he said, "roam about as you please, you have the complete hospitality of the Castro camp. Good luck."

As we took leave of Castro, we were placed in the hands of a diminutive Friar Tuck, literally a merry priest, with sparkling eyes and a desire to help, and in sparse English he said he would take us for the night to his church quarters at the top of a high hill.

From his window there was a magnificent view of the city of Santiago, twenty miles away. When Santiago fell, it was explained, that would be the beginning of the end of Batista, for this was a port of outlet for 80 percent of Cuba's economy, mostly the sugar export.

The priest, father Bernardo Solis, said on the way:

"Sh-hh, I have a secret supply of water. You may have a bath."

He didn't feel it was selfish, he said, to have some water about the church. He took me to his quarters.

I saw a simple room, with a desk in great disarray, books on the desk in four languages. In this little room, near the main chapel, I got undressed, took a bath, and was given a tangerine to dine on.

"Don't use too much water if you can help it, please," he pleaded.

I assured him I was a partisan, albeit a sweaty and dusty one right now, and the water would be preserved.

I finished the bath and ran a grimy towel over my body. It wasn't exactly like the Hotel Nacional or the Park Lane in New York, but I felt better.

I stepped outside the El Cobre Monastery, hungry as a bear and a little weary of the sight of the numerous tangerine trees. There he was, a fine rooster roaming about the yard, living fine on Cuban worms. I tried to grab him.

While going for the red-combed fellow, I wondered whether I was desecrating church property in any way. I reconsidered, let him alone.

In the morning I dined on a banana—better fare than most were having, I understood—took a slug of rum and prepared for the new day of photography, observation and interviewing of aides to Castro.

The photographer was shooting everything in sight, taking pictures as fast as he could reload his camera: photos of rebels, their arms, meetings; Cubans living in their huts; shots of the bearded boys carrying guns; priests busily running in and out of Castro's headquarters.

What kept Castro busy was that negotiations were on for the surrender of Santiago. I hung around the Central America sugar mill, waiting for any chance I could get to see him. I knew what was going on inside.

Castro and his staff were closeted with a Santiago priest, Padre Guzman. The priest was an intermediary, not wearing a priest's frock. He was from the army chief of Santiago and they were hassling about the surrender of that city. If Santiago fell, there'd be a new government.

What impressed me was the intensive role of the priesthood in Castro's affairs. I learned that his principal advisor was Father Solis. He is a Spaniard from the Asturias, and

Father Solis himself authorized me to say that the church was 100 percent pro-rebel.

So that, while you get pictures in the magazines and newspapers of a Castro leadership made up of this one and that one, with their college backgrounds, or their American training—behind the scenes there is this traditional rooted impact of the same force that has so largely directed the affairs of Latin-speaking countries.

The talks between Castro and Padre Guzman went on for two solid days. Apparently the Batista army people wanted certain conditions from Castro which he was prepared to grant. But Castro didn't want the Batista men to remain in the key positions they were holding, which was what they were holding out for.

Fidel finally got his way. When he came out from this conference he had a very beat look, but there was a glow in his face as if he had gotten what he wanted. His aides looked and acted the same way too.

Barging around in the rebel camp I naturally found my way to the women's corps called the Mariana Grajales Battalion. Mariana was the mother of Antonio Maceo, a Cuban patriot, and the girls in the battalion had been with the Castro force for a long time.

I learned they were armed with bras, low-heeled shoes, no makeup, and guns. All very ascetic, like the bearded men who didn't drink and didn't consort with females while the revolt was on—so it was said.

Most of the girls had a personal reason for being there. A brother or a parent had been shot by the Batistans.

One girl said she'd never marry till the revolt was comlete. Another was in it for revenge, for injuries done to a sweetheart.

Their boots and shoes were pretty well gone, from plenty of walking. They wore slacks, what they called picadores that opened above the boots, a kind of blue jeans garb.

When they joined up with Castro and took to the hills they had to put aside the bobby pins, curlers, all the gadgety stuff that women everywhere find vital.

I can't say that this made exactly a bevy of chorus-type

beauties out of the gals, but they had something that was pretty wonderful, a camaraderie, and fine faces. They were rather grim; they wanted no more tyranny, they said.

"Peace, for God's sake, let our country live, the people be in it without constant threats to our men or land," they prayed.

Not even I can gag up everything I see. What I bumped into among the rebels was serious, truly revolutionary. There had been too much suffering over the whole island.

I felt low when Castro told me what happened to my pilot when he returned to Camagüey only two hours after he left me. Batista's soldiers were waiting there for me to return. They pulled him off his plane and asked him:

"Where did you leave Flynn and his companion?"

I wouldn't know whether he told them or not, but that was all the "trial" he had—30 seconds. They never even gave him a chance to walk to the airport. A tommy gun blew him to pieces, ripping up and down his body.

My photographer, John MacKay, planed back to Havana with scores of pictures, and a new cameraman, John Elliot, arrived.

The weather had been changeable. One day it was horrible, stifling and dusty as you jeeped along the roads; the next day it would pour.

In any small area you saw a variety of verdure, lush green pasture land here and rich green sugar cane ready for harvest right next to it. Then there'd be great patches of parched earth and dust and a look of drought.

Wherever you went, the large tropical cockroaches were doing sentry duty. Surefire, nimble-footed, these Cuban cockroaches were natural guerrillas of the land, hiding behind leaves, beneath beds, under your pillow, crawling into your briefcase.

Castro gave me a surprising amount of his time and attention at just the period when Batista was getting ready to quit Cuba and just as the revolt was at the edge of success.

He asked me about my own life and experience and my

work as an actor, and that led into my giving him some thoughts on delivery, histrionics, how to be effective with an audience. He listened attentively and said that he would try to put some of the advice to work. He intended giving an address to his officers shortly, and he asked me to let him know how he did.

I don't know why but for some reason Steve Allen flashed into my mind as Castro talked and moved around his quarters. Castro is a man who puts an excessive amount of energy into his speech, manner and action, and who, having done this, slumps just as Steve does after a show.

I don't mean to compare him in any sense with a comedian and a performer in the entertainment field—just that one characteristic, reacting in that way after an effort.

Once he has put out every bit of energy, Castro poops. I noticed how his shoulders slumped when he felt it was time to relax. You could visibly see his recharging, like a battery, for the next exertion.

I heard his voice get tired, husky, weak, after a long chat. I thought I tired him out; but actually he ran my pants off for several days, jeeping around.

We talked hot and heavy about many things, and he told of his strategy for defeating the Batista government.

He told me how one of the methods of weakening the government force was to cut electric power. This was a principal part of the strategy which won him the victory.

But it was another thing altogether and a wrong thing, he said, to poison water, which was a government tactic. The idea was to do everything to represent the people and keep their good will, and to develop their appreciation of the rebel movement, not to endanger the public in any way.

Cut off transportation, yes. Break up communication, yes. But no mistreatment of the public, no terrorism.

I asked him why his movement allowed itself to be called a rebel rising instead of a patriot movement. I suggested that the word rebel had an outlaw flavor to it, that they should call themselves patriots. He didn't understand the difference.

I mentioned Jesse James.

"Who is she?" he asked.

I described the notorious outlaw—and Castro said he didn't understand. I then said that his movement looked, in America, as if it was a force directed against a legal authority. That he understood. He stiffened. "I am a doctor of law myself," he said, "and the government has never done anything legal, never."

My effort at semantics got nowhere. As it turned out, it wasn't needed.

We dined together, always pretty lightly. He took no pleasure or interest in his food, it seemed, went about it perfunctorily like a man who, shaving, thinks of other things. His food was about the same as everyone else's, as nearly as I could figure.

Occasionally he had a can of Spanish tuna served to him, but he said he felt he was being overprivileged if he got fare like that. Mostly he ate arroz con pollo—chicken with rice. But you had to look hard to find the chicken.

I tried my damnedest to make him laugh, but it wasn't easy to do so. I gathered that he used laughter rather as a tool in his armory, as a weapon, to work on the spirits of his followers, but he was too involved a man to see ironies, paradoxes, amusements in what he was doing, or in any of the sporting-blood fillips that a visiting actor could get off.

I gathered that one of the items that pleased Castro was the way in which his forces captured the guns of his enemies. He told me how his movement had begun with eight men setting out to defy the government, and they began with no guns. His movement got its guns mostly by capture from their enemies.

And when a man got a gun he kept it in marvelous shape, treating it as a teenager would handle a hot-rod or jalopy, with affection.

While Castro modestly attributed to many others the reason for his movement's growth and the spread of military successes, I saw this scene:

A colonel of police, a hard Batista man, surrendered. I saw this man as he came to Castro's headquarters. He was a brash guy, he spoke good English, and he had been to school in Chicago. Soldiers brought him to the comandante extra well secured because the mob was ready to tear him apart. They knew his record as a terrorist.

But he gave himself up and came over to rebel forces, shaking and trembling, and when he was brought before Castro he said, "I would like to join the movement of the 26th of July," Castro's trademark when the anti-Batista campaign began.

"Not until you have earned it," Castro said.

He gave this colonel a loaded automatic tommy gun with directions to join his force and show his mettle before he could belong to the Castro movement.

On another occasion, at three o'clock one morning, I was awakened from a fitful sleep—I was on a low-lying wooden bench of some sort—when my photographer and I were told that Castro was addressing his officers and we could go and hear him.

We walked from the hilltop in the moonlight down the long hill that led to the sugar mill where Castro held forth. All about there was a gathering of rebel soldiers. They talked frenziedly and in the semi-dark I could see their beards—the trademark of the revolt, the austere bush on the face, symbol of hardness, masculinity, self-denial.

In the mill there was a large room where Castro would speak and we were led inside. Along with us there filed in scores of soldiers and officers. I took up a spot in the rear of the room. Up front, on a rigged kind of platform, was Castro, and he stepped forward.

I am used to hearing good voices and to being associated with men who have timbre and power in their throats. I had given him a few suggestions; now I listened.

Castro had as much power in his voice as anyone I have ever heard say lines for the screen or in the theatre. I believe that this has since been noted by television audiences who have heard his voice, with its confidence and sweep.

Here, by sheer oratory, he held the attention of a crowd of young men—I say young because the Castro movement is largely and has mainly been a youth movement. It dawned on me that he was giving them hell.

They had always fought honorably, he remined them, and they treated their prisoners well, and they hadn't stolen, but by Dios, the discipline was breaking down. Maybe, he said, this was because they'd come down out of the mountains and the scent of victory was in their nostrils, but some things that were going on had to stop! They were drinking beer! Beer, while the cause wasn't yet won!

I hadn't realized that this was such a crime at this end of Cuba. What was I doing here? I better keep under wraps that briefcase with the bit of vodka still in it.

Now he lit into them real good. They were also going out with girls, and these gals weren't even members of the movement. Where in blazes was this going to end? he asked.

His voice ripped through the sugar mill, and even with my meager Spanish I caught the words, "You are failing yourselves!" Even so he had them laughing once or twice, and they'd get tense and rapt as he went serious.

I hadn't been so close to so much virtue in a long time. Not since I entered a church forty-two years earlier, dragged there unwillingly by my mother. I thought of my wives, mistresses and lesser females in the Flynn retinue around the globe. I wondered what the relationship was between celibacy and a successful revolution.

I suppose females do interfere with that dedicated feeling you ought to have during a crusade. I realized I could never have the qualifications to pass the muster of the true Castroite rebel. But what a wonderful way to avoid alimony. Suddenly the comandante grinned, threw up his arms and left the room. His admirers let loose with ear-splitting yells and it was clear to me that they loved him like a mother, father, and brother. It was no Gettysburg Address, I decided, but it was nice to see the boss in good oratorial form.

On New Year's Eve, jeeping about with Fidel Castro, he told me that Batista would quit in a week.

The next morning I was awakened with the cry that he had indeed fled from Cuba, that Santiago fell without a fight.

I woke up my photographer.

"Come on, Johnny, get out of the sack, the thing is over with!"

Just then a hawk-faced captain, with the usual beard and lean and hungry look of the revolutionist, came to me with the message, "Mr. Flynn, Fidel sends me to tell you that to go to Santiago is going to be highly dangerous. You want to go?"

I sure did, I told him, and so did the photographer.

During the day a long convoy of rebel troops formed, stretching for a mile. Jeeps and motorcycles carried the soldiers. Rebel flags made their appearance on poles and trees.

I was in a jeep with the photographer and some Castro men, as the line moved sluggishly toward Santiago. Everybody expected there would be resistance in the city in spite of the flight of Batista. The local Batista men would figure they might as well fight as to be arrested and shot.

We bounced along behind a column that convoyed Fidel himself toward Santiago. We got as far as Central Palma, several miles from Santiago, and we suspected an ambush. The jeeps slowed, and then there was a burst of fire from somewhere.

Everybody went for the ditches. My own view was that the only time to go for a ditch was when planes came and strafed, so I headed instead for cover behind a wall. This building had been shelled and bricks were loose around it.

Something went through my pants, whatever it was. If not a bullet, then a hunk of mortar had been splintered and it shrapneled against my leg. I looked down there and the jeans were pretty bloody. It didn't look bad, and I considered myself to be lucky—so far.

The next day, January 2, there was fighting all over Santiago, plenty of resistance. Once when the fire was quite noisy, I laid down in a gutter and filled up a stenographic pad with notes. My belly was resting uncomfortably in water.

On the morning of the third and the morning of the fourth the local holdouts continued to whiz their bullets around in a nasty way. I managed to get quarters in the Casa Grande Hotel—business as usual, and even special consideration for me—and from my window I could see shooting in the street, also an ambulance hauling away a dead rebel.

It chanced that the hotel wasn't doing a brisk business. I was the only guest and a little lonesome. I alternated between hanging around the hotel and getting out into the streets. My notes for January 4 read: "Must quit—things getting a bit too hot. I'm behind a marble pillar on hotel porch but being only one around here feel lonely—bullets—too many coming too close make me feel that way. Going to make a dash for it inside hotel. Here goes."

It was around this time that it dawned on me they were not shooting film.

Obviously the thing to do was to get the hell out. The set was becoming as nasty as a battle scene worked out by Mike Curtiz. All this time I had made notes, figuring that since I was the only thing like an American war correspondent with Castro, and nobody else was permitted to be with him from stateside, that I had a pretty good news story, and ought to get it to the press.

But there was no communication with Havana, no phones or telegraph now, no planes going between Santiago and Havana.

To complicate matters I couldn't get a haircut. Ever since the rebels decided to grow beards and long hair, the barber business had gone shot to hell. They were as scarce as plane pilots, and some of the barbers began to grow long hair themselves for fear they'd be thought of as Batistans.

In the midst of these problems a tourist guide approached me. He showed me his badge and license. Could he show me around?

"Where can you show me around where there are no bullets flying?" I asked. He happened to be a very fat fellow and he said, "You are in no danger with me. Don't you know everybody loves a fat man?"

I didn't care to make any scientific tests of that bromide in this particular hot test tube.

From time to time Santiagoans ventured out of their

houses to head over to the hotel to take a look at me and to wonder—like me—what I was doing there at this time.

One fellow, a kind of comic, asked me, "How come you looking so young in the movies and so old now? Tell me."

That hurt a little, and for an answer, I gulped some rum.

"Why you no go and act instead of dreenk rum?"

Big laugh from a small audience at my expense, and of course I had no very profound answer. All of it was convincing me, however, that I should get out.

I retired to another part of the hotel and got my shoes shined.

Why is it, I asked myself, that while wars and revolutions go on, you can always get these little details taken care of?

In a religious country like this, I said to myself, there will be a quieter day on Sunday, they will not shoot each other so much.

Sunday came.

But after the noon Mass, and while the bells were still ringing, bullets began flying.

To hell with this, I said to myself, let's go see the Coordinator of Transport for two passes to get to Havana. I made a run for the Administración Civil, as they called it. But there seemed to be no available pilot to get us to Havana where we could tell what we knew and what we saw. Also by now the wound on my shin was nasty looking and needed some dressing and care.

I thought of getting out by jeep, by water. The airport manager at Santiago had a couple of old planes lying around there, government planes. He said if I could fly I could take one out. "Help yourself," he offered.

"You help yourself," I said. "I'm not flying one of those crates." They looked to me as if they'd been built for small boys by that firm that makes Erector sets.

A planeload of exiled Cubans from Venezuela landed, unloaded its cargo, and apparently it was going to go on to Havana from here.

Boy, did I get gallant with a little lady at the airport! She was one of the workers in charge of keeping the airport going, and I begged her to let me on this machine headed westward. I promised her everything except a starring role in my next movie. My charm worked, I held her hand, I beamed down on her like the warm Cuban sun. Lady get me on that plane. She melted, and Johnny Elliot and I got on that plane and we moved swiftly back to Havana.

Returned to the big city I had my leg wound looked after, and it is just possible that a little more was made of it internationally than it deserved.

There is a report around that I put in a half dozen calls to the States to mention my wound and the news of my having been with Castro. That is an absolute lie.

I only put in one.

That was all that was necessary.

Just before I made ready to return to the States I received a wire from a theatrical agent in New York. It was signed Arthur A. Treffeisen, General Artists Corporation.

> IF YOU WIN THE WAR HAVE POSSIBILITY TOP NOTCH
> BROADWAY SHOW CONTACT IMMEDIATELY UPON RETURN
> TO NEW YORK.

IF I win the war. Flynn, of Burma, Berlin, Tokyo! How could he be so naive!

Postscript

THE BIGGEST IRONY in the story of Errol Flynn is that success as a writer came to him posthumously. The recognition he had sought in his early years in Hollywood with his writings, and which soon dwindled into a vain hope, came on a grand scale with his autobiography. He had read and approved all the galleys of *My Wicked, Wicked Ways* and he had every reason to believe it would sell well. It was inevitable that he should write a book about his life. By anybody's yardstick, it had been a complex and colorful life, and he had been making notes for it for years.

In 1957 G.P. Putnam's Sons, New York, gave Flynn a generous advance to write the saga of his life. With his track record as a writer and with a life story more bizarre than any actor in Hollywood, the publisher reckoned it a good gamble. But they did not reckon with his tardiness, nor did they know it was now difficult for him to concentrate on anything for any length of time. Flynn admitted to friends that it was tougher going than he had imagined. That wasn't the only problem.

In Paris in July 1958, Flynn happened to meet Art Buchwald, who wanted to know, as did almost everyone, how the book was coming along. Flynn smiled a little wanly and allowed that he had so far assembled something like fifty thousand words but that he was far from pleased. He told Buchwald, "I lay awake at night plucking at the coverlet wondering what tomorrow's chapter will be. I can't write about myself because I lie to myself. I don't even know they're lies because I believe them. I don't believe in ghost writers. Many of my colleagues who have told all for the right price have less principle about this than I have. I wanted to write the book myself but now I'm willing to give back the advance."

Flynn was not a man noted for giving back money, and Putnam's was not about to let a potential winner slip away. Despite his declaration about having principles, he finally agreed to a ghost writer, albeit on the understanding that the book would appear under Flynn's name, with no mention of a helper. Putnam's hired veteran author and journalist Earl Conrad, who read through all the material Flynn had penned but decided a completely new tack needed to be taken. Late in 1958 Flynn took Conrad with him to his estate in Jamaica and the two men worked together for the next ten weeks. Conrad hired two court stenographers to take down his daily probing and prodding of Flynn—a long, long interviewing, verging on psychoanalysis. With almost a quarter of a million words of notes, Conrad returned to New York and put together what became known as *My Wicked, Wicked Ways.* The end product sounded so much like Flynn that few people suspected the hand of another man. And it did indeed become a best seller.

Looking back on his association with Errol Flynn, Earl Conrad muses, "He was a macrocosm. That is to say he was a convoluted, contradictory enlargement of other men; and through examining him and what had happened to him, you could get insights into the nature of other men, rather like a scientist looking into a microscope at some devilish microbe. It helped me to understand the complicated nature of living as it pertains to all of us. Flynn was a collection of disparate personalities, and he had had too much of everything. Eventually he became a ripped-out-at-the-seams caricature of himself, trying to keep up an image he really didn't want. I noticed he kept no photos of himself and he seemed to avoid looking in mirrors. He told me he would rather have written a few good books than made all his films. Everyone in the world thought they knew Flynn but they didn't—he was isolated by his fame, probably because he was an isolated human being to begin with."

Errol Flynn toward the end of his life found himself with few close friends, partly because he moved about so much, partly because he became bored with people, and largely because he exhausted those around him. "I found that after three or four hours with Errol," says Earl Conrad, "I had to get away from him and be by myself. He was a man on fire—there was so much action and excitement in him."

Flynn was aware of the contradictions of his nature and made many revealing remarks to Conrad for the book, such as, "I want faith, and I am faithless," and "I want to be loved, yet I myself may be incapable of really loving." In Conrad's view there was also a suicidal streak in Flynn. "He seemed to be an expert on drugs. He told me there were six different ways of killing oneself and that an overdose of morphine was the easiest. One of the things he did for a kick was skin diving, going down eighty and ninety feet. One day he came rushing up to me after he had just come out of the water and he said, 'My God, what an escape I've just had. My air tank gave out when I was ninety feet down and I don't know how I got up.' He was elated with the exertion, with the excitement of having survived a hassle with death. That gave him a great kick; he lived on that for the rest of the day. That was typical of Flynn."

Flynn stayed in Jamaica after Conrad left. He said he intended to retire from acting within a year or so and live in the new house he was building on his estate near Port Antonio, and even pointed out the spot where he wished to be buried. He also told Conrad that he wished to form a writing partnership with him and do a number of books together. In the summer of 1959 he went to Hollywood to appear in a TV film called *The Golden Shanty*. The half-hour playlet was filmed in three days and directed by Arthur Hiller. Flynn looked like a much older man than fifty—a sick, older man. He had trouble remembering his lines, even in reading them off cue cards. For all that, says Hiller, "He was still a humorous, likable man with a mischievous air about him. But it was painful to look at him now and remember what a graceful athlete he had been only a few years before."

In the first week of October, Flynn made his last appearance before the cameras. He was a guest on "The Red Skelton Show," playing a gentleman tramp in a comedy sketch. A few days later he took Beverly Aadland with him to Vancouver, British Columbia, where he intended to discuss the sale of his yacht, the *Zaca,* to a Canadian businessman. A price of $100,000 was agreed upon and Flynn then spent several days being entertained by his hosts. On October 14, while being driven to the airport, he complained of great pains in his back. He asked to see a doctor and his hosts took him to the home of a friend, Dr. Grant A. Gould. The doctor administered a pain-killing drug and Flynn soon felt better, although stiff in the back. His mood picked up and he began telling stories about famous Hollywood personalities. After a while he asked the doctor if he might go to the bedroom and lie down for a while. Because of the stiff back, Dr. Gould advised Flynn to lie on the floor. Beverly covered him with a blanket and his last words were, "See you in an hour." She rejoined the others but decided to look in on Flynn about thirty minutes later. She found him lifeless and a blue-gray color. Dr. Gould shot adrenalin straight into Flynn's heart but neither this nor mouth-to-mouth resuscitation had any effect. Flynn was rushed to a hospital and given oxygen but he failed to respond and he was shortly pronounced dead. His body was shipped to Los Angeles by rail and a few days later he was buried at Forest Lawn—a cemetery he had often decried as ludicrous and one in which he hoped he would not end. But he received a respectable Episcopal service, with his ex-boss Jack L. Warner delivering a eulogy and his studio colleague Dennis Morgan singing "Home Is the Sailor."

Had Flynn lived to enjoy the success of *My Wicked, Wicked Ways,* which told more than even his most ardent fans expected, he would also have had to do some explaining. There were relatives and friends from the early years, those who had been of help to him, who wondered why they had received no mention. And there were a few people who strongly objected to being mentioned as he had done. Among them were his mother, ex-wife Lili Damita, Warner Bros., and director Michael Curtiz. These, and others, assailed G.P. Putnam's with protests; consequently *My Wicked, Wicked Ways* appeared in later printings somewhat shorter than the first. Those who had been slighted, or ignored, reasoned that Flynn in his last year was confused in his recollections and thoughts—a fair assumption in view of the excessive use of drugs and alcohol, particularly so in a man with a propensity for blending facts and fiction. Be that as it may, *My Wicked, Wicked Ways* is a remarkable outpouring of recollections and thoughts. With the help of Earl Conrad, Flynn was able to reveal himself in all his complexity, and with considerable candor. Few public figures have chosen to reveal themselves so intimately and almost none have, or could, tell such tales. If nothing else, Errol Flynn stuffed his fifty years like a huge, bulging bag.

But what of Flynn as a writer? In his book *The Young Errol,* John Hammond Moore gives the opinion that he was an entertaining, highly readable writer, who could probably have made a living as a journalist or short-story writer, had he not become a celebrated actor. But Flynn was lazy. "Why spend time and effort learning a trade or a profession when through wit, physical charm, guile, and theft one could shortcut his way to wealth and ease?" Dr. Moore also believes, as do many who knew Flynn, that he became a victim of his own public image: "Hollywood, the publicity staff at Warner Bros., and millions of fans who wallowed vicariously in the alleged sexual exploits of this beautiful man created a monster which eventually triumphed over reality." And whatever talent Flynn may have possessed as a writer was an easy victim of that still lingering, phallic, amusing, and largely false heroic image.

A personal footnote: In an interview I tape-recorded with Flynn about a year before he died, I asked him one very deliberate question. I had been one of his boy idolators and I had learned a great deal about him over the years. Part of what I had learned was that my boyhood hero was much less heroic than the image I had idolized but far more interesting, however sadly, as a complicated, flawed human. And by that time I had come to know him well enough to be able to needle him.

"Errol," I ventured, "you've often been called Huckleberry Flynn, the perennial bad boy. Now, tell me. Do you feel more sinned against than sinning?"

He feigned mock outrage. "Sir, I resent that question. I resent it." Then he laughed and admitted, "No, I contributed. I had a hell of a lot of fun and I loved it—every minute of it."

Like so many things about Errol Flynn, it wasn't quite true. But it sounded marvelous.